MUTUAL FUNDS

AN INTRODUCTION
TO THE CORE CONCEPTS

MUTUAL FUNDS

AN INTRODUCTION
TO THE CORE CONCEPTS

Mark Mobius

BICENTENNIAL
1807
WILEY
2007
BICENTENNIAL

John Wiley & Sons (Asia) Pte Ltd

Other Wiley Editorial Offices

John Wiley & Sons, Inc., 111 River Street, Hoboken, NJ 07030, USA

John Wiley & Sons Ltd, The Atrium Southern Gate, Chichester P019 8SQ, England

John Wiley & Sons (Canada) Ltd, 5353 Dundas Street West, Suite 400, Toronto, Ontario, M9B 6HB,
    Canada

John Wiley & Sons Australia Ltd, 42 McDougall Street, Milton, Queensland 4064, Australia

Wiley-VCH, Boschstrasse 12, D-69469 Weinheim, Germany

Library of Congress Cataloging-in-Publication Data
ISBN: 978-0-470-821435

Wiley Bicentennial logo: Richard J. Pacifico
Typeset in 11points, Galliard by Hot Fusion
Printed in Singapore by Saik Wah Press Ltd
10 9 8 7 6 5 4 3 2

CONTENTS

ACKNOWLEDGMENTS

Numerous commentators and scholars have studied mutual funds around the world and their concepts have provided the stimulus for many of the ideas discussed in this book. There are too many to mention and to thank individually but I hope that I have been able to accurately reflect the body of knowledge available now about mutual funds.

Special thanks go to Dennis Lim, Dr. Thomas Lanyi Yuri Mashintsev, K.C. Chin, Natalia Olynec, Virginia Cheng and Zita Ng for their valuable assistance and comments as well as John Wiley's Janis Soo and Nick Wallwork for their patience and diligence.

The views expressed in this book are solely my own and do not represent those of my employer or any organization to which I am associated.

To help us improve future editions of this book, please email your comments to: jmarkmobius@yahoo.com.

AN INTRODUCTION TO MUTUAL FUNDS

Mutual funds have become an invaluable tool for a wide range of investors, from individuals seeking to save for retirement to sophisticated socialites focused on preserving their assets and businessmen determined to create wealth.

In its most basic form, a mutual fund is a company that pools money from a group of people with common investment goals to buy securities such as stocks, bonds, money market instruments, a combination of these investments, or even other funds. The collected holdings of these securities is known as its *portfolio*. Each share, or unit, represents an investor's proportionate holding of the portfolio and their proportionate entitlement to the income generated by those holdings.

At the beginning of the 21st century, the number of mutual funds in the US exceeded the number of companies traded on the New York Stock Exchange. While they have gained popularity in recent decades, mutual funds are not a new invention. Mutual funds have a long and varied history. The concept of pooling investments that developed in Europe in the late 1700s led to the development of unit trusts, or mutual funds. According to K. Geert Rouwenhorst in *The Origins of Mutual Funds*, during the late 1700s "a Dutch merchant and broker, Adriaan Van Ketwich, invited subscriptions from investors to form a trust...to provide an opportunity for small investors with limited means to diversify.[1]"

English and Scottish investment trusts sold shares to investors in the 1800s. The Joint Stock Companies Acts of 1862 and 1867 in the UK allowed investors to share in the profits of an investment enterprise and limited investor liability to the amount of investment capital devoted to the enterprise. One of the first fund managers, Robert Fleming, formed the Scottish American Investment Trust and invested in the post-Civil War US economy, mainly through US railroad bonds. Many other trusts invested in the US and brought the concept of fund investment across the Atlantic.

---

[1] Rouwenhorst, K. Geert, *The Origins of Mutual Funds*, Yale ICF

FUND TYPES

Mutual funds, or *unit trusts*, are called open-end funds because they are required to buy back shares, or units, from the shareholders at any time at a price based on the current value of the fund's net assets. Mutual funds also offer new shares to the public on an ongoing basis.

Closed-end funds, or *investment trusts*, are another type of fund that issues a fixed number of shares, as in the case of open-end funds. If shareholders want to exit the fund they must sell their shares on the market. Investors who want to purchase shares must also go to the open market to purchase them from existing shareholders since no new shares will be issued by the manager. While shares of open-end mutual funds are redeemed and sold at the net asset value of those shares (i.e. market value of the fund's holdings), the price of closed-end funds depends on market forces. As a result, closed-end fund shares may sell at a premium or discount to their actual net asset value, depending on the supply and demand for those shares.

In addition to mutual funds (unit trusts) and closed-end funds (investment trusts) there are other types of aggregated investments. For example, there are exchange-traded funds, or ETFs, which are designed to mirror the return of a particular market or sector index. The shares of ETFs are traded on stock exchanges at market-determined prices. Investors can buy or sell an ETF through a broker just like the shares of any other company.

There are also unit investment trusts, or UITs. UITs are "unmanaged" US investment companies with a portfolio of securities that have a definite life, as opposed to mutual funds and closed-end funds, which normally do not have a definite lifespan. There are both stock, or equity, trusts and bond, or fixed-income, trusts.

The difference between a UIT and a mutual fund is that, in addition to having a fixed life at which time all the assets will be sold and returned to investors, a fixed portfolio of investment is made at the inception of the UIT and is not changed unless there is a bankruptcy or other corporate change in one of the securities held in the portfolio. Thus it is "unmanaged." The objectives of such UITs can be to provide capital appreciation or dividend income. In the case of UIT bond trusts, they normally pay monthly income from the interest earned on bonds and the proceeds of bonds that have matured and had their principal paid out.

BENEFITS

The benefits envisioned more than 200 years ago remain the same today. Investors are attracted to mutual funds, also known as unit trusts in the UK, for five key reasons:

- Professional management

- Diversification

- Lower cost

- Convenience

- Liquidity

Professional Management

A professional fund manager, also known as an investment adviser, carefully chooses the securities in which the fund invests. The fund manager also normally employs a team of researchers, investment analysts and strategists to provide the detailed market information that needs to be considered when choosing individual stocks and bonds. These decisions are based on a variety of factors, including the fund's investment objectives and risk tolerance. The manager also has access to extensive, real-time information services. Individual investors with more limited means do not have such access. The fund manager and his team are also subjected to a wide range of professional standards and legal restrictions, such as limiting transactions between the adviser and the fund he advises to prevent conflicts of interest.

Diversification

A mutual fund can hold several hundred stocks and/or bonds in its portfolio from different companies and, often, from different industries or regions. This greatly reduces the risk of the poor performance of any one security or business sector disproportionately reducing the value of the fund's assets. Still, lower risk does not mean no risk. For example, if the overall stock or bond market declines, the value of the mutual fund may also drop. The key point here is that by buying a unit in a fund, individuals receive exposure and diversification that they would otherwise not be able to easily and efficiently replicate.

Lower Cost

The costs related to buying shares in a mutual fund are lower than buying individual stocks and bonds on your own to build a diversified portfolio. This is because with mutual funds the costs of accessing extensive research, as well as administrative, operating, and trading expenses, are spread among thousands of investors.

Convenience

With more than 55,000 mutual funds available worldwide, investors have access to a wide variety of investment vehicles that meet different investment goals. They cover many markets, industries and types of securities. The vast array of choices also ensures that investment companies compete for business and provide a myriad of customer services, such as automatic investment plans, online purchases and sales, and asset allocation models. As a result, it is easier to make investment decisions, track performance and keep accurate records.

Liquidity

Mutual funds are also liquid, which means you can redeem your shares at any time, in the case of open-end mutual funds, or sell them in the market, in the case of closed-end funds, or investment trusts. Liquidity of closed-end funds can be a problem and often the price received may not be in line with the actual net asset value of the fund. In the case of open-end funds, however, investors may redeem at any time and at the actual value of the fund investments at that time.

DRAWBACKS

Investing in mutual funds is not without its drawbacks. They include risks similar to those that come with investing in stocks or bonds, such as problems of volatility, delegated control and limited flexibility.

Volatility

When you invest in mutual funds that hold stocks or bonds, the value of your funds changes with the fluctuations in those securities markets. Most mutual funds cannot guarantee a specific return or a return of capital. In most cases, investors must pay sales charges, management fees and other expenses regardless of how the fund performs. If you are very conservative and need an absolute guarantee, you will probably be more comfortable investing in more traditional bank products that pay a guaranteed rate of interest. However, in the long term, investing in mutual funds should give a better rate of return.

Delegated Control

If you want to control the specific stocks and bonds in your portfolio, mutual funds are not for you. Mutual funds are successful because they spread the cost of running a portfolio among many shareholders. Thus they cannot take into consideration the specific needs of individual investors. They also will not satisfy investors who want to actively trade and select the stocks or bonds they want to hold.

Limited Flexibility

If you are fortunate enough to be very wealthy and have millions of dollars to invest, mutual funds may not give the flexibility you need. Many private banks will create specific investment products to cater to your needs. Still, many wealth managers also use mutual funds to fulfill some of the objectives of their wealthy clients, and they frequently make up a portion of a high net-worth individual's wider portfolio. The variety and number of mutual funds offered today can probably meet the need of even the most sophisticated investor.

ORIGINS AND DEVELOPMENT OF MUTUAL FUNDS IN THE US

1924 The first mutual funds, the Massachusetts Investors Trust and the State Street Investment Trust, are established in the US.

1929 Market crash and beginning of the Great Depression.

1933 The Securities Act of 1933 requires registration of all public offerings of new securities, including mutual fund shares. It requires that all prospective investors receive a current prospectus describing the fund.

1934 The Securities Exchange Act of 1934 authorizes the US Securities and Exchange Commission (SEC) to regulate the securities markets. Broker-dealers, including mutual fund principal underwriters and others who sell mutual fund shares, must register with the SEC.

1940 The Investment Company Act of 1940 sets the structure and regulatory framework for the mutual fund industry. It requires mutual funds to keep detailed records, safeguard their portfolio securities and file semiannual reports with the SEC.

The Investment Advisers Act of 1940 requires federal registration of all investment advisers and requires all advisers to meet record keeping, custodial, reporting and other requirements.

1951 The total number of mutual funds exceeds 100.

1971 Money market mutual funds are introduced.

1974 The Employee Retirement Income Security Act (ERISA) creates the Individual Retirement Account (IRA) for workers not covered by employer retirement plans, resulting in a new set of potential investors in mutual funds.

1978 The Revenue Act of 1978 allows the creation of 401(k) retirement plans and simplified employee pensions (SEPs).

1988 The SEC creates a mutual fund fee table rule, which standardizes presentation of fund fees in prospectuses.

1990 Mutual fund assets top $1 trillion.

1992 Brokers start offering "mutual funds supermarkets," which allow investors to buy funds offered by many different investment companies and receive one consolidated statement.

1998 The SEC approves disclosure reforms for mutual funds that require the use of "plain English" fund profiles and improved risk disclosure.

Source: *Investment Company Institute*

INDUSTRY DEVELOPMENT

Open-end mutual funds issue new shares as new money is invested. The first funds of this type were introduced in 1924 in the US. The Massachusetts Investors Trust and the State Street Investment Trust, like today's funds, allowed investors to buy shares in a professionally managed portfolio that included a wide selection of securities. These funds introduced important changes such as the continuous offering of shares, the ability to redeem shares instead of holding them until the dissolution of the fund, and clear investment guidelines and restrictions.

In the early 1900s, the concept of mutual funds was slow to catch on with the general public. Investing directly in individual stocks was more common, with funds managing only an estimated $140 million by the end of 1929. The market crash of 1929 and the Great Depression that followed all but extinguished interest in all types of securities, including mutual funds.

In 1933, new legislation and regulations introduced by the US Congress and the country's newly created Securities and Exchange Commission (SEC) breathed new life into the securities industry and renewed investor confidence in funds.

One of the most important pieces of legislation, the Investment Company Act of 1940, classified and regulated different types of pooled investment vehicles. It set rules for creating, marketing and operating investment companies and their products. It also required funds to obtain approval from the SEC before issuing or selling any shares to the public. This legislation has been improved over the years, requiring funds to disclose costs, risks and other information in a legal document called a prospectus. At the time when the 1940 Act was passed, there were only 68 mutual funds operating in the US. This number grew to 361 by 1970. However, the severe two-year bear market in 1973-1974 stifled interest in funds. During this period, the Dow Jones Industrial Average index tumbled almost 50%, resulting in a flood of investor redemptions.

Prior to the early 1970s, funds mostly focused on investing in stocks. But several events in the mid-1970s spurred the interest of small investors in both money market and bond funds. During the bear market, small investors flocked to Treasury bills as interest rates on six-month bills rose to more than 16%. To reduce demand for bills, the Federal Reserve Board (FRB) increased the minimum purchase to $10,000 from $1,000. As a result, small investors unable to afford the minimum $10,000 investment turned to a newly created product called a "money market mutual fund," which invested in government bills. These funds allowed access to the same high interest rates, but with smaller minimum investment requirements.

Individual investors also started turning to mutual funds when commissions on securities transactions became negotiable in 1975. Brokerages were no longer interested in serving small individual investors because the commissions earned on small trades of stocks and bonds were insignificant compared with those earned from the much larger investments

Figure 1.1 — US Mutual Fund Industry Total Net Assets, Number of Funds, Number of Share Classes And Number of Shareholder Accounts

Year	Total Net Assets (Billions of US Dollars)	Number of Funds	Number of Share Classes	Number of Shareholder Accounts (Thousands)
1940	0.45	68	-	296
1945	1.28	73	-	498
1950	2.53	98	-	939
1955	7.84	125	-	2,085
1960	17.03	161	-	4,898
1965	35.22	170	-	6,709
1970	47.62	361	-	10,690
1971	55.05	392	-	10,901
1972	59.83	410	-	10,635
1973	46.52	421	-	10,331
1974	35.78	431	-	10,074
1975	45.87	426	-	9,876
1976	51.28	452	-	9,060
1977	48.94	477	-	8,693
1978	55.84	505	-	8,658
1979	94.51	526	-	9,790
1980	134.76	564	-	12,088
1981	241.37	665	-	17,499
1982	296.68	857	-	21,448
1983	292.99	1,026	-	24,605
1984	370.68	1,243	1,243	27,636
1985	495.39	1,528	1,528	34,098
1986	715.67	1,835	1,835	45,374
1987	769.17	2,312	2,312	53,717
1988	809.37	2,737	2,737	54,056
1989	980.67	2,935	2,935	57,560
1990	1,065.19	3,079	3,177	61,948
1991	1,393.19	3,403	3,587	68,332
1992	1,642.54	3,824	4,208	79,931
1993	2,069.96	4,534	5,562	94,015
1994	2,155.32	5,325	7,697	114,383
1995	2,811.29	5,725	9,007	131,219
1996	3,525.80	6,248	10,352	149,933
1997	4,468.20	6,684	12,002	170,299
1998	5,525.21	7,314	13,720	194,029
1999	6,846.34	7,791	15,262	226,212
2000	6,964.63	8,155	16,738	244,705
2001	6,974.91	8,305	18,023	248,701
2002	6,390.36	8,244	18,985	251,125
2003	7,414.40	8,126	19,319	260,701
2004	8,106.94	8,044	20,030	269,479
2005	8,905.17	7,977	20,556	277,713

*Number of shareholder accounts includes a mix of individual and omnibus accounts.
Note: Data for funds that invest primarily in other mutual funds were excluded from the series.

Source: *2006 Investment Company Fact Book, Copyright © by the Investment Company Institute (www.ici.org). Reprinted with permission.*

of institutional investors. As a result, brokerage commissions for small investors were higher than those charged to institutional investors such as mutual fund companies.

Industry Growth Accelerates
The amount of money flowing into mutual funds and the number of mutual fund investors soared during the bull market in the 1980s.

The introduction of Individual Retirement Accounts (IRAs) under the Tax Act of 1981 increased awareness of the benefits of mutual funds as vehicles for investing for retirement. Interest rates also began a steady decline in the 1980s. This resulted in higher bond prices, reducing the appeal of money market funds. The mutual fund industry met this new demand by creating other long-term, income-producing funds as well as offering more equity mutual fund products.

In the 1990s, rising equity markets and the increasing popularity of 401(k) retirement plans fueled the growth of the mutual fund industry. Assets held in mutual funds soared to about $7 trillion by the end of the decade from about $1 trillion at the beginning of the 1990s. Assets from retirement plans such as 401(k)s and IRAs rose to more than one-third of all fund assets in 1999 from less than one-fifth in 1990, according to the Investment Company Institute (ICI).

Robust economic and corpo-rate profit growth, low inflation, and relatively low interest rates also created ideal conditions for the growth of the industry. A strong US economy created more than 20 million new jobs by the end of the decade and pushed the unemployment rate to a 30-year low. Inflation fell to its lowest level since the 1960s.

To meet growing demand, fund companies developed new sales channels in addition to sales through brokers and direct sales to investors. Third-party distribution took place through employer-sponsored pension plans, mutual fund supermarkets, fee-based advisers, mutual fund "wrap" account programs and bank trust departments.

Large fund complexes were developed to provide "one-stop shopping" for equity, bond, hybrid and money market funds. For example, in 1992, one stock broker offered a "mutual funds supermarket," which allowed investors to buy funds offered by many different investment companies and receive one consolidated statement. Assets in such mutual fund supermarkets reached an estimated $500 billion by 1999, according to the ICI.

The cost of buying mutual funds also declined significantly due to economies of scale and competition. Purchasing costs declined 25% for equity funds between 1990 and 1998, the ICI said.

Equity funds made up more than two-thirds of the increase in the number of funds since 1990. The variety of equity funds offered also expanded to those focusing on emerging markets, specific industries and geographical regions. Mutual funds became one of the most convenient ways investors could purchase foreign stocks because of the cost and complexity of directly buying stocks not listed on US exchanges. Technology funds, which include those investing in companies associated with the Internet, grew in popularity during the so-called dot-com bubble at the end of the decade.

Mutual Funds in the 21st Century

By year-end 2005, mutual fund assets reached almost $9 trillion in the US compared to $448 million in 1940. Mutual fund assets worldwide were $17.8 trillion at the end of 2005.

As interest in mutual funds soared, so did the scrutiny of regulators. The beginning of the 21st century was marked by increased scrutiny in the US and Europe to ensure that mutual fund investors were treated fairly. There was increased awareness of the need for undertaking complete due diligence of the parent company of an individual fund before investing, as well as the need for increased attention to fund shareholders' rights.

MUTUAL FUND STRUCTURE

In some ways, mutual funds are structured like any other company. A fund sells shares to investors and has officers and directors or trustees. Understanding the structure of a fund gives insight into the internal division of responsibilities, which ultimately protects investors and makes them aware of the various costs associated with the operation of the fund.

Mutual funds require the services and expertise of at least eight entities: a sponsor, underwriters/distributors, a custodian, shareholders, a board of directors, a fund manager, a management company and a transfer agent.

Figure 1.2 — Mutual Fund Structure

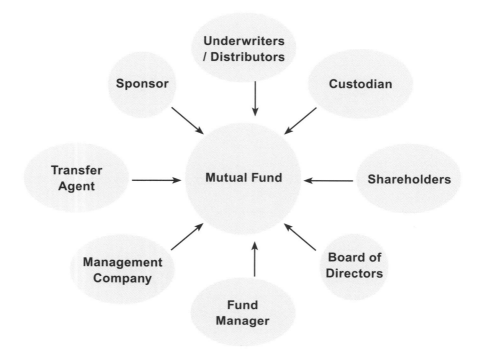

Management Company

Each mutual fund is registered as a separate management company or trust, which is created by a sponsor. A sponsor may decide to put many of its funds under one umbrella and create a *family of funds,* with different investment objectives or with portfolios containing different types of securities. The funds within the family often offer the same services and benefits and allow the management company to attract more of their clients' capital as they try to diversify or change their investment goals.

Sponsor

A sponsor is typically a financial services company such as a mutual fund company, brokerage, bank or insurance company. The sponsor makes the initial investment in the fund and assembles the other third parties needed to operate the fund. In the US, the sponsor must register the fund with the SEC. This registration document will become the prospectus for the fund, which identifies the fund's sponsor, board of directors, investment objectives, types of permitted investments, fees, and risks.

The sponsor can spend several hundred thousand dollars registering the fund and designing corporate documents. Operating the fund also has many costs. Funds incur expenses such as transfer agent and custodian fees, as well as accounting and other business expenses to service shareholders and meet the regulations governing the fund.

Shareholders

The fund is managed for the benefit of investors who buy its shares. Investors are given detailed information about the fund through its prospectus, as well as through periodic and annual reports. By studying these documents, shareholders can determine whether the fund has met its goals and followed its investment strategies.

Mutual fund shareholders have the right to vote to elect directors, and they must also approve changes to the terms of the fund's contract with the *fund manager,* who manages the fund's assets. The approval of the majority of the fund's shareholders is normally needed to change the fund's objectives or major policies.

Board of Directors

Shareholders elect a board of directors to oversee the management of the fund and the work of the portfolio manager. The board ensures that the fund manager's investments adhere to the fund's objectives and votes on renewing the fund manager's contract and any changes to his fees. Directors earn fees that are specified in the fund's prospectus.

Fund Manager

The fund manager, also sometimes known as the investment adviser, invests the fund's assets according to the fund's stated investment objectives by researching and choosing specific securities that will be bought or sold in the portfolio. As a professional money manager, the fund manager provides knowledge and expertise beyond the scope of the average investor. This service offers small investors an economical way to access research and expertise similar to that available to large institutions and high net-worth individuals.

The adviser is often not an individual, but a wholly owned subsidiary of the sponsor or an outside investment management company. The organization of an investment advisory firm can take many forms. At some companies a fund manager oversees just one fund, while at others he manages more than one fund in related sectors or with similar objectives. When there is a team managing a fund, one or two are appointed lead managers. They often direct the work of junior managers, researchers and analysts.

The fund managers often visit many of the companies they are researching and use computer models to choose securities for their portfolios. They also have access to sophisticated fund analysis tools and real-time financial information services from various data sources. The investment advisory company earns a management fee, while individual fund managers may receive a salary plus a bonus based on the fund's total return.

When investing in a fund, it is important to gather information about the manager's record and experience. The fund's prospectus provides these details, including how long the manager has run the fund, the manager's education, and other funds managed by the adviser. This information can be used to assess the manager's skills. Does he have experience in bull and bear markets? What returns did he produce relative to the benchmarks during both peaks and troughs in the market? The safest choice is an experienced fund manager with consistent results during both market highs and lows.

Fund management companies often market their most successful fund managers as celebrities in their advertising and promotional materials. This is often a good marketing tool. However, the company then risks having clients follow their star to a new fund company if he or she leaves.

Underwriters/Distributors

Investors buy and redeem fund shares either directly or through a third party called the principal underwriter or distributor. The distributor is essential to the fund's success because it is responsible for attracting investors to the fund. As competition increases in the industry, based on service and performance, the distributor/underwriter's role is becoming more important. To market the fund, the distributor prepares sales material, brochures and advertisements. Incentive systems may also be organized to encourage various sales agents to promote sales. The distributor can either sell shares directly or through selling groups of brokers, financial planners, banks, insurance companies, or through mutual fund supermarkets.

"Son, there are five basic elements; earth, air, fire, water, and mutual funds."

A DAY IN THE LIFE OF A FUND MANAGER: MARK MOBIUS

Belgrade, Serbia

07:00 The phone rings. It's my morning wakeup call. I get out of bed and turn on the broadband connection for my laptop computer and begin downloading e-mails. There are at least 100 messages waiting for me as our offices in Asia have been working for a number of hours.

07:30 Morning exercise. My hotel has a small gym with a stationary bicycle. I cycle for half an hour while reading the latest financial magazine. I always stay in hotels with either good gyms or in locations with large gyms within walking distance. Another important consideration is good broadband Internet access. Unfortunately, many hotels in emerging markets don't provide both, or even one, of these features. Here in Serbia, the choices were limited, and we had to make do with a hotel with a small gym and quite slow Internet access.

While exercising I skim the financial magazines for articles on emerging markets and specific companies in which we might be invested or which we could be studying for investment.

Of course, the benefit (and problem) of us fund managers is that we must be interested in anything and everything, since the range of businesses in which we could invest is virtually unlimited. Even fashion magazines may have something of interest.

08:30 I quickly shower, dress and go downstairs to a breakfast meeting with a local consumer goods company. We are thinking of making a private equity investment in the company and want to learn more about it and, particularly, how it plans to finance its expansion.

09:30 I visit a local construction company at its Belgrade headquarters. As we haven't invested in Serbia yet, this is an exploratory meeting. We want to understand how the management operates, what its plans are, and how the company is structured.

More importantly, we want to see how the company is surmounting the past Communist mentality and moving to a modern and business-like, profit-oriented focus. My associate from Poland was not impressed and said that he would veto investing in the company because he saw that it had not yet rejected the state-controlled mentality. He saw the same problem in Poland and found (through hard experience) that investments in such companies were disasters.

11:00 We meet with a pharmaceutical company that is on the list of companies to be privatized. We are particularly interested in speaking with the research scientists who are developing new drugs. There is good brain power in Serbia and possibilities of new drug developments that could turn into blockbusters.

12:00 I have a lunch meeting with officials from one of the country's major banks. We are interested in getting their views on the government's privatization plans and macroeconomic policies. Were the government's budgetary policies leading to higher or lower debt? Was the money being spent wisely or was there lots of "leakage" so that there is no efficient allocation of resources? What are the bank's policies regarding loans? What percentage of loans were to the private sector as compared with government loans or purchases of government bonds? Do the laws protect the lender or the creditor? Is it difficult to legally collect loans?

13:30 I visit the factory of a dairy products company with my team. Since we have visited a number of dairy products factories around the world, we are looking for the telltale signs of unsanitary conditions, poor work-flow and general disorganization. In this case we are impressed; the factory is operated in good order.

15:00 Meeting with executives of a confectionary company. We are looking for consolidation possibilities because the industry is fragmented, with thin margins and high competition. We want to find out whether the management is interested in merging with other companies so that we could make an investment in a combined operation with larger market share and better profit margins.

16:30 Back to the hotel for a conference call with an institutional investor located in the US. Our investors want information regarding the progress of their investments. Typical questions include: Where are we finding bargains? What about performance? Why are we down or up? What are we doing about it? What about the general organization or our operations? Are there any changes that could impact our performance? We respond thoughtfully, always taking care not to breach any confidences.

17:30 I start answering e-mails again. Another 200 messages have piled up from our offices in Eastern Europe, Africa and Latin America. Also, there are some e-mails starting to come in from our corporate officers in the US.

18:30 I meet my team members for dinner to discuss today's company visits. Since we don't have an office in the Balkans, the analysts from Russia and Poland cover Serbia. During dinner we discuss our general impressions of the day's visits and focus on those companies in which we might invest.

The next step is for the analysts to prepare detailed documentation and analysis of the companies we have decided to target for possible future investment. While the final decisions for allocating investments are the responsibility of the manager, the research is a team effort and frequent discussions can lead to a consensus. We realize that no one person has all the wisdom and that the combined efforts of all our staff yield the best results.

20:00 I hold a conference call with my team of over 25 analysts located all over the world: Korea, China, Singapore, India, Turkey, Poland, Russia, South Africa, Brazil and Argentina.

21:30 I answer e-mails and download additional messages coming into my inbox. I also review company research and study the portfolio allocation recommendations made by analysts around the world.

23:00 I go to sleep. I will be flying to Istanbul the next day with three analysts.

Custodians

Mutual funds must place their portfolio securities and cash with a custodian bank for protection. These securities must be separated from the bank's assets to protect them in case the custodian goes bankrupt. The portfolio manager does not have physical possession of the assets it manages and does not have control of them other than to direct investments, provided that investments are within the scope and limitations outlined in the prospectus.

If the management company were to shut down, the fund's assets would be liquidated by the bank and distributed to shareholders, or transferred to another fund manager selected by the board of directors and approved by the shareholders.

Transfer Agents

Mutual funds also use third parties called transfer agents to keep records and distribute information. Transfer agents calculate and distribute dividends, maintain account records, and prepare and mail shareholder account statements, as well as other shareholder information. Some also manage customer service departments to provide fund information and answer shareholder questions. For some mutual funds, custodian banks play the role of transfer agent, while other funds hire an outside organization to perform these functions.

Mutual Fund Organizations

Athough we have described above all the specific functions required for a mutual fund to operate, many of these functions are undertaken by large mutual fund organizations with a number of divisions able to carry out a number of those functions. For example, there are firms that create and sponsor mutual funds; underwrite and distribute; undertake the transfer agency functions, and finally have fund managers who actually make the investment decisions.

 SUMMARY ————————————————————————————

Mutual funds, also known as unit trusts, provide investors with professional portfolio management, diversification, cost savings and a wide array of choice. The funds bring together a large group of investors that pool money to buy stocks and bonds or other securities and share the costs involved.

In the US, the first mutual funds, which issued new shares to investors as new money was invested, were created in 1924. A series of legislative changes increased regulation of the industry and fueled interest in mutual funds after the Great Depression. The amount of money invested in mutual funds started to soar in the 1980s with the growth of defined contribution plans used for retirement savings. New channels of distribution — such as fund supermarkets — and the growth of information available online also raised awareness of the benefits of fund investing.

Mutual funds are registered as separate companies, with their own directors and shareholders. Sponsors make the initial investment, register the fund, and organize the third parties needed to run the fund. Shareholders receive regular information about the fund and vote to make changes and elect directors. The board of directors oversees the management of the fund. The fund manager researches and chooses the specific securities to be bought and sold by the fund. The principal underwriter is responsible for attracting investors to the fund. Transfer agents keep records and distribute information to fund managers and investors. The custodian is responsible for the safekeeping of the securities and cash of the fund.

One has to distinguish open-end from closed-end fund types; the former redeem shares at any time, while the latter issue a fixed number of shares that trade on a stock exchange. A unit investment trust buys and holds a fixed portfolio of stocks until a specific date, when investors can receive their share of the assets. An exchange-traded fund is an open-end fund or a unit trust that trades its shares on stock exchanges like an equity security.

QUICK QUIZ

1. What are the five key benefits of investing in mutual funds?

2. Describe some profiles of investors who should not invest in mutual funds.

3. Name four key pieces of legislation that regulate the mutual fund industry. List at least one change made by each.

4. Mention three developments that have fueled the growth of the mutual fund industry during the past 25 years.

5. Identify the key roles and responsibilities of the fund's sponsor, shareholders, board of directors, investment adviser, principal underwriter, custodian and transfer agent.

6. How do mutual funds differ from other types of funds? Name two other types of funds and describe them.

TYPES OF MUTUAL FUNDS

2

Mutual funds come in all shapes and sizes and can vary significantly in terms of their composition and investment objectives. To choose the right fund, it is important to understand whether the fund's objectives match an investor's goals. Of course, everybody wants to make more money, but different individuals want their investments to work for them in different ways. Whether saving for retirement, a new home, a child's education or a dream vacation, there are funds that can match different needs, time horizons and risk profiles.

To choose an appropriate fund, investors must be able to clearly understand the different types of securities within fund portfolios, the investment objectives adopted by specific funds and the strategies used by fund managers to meet these goals.

As indicated by Figure 2.1, the number of mutual funds has grown dramatically, increasing by almost eight times between 1984 and 2004. In 2004, equity funds represented the largest number with half of the total, followed by bond funds, money market funds and hybrid funds (funds with both equities and bonds).

TYPES OF FUNDS

Equity Funds

Equity funds, possibly the most popular type of fund, invest in equities (also called stocks), which represent a share of ownership in a company and its profits. Mutual funds offer a low-cost way to build a diversified portfolio of stocks and gain access to the skills of professional money managers. Owning a large number of stocks as part of a fund minimizes the effect of any single stock's decline.

Equity funds make money for investors in three different ways:

- Dividends
- Capital gains distributions
- Share price appreciation

The combination of these elements is called the *total return* of the fund.

Figure 2.1 — Number of Mutual Funds by Type of Fund, 1984 and 2004

	1984	2004
Equity Funds	459	4,547
Hybrid Funds	89	510
Bond Funds	270	2,041
Money Market Funds	425	943
Total	1,243	8,041

Note: *Data for funds that invest in other mutual funds were excluded from the series.*

Source: *2006 Investment Company Fact Book, Copyright © by the Investment Company Institute (www.ici.org).*

Equity Fund Categories

Equity funds and the shares they invest in are categorized depending on different features such as the size of the company, dividend history, potential for capital appreciation, and reactions to economic changes.

Company Size

Capitalization, also known as market capitalization or market cap, is the total market value of a company's outstanding stock. The market value is determined by multiplying the number of common shares by the current price of a share. Companies are defined as large-cap, mid-cap, small-cap or micro-cap depending on the value of their capitalization.

- Large-cap: companies that generally have a market cap of more than $10 billion. The largest and most successful companies are often called blue chips, named after the most valuable chips in a casino poker game.

- Mid-cap: medium-sized companies with capitalization of between $2 billion and $10 billion.

- Small-cap: small companies with market values of between $300 million and $2 billion.

- Micro-cap: companies whose common shares have a total market value of less than $300 million. The shares of these companies are usually less liquid.

The measures used to define the size of a company in terms of capitalization vary among investment companies. The figures used above give a rough idea of how they are categorized. It is important to note that market cap sizes can be much smaller in less developed markets. For some emerging markets, for example, a market cap of $300 million could be considered large.

Why is capitalization important? Depending on market phases, smaller companies can sometimes be more volatile but produce greater total returns. Larger companies' shares may fluctuate less and produce lower returns than smaller companies' shares. Also, smaller companies would tend to be less liquid than larger one.

 TERMINOLOGY

GROWTH STOCKS — *Growth stocks are shares of companies that are growing rapidly because of the expanding market share for their products, and have had steady increases in sales and profits. Although these stocks are likely to be more expensive than the so-called value stocks (i.e. they may have a higher price to earnings ratio, higher price to book value ratio, and lower dividends), their prices may have dramatic increases for as long as they sustain their growth. These types of companies usually reinvest their earnings in the company and pay low or no dividends.*

INCOME STOCKS — *Income stocks usually pay a high portion of their earnings to shareholders in dividends. Conservative investors tend to favor these stocks, and they usually buy and hold them for a long period of time. As a result, the prices of these types of stocks do not usually have wide price fluctuations.*

VALUE STOCKS — *Value stocks are stocks that are considered to be under valued compared to their profits and assets. The earnings of such companies usually grow slowly compared to growth stocks, and some fund managers choose them because they feel markets do not fully recognize the potential of such companies for greater profits.*

Fund Objective
The categories of growth and income are usually further spliced to differentiate funds depending on how much risk they take to earn greater returns. These are called the fund's investment objective.

Growth
Funds with a growth objective invest primarily in large- and mid-cap companies whose share prices are expected to rise. Dividend payments are not a primary consideration. Some growth funds invest in small-cap stocks or companies in an industry or sector, such as biotechnology, with growth and greater earnings potential. There is a wide range of definitions of growth stocks among fund managers. As a result, some growth funds are more volatile than others depending on the manager's investment style. (For more information on investment styles see Chapter 4.)

Aggressive Growth

Aggressive growth funds invest in growth-oriented company shares whose market prices are expected to rise rapidly. These companies are typically mid- and small-cap. The fund manager may also invest in initial public offerings (IPOs); an IPO is the process by which companies raise capital by selling shares to the public for the first time.

Aggressive growth funds can focus on specific sectors or industries and use more speculative strategies. They can change strategies frequently and trade stocks more often than more conservative funds. These types of funds tend to show major gains during market rallies, but their prices can also tumble when the market declines.

Capital Appreciation

A capital appreciation fund tries to make money by investing in stocks whose prices are expected to increase due to a wide variety of factors (e.g. earnings growth), or simply because the shares are trendy among investors. Managers of these funds often trade frequently and use riskier strategies such as buying options, which are exchange-traded contracts that give the buyer the right to buy or sell an asset at a set price on or before a given date.

Equity Income/Dividend

Equity income or dividend funds generally invest in companies that pay a substantial percentage of their earnings in dividends. These companies typically have a long history of paying dividends and tend to increase dividend payments over time.

Growth and Income

Growth and income funds choose stocks that offer both capital appreciation as well as steady and increasing dividends. These types of funds have the potential to provide more capital appreciation than an income fund, but are less volatile than capital appreciation funds.

Value

Value funds often invest in companies that have been overlooked by the market. The shares of these companies usually have cheap price to earnings ratios. They may also look cheap relative to a benchmark such as the company's competitors.

Geography
International/Global

International funds can invest in any country except the fund's home country. For example, an international fund being sold in the US would not invest in the US. *Global* funds can invest in all countries, including the home country. This group of funds is usually focused on capital appreciation rather than dividend payments. Some international funds are further categorized according to specific geographical focuses. These include country or region-specific funds, emerging market funds, European stock funds, and Pacific stock funds, among many others.

Global funds often have between one quarter to half of their assets in their home country. Some investors see this as a way to protect themselves from foreign currency fluctuations and volatility in foreign markets. Still, because the mixture of foreign and domestic shares within a global fund changes, it can be difficult for an individual investor to set a long-term allocation of funds between both groups of stocks.

It is important to examine a particular international fund's country exposure to understand whether it prefers a few markets, a specific region, or whether it has a broader focus. Another key consideration is the fund's currency-hedging policy. When fund managers buy foreign stocks, they are also, in effect, investing in the country's currency. If the Japanese yen strengthens against the US dollar, a fund can make a gain even if its Japanese holdings do not appreciate. Some fund managers protect themselves from currency fluctuations by hedging, trading their exposure to foreign currencies for US dollars.

Emerging Markets

Among international funds, emerging market funds have gained popularity in recent years because of the large gains seen in certain markets. With many countries in the early stages of economic development and with underdeveloped capital markets, there is often great opportunity for growth and profit. In recent years, some international funds posted amazing returns of 100% or more in a single year.

Of course there is a price to be paid for the opportunity to access such astounding gains — the very real threat of major losses. The Morgan Stanley Capital International Emerging Markets Index (MSCI EMI), a key benchmark for such funds, gained 64% in 1999 and tumbled 32% in 2000.

Definitions of "emerging markets" vary, but the most commonly used is: all countries designated by the World Bank as "low and middle income," based on per capita income. Countries with per capita incomes of less than about $10,000 per year are normally included in this category.

Of course there are some unusual cases, such as Hong Kong. While it is often considered "developed," with one of the world's major stock exchanges, Hong Kong is included in the "emerging" category because it became part of China after the 1997 handover. In the case of Singapore, the companies listed on the exchange often have the largest part of their profits, earnings and/or operations in emerging countries such as Indonesia, China and Thailand. As a result, the city-state is also often listed as an emerging market for the purposes of fund management.

Currently, the emerging market countries comprise: all of Latin America, all of Africa, all of Eastern Europe, Russia and the former Soviet Union, and all of Asia except Japan, Australia and New Zealand.

Industry
Sector Funds
Sector funds are mutual funds that invest in a specific industry or sector. The sectors vary, but the leading funds usually focus on one or two industries. Key examples are technology funds in the late 1990s.

Of course the downside of such outsized rises is greater risk. At the end of 1999, nine of the 10 funds with the best 10-year returns were technology funds, according to Morningstar. By early 2002, only two were in the top 10. These types of funds are affected more by the risks associated with a specific industry than by the fluctuations of the overall stock market.

Many investors discover specific sector funds just as the area is about to cool off, because people tend to buy funds that already have posted impressive gains. These types of funds are often launched when the sector is already considered to be booming — the best time to attract the most investors, but often the worst time for the fund manager to invest. They are also usually more expensive than other funds because managers need more in-depth research to gain expertise in a certain industry.

Sector funds are often useful when included to help diversify an investor's portfolio that is already heavy on other industries.

Some popular types of sector funds include:

Technology: These funds invest in shares of companies that develop, distribute or service technology-related processes, including companies that produce computer chips, hardware and software.

Communications: These funds invest in shares of manufacturers of telecommunications equipment and service providers.

Financial services: These funds invest in shares of financial services companies, such as banks, brokerages, insurance companies and mutual fund companies. The funds could be affected by interest rate changes.

Health care: These funds invest in shares of health care companies, such as hospitals, pharmaceutical companies, drug-makers, biotechnology firms and health insurance companies.

Natural resources: These funds invest in shares of companies that explore, mine, distribute or process natural resources such as oil, metals, timber and coal.

Precious metals: These funds invest in shares of companies that mine, process or distribute precious metals such as gold, silver and platinum. The earnings of these companies are linked to the market price of the precious metal. The value of these funds may fluctuate more than the prices of the metals themselves.

Utilities: These funds invest in shares of public utilities companies such as electricity, gas and telephone companies.

Real estate: Real estate funds are an interesting addition to a portfolio because they have a lower correlation to the stock market, making them attractive when large-cap stocks are down. Real estate funds tend to be negatively correlated to bonds. Most real estate funds invest in real estate investment trusts (REITs), which are required to pay out most of their income as dividends to shareholders. These payouts tend to boost returns when the market is high and buffer losses when the market drops.

Fund of Funds

A fund of funds is a mutual fund that aims at investing in a group of top-performing funds. Ideally, this type of fund should offer diversification and asset allocation among different asset classes, sectors and countries, regardless of short-term market trends. Instead of having to research specific funds and study fund managers' records, a fund of funds does the legwork for you. It chooses the funds with the best records that fulfill a specific investment objective. Some funds of funds also target a specific retirement date and gradually move assets into more conservative income-producing securities as you get closer to retirement.

This type of one-stop shopping can be appealing, but there are several disadvantages that can affect performance. When investing in a fund of funds, investors could be charged with two sets of fees — first, the management fees and other charges that the fund requires, and second, the same expenses the underlying funds charge your fund. These charges are outlined in the fund's prospectus. Some companies avoid these double charges by creating a fund of funds using the funds in their own company's family of funds.

Alternatives to Mutual Funds
Closed-end Funds

A closed-end fund (known in the UK as an investment trust) is another type of fund that has some qualities of stocks and some characteristics of mutual funds. Like mutual or open-end funds, closed-end funds create a portfolio of assets with money from investors. But a closed-end fund usually issues shares to the public only once and has a fixed number of outstanding shares. It does not continually issue or redeem shares like a mutual fund. The value of one share of this pool is called the fund's net asset value (NAV), just like with mutual funds. Like stocks, closed-end funds trade on exchanges or the over-the-counter market. As a result, closed-end funds can have another price, known at the market price, besides their NAV. The market price is the price at which investors buy and sell shares of the closed-end fund.

Closed-end funds and *closed funds* are not the same. A closed fund is an open-end mutual fund that has stopped accepting new money, either permanently or temporarily.

Typically, closed-end funds invest in securities of foreign countries or specialized sectors because these assets have relatively lower liquidity than those traded on major stock exchanges. Since closed-end funds are traded on an exchange, it is easier for investors to have access to these illiquid assets.

Also, in a downturn, closed-end fund managers can still maintain their portfolio allocations because they are not required to redeem shares on a daily basis like mutual funds. This is an advantage because the securities in the fund's portfolio, which trade infrequently, would be harder to sell on demand. Instead, as investors sell the fund's shares on the exchange, the market value would be driven down to a deep discount to the NAV of the securities in the portfolio. In a mutual fund, the manager would have to liquidate some positions if the redemptions exceeded the cash in the fund.

As with any publicly traded company, closed-end fund shares are sold in an initial public offering (IPO). The initial price is based on the value of the securities in the portfolio plus an additional underwriting charge, which can be as large at 7%.

Closed-end funds can trade at a premium, discount or, rarely, exactly equal to their NAV. The shares of these funds often trade at a discount to their NAV. The ability to buy at a discount is a key benefit of the closed-end structure for investors. If held for a long period of time, the price may eventually return close to the fund's NAV. This price increase, combined with any dividends or interest, can provide a higher-than-average rate of return. This is particularly attractive to bond investors because funds pay out income based on their shares' NAV rather than the market price.

If a closed-end fund is trading at a big premium to its NAV, its board of directors and shareholders can raise more money through a rights offering, which would enable the shareholders to buy shares at the NAV and a discount to the market price at a specific time. If the fund is selling at a big discount to its NAV, the fund may be converted to an open-end structure. When the fund is converted, its price will be the same as its NAV. The difference between the discounted market price and the NAV would be a gain for the holders of the once closed-end fund.

Closed-end funds are less popular than mutual funds due to a variety of factors. With mutual funds, the pricing of the fund is more certain, while a closed-end fund may trade at a premium or discount to its NAV. Mutual funds often have more money to invest than closed-end funds because they continually accept new capital from investors by issuing more shares. This gives a mutual fund greater flexibility to purchase more company shares in different sectors.

Passively Managed Funds
Index Funds
Index funds, also called tracker funds or passively managed funds, try to

replicate the performance of a specific index, such as the Standard & Poor's 500 index. They do this by investing in the securities, or a representative sample, of the same companies that make up an index.

These funds must be fully invested at all times and hold very little or no assets in cash. While the allocations of the fund rarely change, if the composition of the index it follows changes, the fund must also adjust its portfolio.

Beyond large-cap stocks, the effectiveness of indexing varies depending on investing styles. The following are some examples of types of index funds:

Global Equity: These seek to mirror the performance of global equity indexes. The administrative costs of this type of index fund may be higher because markets in some of these countries are relatively illiquid. Foreign exchange risk is another consideration when considering this type of fund.

Actively managed emerging markets funds have more choice in terms of assets and may decide against investing in some countries that are experiencing a downturn, or political or economic instability. When following the index, a passive fund does not have this option.

Enhanced index fund: This is a fund that tries to beat the performance of an index rather than follow it. The fund's objective may be to outperform its benchmark index by say 0.1% or as much as 2%. The manager constructs the portfolio in various ways to meet these targets. For example, he may buy all the stocks in the index, but give particular companies or industries greater weighting. The manager may also buy most of the shares in an index and substitute some of the stocks with shares with similar capitalization and characteristics that he sees as undervalued or about to appreciate. He may also use options and futures to meet performance targets. Because enhanced index funds are actively managed, they trade more often and have higher transaction costs and management fees than traditional index funds.

Small capitalization index fund: In the US, this type of fund tracks a small-cap index, which includes companies with a capitalization of less than a certain amount.

Total market index fund: In the US, this type of fund tries to replicate the performance of an index that includes all listed stocks or, at least, most of the listed stocks in a market. Such indexes are considered one of the broadest measures of the overall stock market. For example, one index includes shares of more than 7,000 companies that trade on the New York Stock Exchange, American Stock Exchange (AMEX) and NASDAQ. Because the index has such a wide scope, it reflects the general performance of mid- and small-cap stocks, because there are more of them in the index than large-cap shares.

Exchange Traded Funds

Another type of passively managed fund is exchange traded funds, or ETFs. By 2006, these funds had attracted about $312.8 billion in assets, compared with about $9 trillion in traditional mutual funds, according to the Investment Company Institute. Like mutual funds, ETFs invest in securities. But in contrast to mutual funds, which investors can buy or sell only at the price at the close of the day, ETF's trade on stock exchanges just like stocks and closed-end funds. They can be purchased or sold at any time throughout the day.

ETFs usually try to mimic indices for a specific sector, country or the general market. Since 2000, large investment companies have come up with many new versions with names like SPDRs ("spiders"), HOLDRs, iShares, Diamonds, and Qubes.

There are some disadvantages to ETFs. Because ETFs trade like stocks, there can be a difference between their share price and the net asset value of their holdings. Still, managers of these funds often use methods such as arbitrage to make up the difference.

The lower costs enjoyed by investors can also be offset by the price of the broker's commissions charged when an investor buys or sells an ETF, just like a stock. If an investor makes regular payments into this type of fund over time, brokerage costs could end up exceeding the costs associated with investing in a regular index mutual fund.

Hedge Funds

The history of hedge funds dates back to the 1950s, when a small number of funds were set up with the ability to benefit not only from rising stock prices, but also from falling stock prices. These funds were able to use short-selling strategies, meaning selling borrowed securities in the hopes of buying them back later at a lower price and returning them to the lender.

Typically hedge funds have been reserved for very wealthy individuals and institutional investors. However, in recent years the number of hedge funds has exploded to more than 8,000 worldwide.

A few hedge funds have grabbed media headlines over the years, fueling a general perception that hedge funds are extremely risky because of high levels of gearing and the use of highly speculative investment strategies. However, the majority of hedge funds are created to offer investors low volatility and returns that are not correlated to any specific market. These qualities have made hedge funds attractive to large institutional investors such as pension funds. Entry levels are gradually being reduced, allowing some private investors to participate.

Bond Funds

Bond funds generally have lower volatility than stocks and can offer higher yields than money market funds. They are less popular than stock funds because they typically produce lower returns, but are often good options for conservative investors with low risk tolerance.

The main source of returns for bond funds is income payments from the fixed income securities in their portfolio rather than capital gains. Bond prices are directly influenced by changes in interest rates. As interest rates rise, bond prices fall, and vice versa. Bond prices stay relatively stable compared with stocks because interest rates usually do not change as often as companies report news that can affect their earnings.

Bond funds are also considered safer than stock funds because there is a lower chance an investor will lose his investment, and because issuers must pay interest and principal on the due date. When a company gets into financial trouble, bondholders have first access to assets and must be paid off in full before stockholders receive anything.

Governments or corporations issue bonds as a way of raising money. Their maturity refers to the date at which investors will be paid back. Bond funds can hold hundreds of individual bonds and are generally categorized by the average maturity of the bonds in their portfolio.

Short-term bond funds invest in bonds maturing within a few years. Intermediate-term bond funds hold bonds that mature within five to 10 years, while long-term bond funds hold bonds that mature in over 10 years.

Individual investment companies categorize their bond funds according to their own particular guidelines, so it is important to check the average maturity of a fund that says it holds intermediate-term bonds or some other category, before comparing performance with another bond fund in the same category. Longer-term bonds tend to pay higher yields than shorter-term bonds because they usually see greater price declines when interest rates rise.

Interest Rate Sensitivity

A bond fund's interest rate sensitivity is measured by *duration*, a more useful measure than maturity. For every 1% change in interest rates, the value of the bond fund should change by the duration of that fund. For example, when a bond fund has a duration of 10 years and interest rates rise by 1%, the value of the bond fund should decline. The shorter the bond duration, the less it is affected by changes in interest rates.

Creditworthiness

Bond funds are also categorized in terms of their creditworthiness. Credit rating agencies such as Fitch, Moody's and Standard & Poor's (S&P) rate bonds based on their credit quality and likelihood of default. Bonds with an AAA or AA rating by S&P are considered high-grade, and have little chance of default. These bonds, together with those rated A or BBB, are called investment-grade bonds. Funds holding BB or lower-rated bonds are known as junk bond funds or high-yield funds. These funds see a higher number of defaults but offer higher yields as compensation for the risk.

Bond Types

Bond funds are also differentiated by which type of organization issues the bonds they hold.

US Government Bonds

These are considered the safest types of bonds because they are backed by the US Treasury, which has never defaulted on a loan. As a result, US government bonds are considered AAA, the highest rating.

> **Treasury bills:** have a maturity of one year or less and have a fixed rate of interest. A treasury note has a maturity of one to 10 years, while a treasury bond has a maturity of 10 to 30 years. They also have a fixed interest rate.

> **Treasury inflation-protected securities (TIPS):** have a fixed interest rate, but investors' principal is adjusted every six months by a percentage equal to the rise and fall of the Consumer Price Index (CPI). TIPS are designed to protect investors from inflation risk, the possibility that the money invested will be worth less due to inflation when the bond matures.

> **Treasury STRIPS:** are US government zero-coupon bonds, meaning they do not make periodic interest payments. Instead they are sold at a discount and mature at par value. The difference between the discounted price and par value is the interest received on the investment at maturity.

Municipal Bonds

Municipal bonds are state and local government bonds that are exempt from federal taxes and exempt from state income taxes for those who reside in the state that issued them. These bonds often pay lower rates of interest than Treasury bonds because of their tax benefits.

Mortgage-backed Bonds

Also considered relatively safe are mortgage bonds backed by government agencies. These bonds are made up of a pool of home mortgages. The risk related to these bonds is that mortgage holders will prepay their mortgages, reducing the amount of interest paid to the bondholders. As a result, the prices of mortgage-backed bonds are often somewhat lower than Treasury bonds and their interest payments are a bit higher.

Government National Mortgage Association (GNMA): This agency, also known as "Ginnie Mae," issues debt securities that are backed by a pool of mortgages insured by the Veterans Administration (VA) and the Federal Housing Authority (FHA). These certificates make monthly payments that include both interest and return of principal.

Federal National Mortgage Association (FNMA): Commonly known as "Fannie Mae," this agency issues debt securities backed by a pool of insured mortgages (VA and FHA insured) and conventional home mortgages. These securities pay interest and principal monthly.

Federal Home Loan Mortgage Corporation: Also called "Freddie Mac," this agency issues debt securities backed by a pool of conventional home mortgages that it buys from banks. It makes monthly payments of both interest and principal.

Corporate Bonds

Corporate bonds typically offer the highest interest payments because they are considered the riskiest type of domestic bond. Corporate bonds with credit ratings of BB and below are considered junk bonds, which are also known as high-yield bonds.

International Bonds

International bonds are issued by foreign companies and governments. International bonds denominated in local currency can carry more risk because their interest payments can be offset by changes in currency prices.

Money Market Funds

Money market funds are probably one of the safest instruments for holding cash temporarily. These are mutual funds that invest in the short-term debts of companies and governments; they usually have higher returns than bank accounts.

Money market funds invest in low-risk, high-quality debt securities such as Treasury bills, banker's acceptances, repurchase agreements, short-term debts of US government agencies, commercial paper, and negotiable certificates of deposit.

While the prices of bonds and stock funds fluctuate in value, money market funds often try to keep their NAV, the daily value of a single share constant. The money manager does this by buying debt securities, which trade at a discount to their face value, when they have between one day and 90 days left to maturity. The difference between the discounted purchase price and the face value at maturity is the interest an investor earns. The interest is low because of the short time to maturity.

They offer a low-risk vehicle for short-term investments that need to be liquid. These funds are often used as temporary places to deposit money before it is invested in other securities. Some investors gradually withdraw money from these money market accounts as they find opportunities in stock and bond funds. Once an investor has established a money market fund with a particular mutual fund company, he can normally invest in other funds within the same family without additional paperwork.

There are some risks associated with money market funds. Inflation could chip away at investment returns over time. In the US, these funds are also not insured by the Federal Deposit Insurance Corporation (FDIC), which insures bank deposits up to a certain amount. However, federally insured banks do offer money market deposit accounts, which are savings accounts that pay money market rates. Still, these rates may be lower than those offered by better money market funds because of higher expenses. The Securities Investor Protection Corporation (SIPC) also insures money market investments in case the brokerage firm that holds the shares goes bankrupt.

It is important to remember that yields among funds can vary significantly because of expenses. Some sweep money funds, which are used as default vehicles that brokerage firms will "sweep" unused money into, can be subject to high fees, which, of course, reduce the total return.

"If I could pick just one keepsake, I think it would be the mutual funds."

Types of US Money Market Funds

Tax-exempt money funds: These invest in US municipal securities with short maturities of 30 to 90 days. The interest income earned is exempt from federal income taxes, but is subject to state and local taxes.

US Treasury money market funds: These invest in short-term US Treasury bills (T-bills). These funds are subject to federal taxes but not to state or local taxes.

US Government money market funds: These buy Treasury bills, federal agency notes and repurchase agreements with up to 90 days to maturity. Federal agency notes are debt securities issued by organizations such as the Federal National Mortgage Association (FNMA) and the Federal Home Loan Mortgage Corporation (FHLMC). They are subject to federal taxes but may be exempt from state taxes.

Other money market funds invest in a large pool of holdings of corporate investment grade debt such as commercial paper, debentures, mortgage bonds and equipment trust certificates.

Hybrid Funds

Hybrid funds invest in both stocks and bonds. These funds are seen as less risky than stock funds and may perform better than pure bond funds. The amount of risk associated with a specific hybrid fund depends on the mix of stocks and bonds in its portfolio and the fund manager's ability and skill in changing the allocations. Hybrid mutual funds may be categorised as "balanced funds" or "asset allocation funds."

Balanced Funds

Balanced funds invest in a percentage of stocks, bonds and cash equivalents. A common allocation would be 60% of the fund's total net assets in stocks and 40% in bonds.

Asset Allocation Funds

An asset allocation fund also invests in stocks, bonds and cash equivalents. However, the fund manager can adjust the mix of different investments according to changing market conditions and his economic expectations. The manager moves the fund's assets between stocks and bonds in order to get the best performance.

 SUMMARY

Mutual funds can be effective tools for fulfilling a variety of financial goals such as a university education, buying a new home and enjoying retirement. The key to achieving these goals is understanding the purpose of the investment, the investor's time frame and risk tolerance. These help determine what types of securities to include in a portfolio and the most appropriate investment style.

Mutual funds are categorized according to their objectives, facilitating the identification of the right match for an investor. Some conservative funds focus on regular income from dividends, while others will take on significant risk to try to achieve greater growth. These objectives are further spliced to create many different funds in between these extremes.

With so many fund objectives available, creating a diversified portfolio or investing in a very specific industry or region is easily achievable. If an investor wants exposure to a particular sector such as real estate, biotechnology or energy, a sector fund would be the right choice.

Investors often move into bond funds as they move closer to retirement, in order to reduce risk and volatility. While less volatile than stock funds, bond fund risk levels depend on their sensitivity to interest rates and the creditworthiness of the issuer. Money market funds are also used to stash emergency cash or as a place to hold money while awaiting new investment opportunities.

 QUICK QUIZ

1. On a given day, Company XYZ has 10.13 billion shares outstanding and the company is trading at $23 per share. What is the market capitalization?

2. Company ABC has a market cap of $1 billion. Is this considered a large-cap, mid-cap, small-cap or micro-cap company?

3. Company ABC has for the past three years paid out an annual dividend of 5%. During the period, its stock price has been range-bound between $18 and $21 and the price-earnings ratio has been in line with its peers. Would this company be considered a growth stock, income stock or value stock?

4. Why would an investor choose an actively managed emerging markets fund rather than a passively managed one?

5. How is the pricing of closed-end funds different from mutual or open-end funds?

6. Assume you are working as a financial adviser to a client who wants to invest in mutual funds. Before you make recommendations, what are some of the relevant questions you would ask?

7. Mr. Smith is going through his mutual fund portfolio and looking at results for the past year. His "US Blue-Chip" fund in US dollars is up by 8% and his "Japanese Equity Fund" in yen is up by 20%. During the past year the US dollar has weakened by 15% against the yen. In US dollar terms, which of the two funds has performed best?

MAKING SENSE OF MUTUAL FUND DOCUMENTS

3

M utual fund companies send out many reports filled with hundreds of pages of detailed information often needed to fulfill regulatory disclosure rules. Wading through all of the legalese can be tedious and not always useful. This chapter explores the key information an investor must focus on to understand a fund's investment policies, what it owns, who manages it, and its performance record.

PROSPECTUS

The most important document for a mutual fund is the prospectus, which explains the fund's:

- investment objectives

- strategy

- risks

- costs

- management

- performance history

- procedures for opening an account and buying and selling shares

Many prospectuses describe more than one fund within a family of funds. This saves the mutual fund company the cost of printing separate reports for funds run by the same management team or with similar objectives.

Investment Objectives

The investment objective describes a mutual fund's purpose. It explains issues such as whether the fund is trying to provide regular income or to make money over the long term. These are a general set of guidelines the fund uses to invest investors' money. This section is often quite broad.

Strategy

The strategy section describes the types of stocks, bonds or other securities in which the fund will invest to fulfill its objective. For equity funds, this section will explain the types of companies the fund is interested in buying, such as small companies that are growing quickly or large and well-established firms. Bond funds will describe in this section whether they hold corporate bonds or Treasuries or a combination of different types of bonds. The section will also explain whether the fund can invest in foreign securities. It will list any restrictions imposed upon the fund. The strategy should also explain how the fund manager decides which securities to buy and sell.

Risks

Investing in a fund always has risks and the prospectus must explain them in detail. For example, emerging market funds typically describe the risks associated with emerging economies such as currency fluctuations, market volatility, government involvement in the private sector, and less liquidity than in developed countries. Funds that invest in smaller and mid-sized companies will discuss how these stocks may have greater price volatility than larger companies. Funds will also explain their hedging policies and use of derivative securities. Bond funds explain the credit rating of the bonds they invest in and the possible effects of changes in interest rates.

In the US, the SEC requires that the fund company provide a bar chart that must show the annual total return for the fund for the previous 10 years or since inception. It must show the fund's average annual return for the past one, five, and 10 years, and how these compare to a broad measure of market performance. The fund must also show the highest and lowest quarterly return it has achieved over the 10-year period. This section may also provide examples of how the fund has performed in both bull and bear markets or, for bond funds, during periods when interest rates have changed.

Investment Adviser

This section gives details about the people that manage the investments of the fund. It often gives background information about the company, which can be an outside management firm, and the specific individuals that decide which securities to buy and sell for the fund's portfolio. It also usually lists the names and experience of the fund managers. Sometimes it only mentions a "management team" and provides further details in the fund's "Statement of Additional Information" or annual report. More information is often provided on the company's website. It is important to note how long the fund manager has been overseeing the fund and whether he is responsible for its past record. A look at other funds previously or currently managed by the current fund manager also gives insight into his style and experience.

EXAMPLE
ONE FUND PROSPECTUS DESCRIBES THE RISKS LIKE THIS:

This bar chart and table show the volatility of the Fund's returns, which is one indicator of the risks of investing in the Fund. The bar chart shows changes in the Fund's returns from year to year over the past nine calendar years. The table shows how the Fund's average annual total returns compare to those of a broad-based securities market index. Of course, past performance (before or after taxes) cannot predict or guarantee future results.

CLASS A ANNUAL TOTAL RETURNS

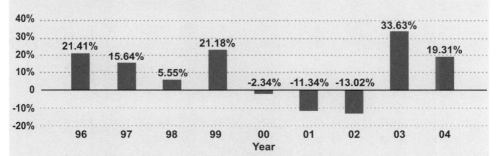

| Best Quarter: | | | Q2 'Q3 | 18.81% |
| Worst Quarter: | | | Q3 'Q2 | -20.92% |

	1 Year	5 Years	Since Inception (5/8/95)
Fund - Class A[2]			
Return Before Taxes	12.45%	2.50%	7.64%
Return After Taxes on Distributions	12.51%	1.84%	6.50%
Return After Taxes on Distributions and Sale of Fund Shares	8.66%	1.80%	6.06%
MSCI EAFE Index[3]	20.70%	-0.80%	5.58%

(Index reflects no deduction for fees, expenses or taxes)

EXAMPLE
INVESTMENT ADVISER SECTION

Management

ABC Advisers, is the Fund's investment manager.

The Fund is managed by a team of dedicated professionals focused on investments in equity securities. The portfolio managers of the team are as follows:

Mr. X, CFA, Executive Vice President of ABC Advisers

Mr. X has been a manager of the Fund since 2002. He has primary responsibility for the investments of the Fund. He has final authority over all aspects of the fund's investment portfolio, including but not limited to, purchases and sales of individual securities, portfolio risk assessment, and the management of daily cash balances in accordance with anticipated management requirements. The degree to which he may perform these functions and the nature of these functions, may change from time to time. He joined XYZ investments in 1993.

Mr. Y, CFA, Senior Vice President of Investment Counsel

Mr. Y has been manager of the Fund since 2004, providing research and advice on the purchases and sales of individual securities, and portfolio risk assessment. He joined XYZ Investments in 1998.

Ms. Z, CFA, Vice President of ABC Advisers

Ms. Z has been a manager of the Fund since 2000, providing research and advice on the purchase and sales of individual securities, and portfolio risk assessment. She joined XYZ investments in 1990.

Costs

Investing in mutual funds costs money and fees vary from fund to fund. Investment companies are required to list the costs related to owning a fund in the prospectus. This includes the sales commission the fund charges, if any, for buying and selling shares. It also tells you the management fees and operating expenses deducted each year to cover the costs of running a fund. It may even include the estimated cost of owning the fund over several time periods, assuming you invested, say, $10,000 at the beginning of the year.

CASE STUDY: ONE FUND DESCRIBES ITS STRATEGY IN THIS WAY:

Main Investment Strategies

Under normal market conditions, the Fund invests primarily in equity securities of companies that trade on a securities exchange or in the over-the-counter market. An equity security, or stock, represents a proportionate share of the ownership of a company; its value is based on the success of the company's business, any income paid to stockholders, the value of its assets, and general market conditions. Common stocks and preferred stocks are examples of equity securities.

The Fund may invest in securities of companies of any size market capitalization (share price multiplied by the number of common shares outstanding), including a significant portion of its assets in companies falling within the mid-cap (less than $8 billion) range. The Fund may invest a portion of its assets in foreign securities and small-cap companies.

The Fund's manager is a research-driven, fundamental investor, pursuing a growth strategy. As a "bottom-up" investor focusing primarily on individual securities, the manager chooses companies that it believes are positioned for above-average growth in revenues, earnings or assets. The manager relies on a team of analysts to provide in-depth industry expertise and uses both qualitative and quantitative analysis to evaluate companies for distinct and sustainable competitive advantages that are likely to lead to growth in earnings and/or share price. Advantages such as a particular market niche, proven technology, sound financial records, strong management, and industry leadership are all factors the manager believes point to strong growth potential.

In choosing individual equity investments, the Fund's manager also considers sectors that have growth potential and fast-growing, innovative companies within these sectors. Consequently, the Fund, from time to time, may have significant positions in particular sectors such as technology.

Temporary Investments

When the manager believes market or economic conditions are unfavorable for investors, the manager may invest up to 100% of the Fund's assets in a temporary defensive manner by holding all or a substantial portion of its assets in cash, cash equivalents or other high quality short-term investments. Temporary defensive investments generally may include short-term US government securities, commercial paper, bank obligations, repurchase agreements, money market fund shares, and other money market instruments. The manager also may invest in these types of securities or hold cash while looking for suitable investment opportunities or to maintain liquidity. In these circumstances, the Fund may be unable to achieve its investment goals.

This section of the prospectus also shows how a fund's annual operating expenses (ratio of total expenses to average net assets) have changed over time.

Financial Information

A chart known as "financial highlights" gives the fund's total return for each of the past five years or since inception. It also provides year-end net asset value (NAV) figures, the price per share of the fund. Some funds provide additional charts showing how the fund has changed in value over time or a table comparing the fund's performance to benchmark indexes. It is important to note the types of benchmarks chosen by the fund company to ensure they fit the fund's objectives.

Shareholder Information

This section describes how the fund's shares are priced, how a shareholder buys and sells shares, the fund's policy on dividends and capital gains, and the tax implications of investing in the fund. It may also discuss measures the fund has taken to discourage frequent trading, which adds costs to the management of the fund. These may include limits on the number of trades, minimum holding periods, restrictions on transaction requests made by telephone or e-mail, and special fees.

SHAREHOLDER REPORTS

Mutual funds may produce shareholder reports quarterly, semi-annually or annually. These reports give valuable information on how the fund performed over a specific period and the reasons for the performance. They also list all the investments the fund has made in stocks, bonds and other securities. In addition, shareholder reports include financial information such as the fund's costs and profits. Investors should focus on a few key sections of these reports to pull out valuable information that could affect their investment decisions.

EXAMPLE
DESCRIBING RISKS

One fund, which seeks capital appreciation by investing in securities of companies outside of the US, describes the risks associated with investing in the fund this way:

Main Risks
Stocks
Although this may not be the case in foreign markets, in the US, stocks historically have outperformed other types of investments over the long term. Individual stock prices, however, tend to go up and down more dramatically. These price movements may result from factors affecting individual companies or industries, or the securities market as a whole. A slower-growth or recessionary economic environment could have an adverse effect on the price of the various stocks held by the Fund. Value stocks are considered "cheap" relative to the company's perceived value. They may not increase in price, as anticipated by the manager, if other investors fail to recognize the company's value and do not bid up the price, the markets favor faster-growing companies, or the factors that the manager believes will increase the price of the security do not occur.

Foreign securities
Investing in foreign securities, including depositary receipts, typically involves more risks than investing in US securities. Certain of these risks also may apply to securities of US companies with significant foreign operations. These risks can increase the potential for losses in the Fund and affect its share price.

Currency exchange rates. Foreign securities may be issued and traded in foreign currencies. As a result, their values may be affected by changes in exchange rates between foreign currencies and the US dollar, as well as between currencies of countries other than the US. For example, if the value of the US dollar goes up compared to a foreign currency, an investment traded in that foreign currency will go down in value because it will be worth fewer US dollars.

Political and economic developments. The political, economic and social structures of some foreign countries may be less stable and more volatile than those in the US. Investment in these countries may be subject to the risks of internal and external conflicts, currency devaluations, foreign ownership limitations and tax increases. It is possible that a government may take over the assets or operations of a company or impose restrictions on the exchange or export of currency or other assets. Some countries also may have different legal systems that may make it difficult for the Fund to vote proxies, exercise sharholder rights, and pursue legal remedies with respect to its foreign invest-ments. Diplomatic and political developments, including rapid and adverse political changes, social instability, regional conflicts, terrorism and war, could affect the economies, industries, securities and currency markets, and the value of the Fund's investments, in non-US coun-tries. These factors are extremely difficult, if not impossible, to predict and take into account with respect to the Fund's investments.

Trading Practices. Brokerage commissions and other fees generally are higher for foreign securities. Government supervision and regulation of foreign stock exchanges, currency markets, trading systems and brokers may be less than in the US. The procedures and rules governing foreign transactions and custody (holding of the Fund's assets) also may involve delays in payment, delivery, or recovery of money or investments.

Availability of information. Foreign companies may not be subject to the same disclosure, accounting, auditing and financial reporting standards and practices as US companies. Thus, there may be less information publicly available about foreign companies than about most US companies.

Limited markets. Certain foreign securities may be less liquid (harder to sell) and more volatile than many US securities. This means the Fund may at times be unable to sell foreign securities at favorable prices.

Geographic concentration. Since the Fund may invest a significant portion of its assets in particular regions of the world, including Western Europe, it may be more sensitive to economic, business, political or other changes affecting issuers of securities in the region, which may result in greater fluctuation in the value of the Fund's shares.

Sector or industry focus
To the extent that the Fund has a significant portion of its assets in the equity securities of one or more sectors or industries at any time, the Fund will face a greater risk of loss due to factors affecting a single sector or industry than if the Fund always maintained wide diversity among the sectors and industries in which it invests. For example, investments in the financial services sector, which includes such issuers as commercial banks, insurance companies and finance companies, involve risks due to

factors such as governmental regulations, possible deterioration of the underlying credit quality of the loans in the issuers' portfolios, and losses when borrowers are unable to meet their loan obligations.

More detailed information about the Fund, its policies and risks can be found in the Fund's Statement of Additional Information (SAI).

 TERMINOLOGY

RATIO OF NET INVESTMENT INCOME TO AVERAGE NET ASSETS — *shows the ratio of annual dividends that the fund is paid from companies, in which it is invested, to the net asset value of the fund.*

TURNOVER RATE — *shows how often the fund trades its securities. It measures the percentage of the portfolio's holdings that has been traded over the year. A rate of less than 30% usually shows the fund has a buy-and-hold strategy. A high turnover of more than 100% denotes a manager that trades frequently.*

Chairman's Letter

One of the first sections of a shareholder report is a letter from the chairman and/or president of the company that runs the fund. The best letters explain the economic conditions prevalent during the report time period to help put the fund's performance in perspective. This section often gives a good overview of general market trends that provide a sound understanding of the investment environment beyond day-to-day market fluctuations.

Some annual reports will compare the fund's performance to relevant benchmarks or comparable funds to show whether the fund has met or exceeded these measures. It is not usually a concern if a fund underperforms a benchmark slightly over a short period such as six months or a year. Investing in mutual funds is usually for a longer period and more extensive historical comparisons may be more relevant. It is important to note whether the comparison is being made to a true peer.

Fund Manager's Letter

The fund manager's letter is much more specific than the chairman's letter and usually explains the most recent changes made to a portfolio and the reasons for reallocations. An effective letter will discuss individual stocks or

EXAMPLE
SAMPLE OF A FINANCIAL
HIGHLIGHTS SECTION:

Financial Highlights
This table presents the Fund's financial performance for the past five years. Certain information reflects financial results for a single Fund share. The total returns in the table represent the rate that an investor would have earned or lost on an investment in the Fund assuming reinvestment of dividends and capital gains. This information has been derived from the financial statements audited by Auditor XYZ whose report, along with the Fund's financial statements, are included in the annual report, which is available upon request.

CLASS A — *Year Ended September 30*

	2005	2004	2003	2002	2001
Per share operating performance (for a share outstanding through the year)					
Net asset value, beginning of year	$22.01	$20.17	$15.37	$18.76	$28.60
Income from investment operations:					
	2005	**2004**	**2003**	**2002**	**2001**
Net investment income (loss)*	(0.01)	(0.09)	(0.06)	0.03	0.44
Net realized and unrealized gains (losses)	2.98	1.93	4.86	(3.11)	(9.70)
Total from investment operations	2.97	1.84	4.80	(3.08)	(9.26)
Less distributions from:					
Net investment income	—	—	—	(0.29)	(0.58)
Tax return of capital	—	—	—	(0.02)	—
Total distributions	—	—	—	(0.31)	(0.58)
Redemption fees	—°	—°	—	—	—
Net asset value, end of year	$24.98	$22.01	$20.17	$15.37	$18.76
Total return[b]	13.49%	9.12%	31.23%	(16.83)%	(32.86)%
Ratios/supplemental data					
Net assets, end of year (000's)	$628,732	$640,120	$558,687	$413,309	$530,074
Ratios to average net assets:					
Expenses	1.00%	0.97%	1.04%	1.00%	0.95%
Net investment income (loss)	(0.02)%	(0.41)%	(0.40)%	0.13%	1.93%
Portfolio turnover rate	17.26%	14.93%	13.68%	8.11%	4.07%

*Based on average daily shares outstanding.
[b]Total return does not reflect sales commissions or the contingent deferred sales charge.
° Amount is less than $0.01 per share.

bonds that the fund owns and the countries or industries in which it invests. It may also describe the obstacles and drivers for the fund's performance. The fund manager's letter may also discuss his strategy and the future outlook.

Fund Performance

Investors should focus on the performance section to understand how the fund is doing. A shareholder report will compare the fund's performance to a relevant benchmark in a chart or a graph. A quality shareholder report will also explain the fund's performance over many different time frames, in both bull and bear markets.

The performance section may also show the results of a hypothetical investment so investors may better understand the possible results of an actual investment in the fund.

The fund performance page of reports will include the different classes of shares. For example, the fund may have four classes of shares: Class Z, Class A, Class B and Class C, each with different sales charges and other conditions. Therefore the performance of the different classes will differ.

Portfolio Holdings

Shareholder reports often list the fund's largest holdings and give some details about these companies and why the manager chose them for the fund. Some funds also give charts explaining how the portfolio is allocated according to industries or countries.

This section also gives a complete list of the fund's holdings, including

EXAMPLE
EXCERPT FROM A SAMPLE FUND
MANAGER LETTER

"Our bottom-up investment strategy frequently results in a portfolio that has a very different geographic and industry mix compared to the Fund's benchmark, the MSCI World Index. In particular, the Fund was substantially overweighted in the UK and underweighted in the US. Both factors positively contributed to Fund performance during the year under review. Strong stock selection and an overweighted position in the aerospace and defense industry also helped the Fund's relative performance. For example, XYZ company appreciated in value 70%, while ABC company rose 50%. Another strong performer was DEF. We purchased the company's shares in 2002 and 2003 at an average price of $30.86 per share, at a time when there was widespread pessimism about the outlook for global commercial aircraft sales. The Fund sold its stake in DEF during the period at an average price of $62.78 per share....

Despite the Fund's strong performance during the year, there were detractors, including a number of the Fund's Japanese investments. Japanese equity markets have underperformed those in the US by a wide margin in the past 10 years. Consistent with our strategy, we found opportunities to invest in companies we believe were undervalued on a five-year view. As a result, exposure to the Japanese market increased from 7.1% of the Fund's total net assets one year ago to 10.6%"

stocks, bonds and cash. It is a useful place to find out whether the fund is focused on a few companies or many different ones within a specific industry. If the section on investment objectives is too vague, reading the portfolio holdings section will give a more thorough description of the fund's true focus. By examining the large number of securities owned by a fund, it becomes clear how mutual funds diversify investments.

Financial Information
The fund's annual report ends with pages of financial statements. While there are a lot of data to sift through, one key area to look at is the fund's "Selected Per Share Data." This is often located towards the end, before the explanation of accounting practices. This section gives the fund's NAV,

EXAMPLE
FEES CHARGED BY A GLOBAL BOND FUND

Fees and Expenses

This table describes the fees and expenses that you may pay if you buy and hold shares of the Fund.

SHAREHOLDER FEES *(fees paid directly from your investment)*

	Class A	Class C
Maximum sales charge (load) as a percentage of offering price	4.25%[1]	1.00%
Load imposed on purchases	4.25%[1]	None
Maximum deferred sales charge (load)	None[2]	1.00%
Redemption fee on shares sold within 7 calendar days following their purchase date[3]	2.00%	2.00%

Please see "Choosing a Share Class" for an explanation of how and when these sales charges apply.

ANNUAL FUND OPERATING EXPENSES *(expenses deducted from Fund assets)*

	Class A	Class C
Management fees	0.45%	0.45%
Distribution and service (12b-1) fees	0.25%	0.65%
Other expenses (including administration fees)	0.35%	0.35%
Total annual Fund operating expenses	1.05%	1.45%

1. The dollar amount of the sales charge is the difference between the offering price of the shares purchased (which factors in the applicable sales charge in this table) and the net asset value of those shares. Since the offering price is calculated to two decimal places using standard rounding criteria, the number of shares purchased and the dollar amount of the sales charge as a percentage of the offering price and of your net investment may be higher or lower depending on whether there was a downward or upward rounding.

2. There is a 1% contingent deferred sales charge that applies to investments of $1 million or more and purchases by certain retirement plans without an initial sales charge.

3. The redemption fee is calculated as a percentage of the amount redeemed (using standard rounding criteria), and may be charged when you sell or exchange your shares or if your shares are involuntarily redeemed. The fee is retained by the Fund and generally withheld from redemption proceeds. For more details, see "Redemption Fee" section.

Example

This example can help you compare the cost of investing in the Fund with the cost of investing in other mutual funds. It assumes:

• You invest $10,000 for the periods shown;

• Your investment has a 5% return each year; and

• The Fund's operating expenses remain the same.

Although your actual costs may be higher or lower, based on these assumptions your costs would be:

	1 Year	3 Years	5 Years	10 Years
If you sell your shares at the end of the period:				
Class A	$528[1]	$745	S980	S1,653
Class C	$248	$459	$ 792	$1,735
If you do not sell your shares:				
Class C	$148	$459	$792	$1,735

1. Assumes a contingent deferred sales charge (CDSC) will not apply

expense ratio and turnover ratios annually for the past five years. A change in turnover rates may signal a shift in the fund manager's strategy.

Investors will also be interested in the explanation of the fund's expenses in the Statement of Operations. The amount of unrealized or undistributed capital gains is found in the Statement of Assets and Liabilities. This is important if the investor is subject to capital gains tax. When the fund sells shares that have risen in price, it realizes gains. Investing in a fund with a high number of unrealized gains may bring a high tax bill down the line.

Footnotes
Footnotes in the shareholder report often contain some of the most valuable information. Do not gloss over them! Investors may find out the fund is hedging currencies or shorting stocks. Footnotes may also give details about stocks that may be illiquid and cannot be sold quickly.

Statement of Additional Information
While it is not routinely sent out to shareholders, a Statement of Additional Information (SAI) can be a valuable source of information for investors in US funds. Investors can request it from fund management companies. These documents can give much more detail than a prospectus or annual report about what the fund is allowed to invest in and what restrictions are placed upon the fund.

The SAI also gives details about the board of directors and how they are compensated. It includes information about the committees of the board, board members' ownership of shares in the fund they oversee, and the code of ethics relating to the fund. The SAI discloses if anyone controls the fund by owning more than 25% of its voting securities. It also lists any principal holders, who hold 5% or more of the shares.

The SAI also provides more detailed information about the people responsible for managing the fund. It includes the other accounts managed by these individuals, total assets under management, and any conflicts of interest in managing the fund or others. It gives a description of how the fund manager is compensated, including benchmarks based on portfolio performance to help determine pay, as well as the portfolio manager's ownership of the fund's securities. The SAI also gives more details about how the fund spends money, such as payments for brokers and marketing.

Fact Sheet
Perhaps the first information an investor will see when doing research on investment opportunities is the mutual fund's fact sheet. This is usually a one- or two-page information sheet that is a quick snapshot with the key facts about the fund. Fact sheets are a great place to start when considering whether a fund is worth including in a portfolio. They are

OPINION
THE IMPORTANCE OF TECHNOLOGY

It's abundantly clear that the Internet has tremendous potential as a tool of investor information and education. The question is: How can we take the fullest advantage of it to improve the accessibility, utility and quality of the information we provide?

I believe a key benefit of the Internet is that it provides a means for dealing with the conflicting pressures that have continually afflicted fund disclosure. The dilemma we face is that the more disclosure that regulators mandate, the more difficult it is to make information easy to understand. On the other hand, the more we might try to make the information understandable, the more difficult it would be to include all of the detail that some market participants require.

As we think about the current disclosure system, one thing is clear: One size fits none.

The Internet offers a solution. It's called choice. Investors can get the information they need, in a form they are likely to use. And we can still provide more detailed information to those investors — or other marketplace participants — who want it. We can inform millions of average investors more effectively.

For a start, we can begin to move forward on providing investors with interactive data. SEC Chairman Christopher Cox has emphasized that this can help put investors "in the driver's seat." The Commission's initiative to advance eXtensible Business Reporting Language, or XBRL, is designed to accomplish this objective — facilitating automated search, retrieval, and analysis of tagged data over the Internet.

To date, the SEC's XBRL initiative has focused principally on financial data. But when it comes to mutual fund disclosure, financial statements are not the source of information that is most useful to investors. To allow mutual fund investors to reap the benefits of XBRL, we need a custom-designed taxonomy that goes beyond financial data.

There's a growing consensus that it's time to make the fullest use of the technology available so that investors have the information they need, all the information they want, in the format that makes it as valuable as possible for them. The Institute looks forward to working with the Commission and all stakeholders to achieve this goal.

Source: Stevens, Paul Schott. *"Using the Internet to Better Inform Investors,"* Mutual Funds and Investment Management Conference, Phoenix, AZ: March 20, 2006. Reprinted with permission from the Investment Company Institute.

EXAMPLE
SAMPLE ANNUAL REPORT
PERFORMANCE PAGE

Performance Summary as of 12/31/05

Your dividend income will vary depending on dividends or interest paid by securities in the Fund's portfolio, adjusted for operating expenses of each class. Capital gain distributions are net profits realized from the sale of portfolio securities. The performance table and graphs do not reflect any taxes that a shareholder would pay on Fund dividends, capital gain distributions, if any, or any realized gains on the sales of Fund shares. Total return reflects reinvestment of the Fund's dividends and capital gain distributions, if any, and any unrealized gains or losses.

Price and Distribution Information

CLASS Z		CHANGE	12/31/05	12/31/04
Net Asset Value (NAV)		+$1.14	$21.59	$20.45
Distributions (1/1/05 - 12/31/05)				
Dividend Income	$0.4874			
Short-Term Capital Gain	$0.4241			
Long-Term Capital Gain	$0.7822			
Total	**$1.6937**			
CLASS A		CHANGE	12/31/05	12/31/04
Net Asset Value (NAV)		+$1.14	$21.61	$20.47
Distributions (1/1/05 - 12/31/05)				
Dividend Income	$0.4269			
Short-Term Capital Gain	$0.4241			
Long-Term Capital Gain	$0.7822			
Total	**$1.6332**			
CLASS B		CHANGE	12/31/05	12/31/04
Net Asset Value (NAV)		+$1.08	$21.17	$20.09
Distributions (1/1/05 - 12/31/05)				
Dividend Income	$0.2795			
Short-Term Capital Gain	$0.4241			
Long-Term Capital Gain	$0.7822			
Total	**$1.4858**			
CLASS C		CHANGE	12/31/05	12/31/04
Net Asset Value (NAV)		+$1.12	$21.51	$20.39
Distributions (1/1/05 - 12/31/05)				
Dividend Income	$0.2833			
Short-Term Capital Gain	$0.4241			
Long-Term Capital Gain	$0.7822			
Total	**$1.4896**			

The Fund paid distributions derived from long-term capital gains totaling 78.22 cents ($0.7822) per share in June and December 2005. The Fund designates such distributions as capital gain dividends per Internal Revenue Code Section 852(b)(3)(C).

Performance

Class A: 5.75% maximum initial sales charge; Class B: contingent deferred sales charge (CDSC) declining from 4% to 1% over six years and eliminated thereafter; Class C: 1% CDSC in first year only. Cumulative total return excludes sales charges. Average annual total return and value of $10,000 investment include maximum sales charges.

CLASS Z	1-YEAR	5-YEAR	INCEPTION (8/19/97)
Cumulative Total Return	+14.14%	+92.50%	+254.10%
Average Annual Total Return	+14.14%	+14.00%	+16.31%
Value of $10,000 Investment	$11,414	$19,250	$35,410

CLASS A	1-YEAR	5-YEAR	INCEPTION (8/19/97)
Cumulative Total Return	+13.82%	+89.22%	+244.75%
Average Annual Total Return	+7.27%	+12.26%	+15.12%
Value of $10,000 Investment	$10,727	$17,832	$32,493

CLASS B	1-YEAR	5-YEAR	INCEPTION (8/19/97)
Cumulative Total Return	+13.03%	+83.20%	+148.84%
Average Annual Total Return	+9.03%	+12.62%	+13.92%
Value of $10,000 Investment	$10,903	$18,120	$24,884

CLASS C	1-YEAR	5-YEAR	INCEPTION (8/19/97)
Cumulative Total Return	+13.06%	+83.13%	+226.60%
Average Annual Total Return	+12.06%	+12.86%	+15.19%
Value of $10,000 Investment	$11,206	$18,313	$32,660

Performance data represent past performance, which does not guarantee future results. Investment return and principal value will fluctuate, and you may have a gain or loss when you sell your shares. Current performance may differ from figures shown.

(con't)

Total Return Comparision for Hypothetical $10,000 Investment[1]
Total return represents the change in value of an investment over the periods shown. It includes any current, applicable, maximum sales charge, Fund expenses, account fees and reinvested distributions. The unmanaged indexes include reinvestment of any income or distributions. They differ from the Fund in composition and do not pay management fees or expenses.

Class Z (8/19/97 - 12/31/05)

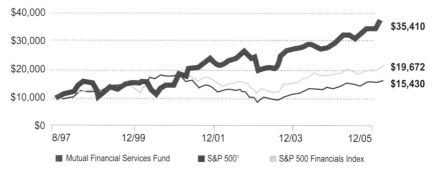

■ Mutual Financial Services Fund   ■ S&P 500[1]   ▨ S&P 500 Financials Index

Average Annual Total Return

Class Z	12/31/05
1-Year	+14.14%
5-Year	+14.00%
Since Inception (8/19/97)	+16.31%

Class A (8/19/97 - 12/31/05)

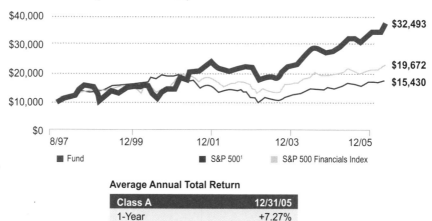

■ Fund   ■ S&P 500[1]   ▨ S&P 500 Financials Index

Average Annual Total Return

Class A	12/31/05
1-Year	+7.27%
5-Year	+12.26%
Since Inception (8/19/97)	+15.12%

(con't)

Class B (1/1/99 - 12/31/05)

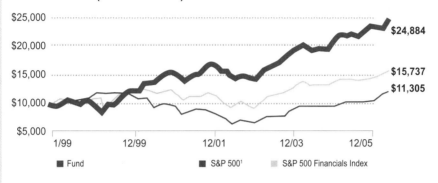

$24,884

$15,737

$11,305

| | Fund | ■ S&P 500[1] | ▨ S&P 500 Financials Index |

Average Annual Total Return

Class B	12/31/05
1-Year	+9.03%
5-Year	+12.62%
Since Inception (1/1/99)	+13.92%

Class C (8/19/97 - 12/31/05)

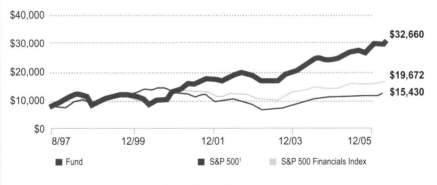

$32,660

$19,672

$15,430

| | Fund | ■ S&P 500[1] | ▨ S&P 500 Financials Index |

Average Annual Total Return

Class C	12/31/05
1-Year	+12.06%
5-Year	+12.86%
Since Inception (8/19/99)	+15.19%

(con't)

usually posted on the company's website monthly or quarterly, but they are not routinely mailed out to clients or required by regulators.

Fact sheets include a summary of the fund's investment objectives and other important data such as the launch date, fund size, fund manager's name, minimum investment, base currency, fees, benchmark, the rating it received from research companies, and the ticker symbol it uses for trading.

The fact sheet gives the names of the fund's largest holdings and their size relative to the fund's assets. Annual performance is often shown in a graph compared with a benchmark and a chart shows returns over one month, three months, six months, one year, three years or more, and since its launch.

This document often includes pie charts showing allocations by sector and by region or country. It could also contain a brief report by the fund manager, discussing its performance, recent portfolio changes and current positions.

INFORMATION GATHERING

Investors can request a prospectus, fact sheet, SAI or annual report directly from the investment company by phone, from brokers, or by e-mail. Many of these documents can also be easily downloaded from company websites. In the US, all mutual fund companies file prospectuses and shareholder reports with the SEC.

EXAMPLE
STATEMENT OF INVESTMENT

	INDUSTRY	SHARES	VALUE
Common Stocks 92.1%			
Bermuda 1.6%			
*Accenture Ltd, A	IT Services	3,395,700	$ 82,855,080
ACE Ltd.	Insurance	3,700,000	164,317,000
XL Capital Ltd., A	Insurance	2,600,000	180,700,000
			427,872,080
Canada 2.1%			
Barrick Gold Corp.	Metals & Mining	8,000,000	209,609,635
BCE Inc.	Diversified Telecommunication Services	12,325,460	322,526,670
			532,136,305
Denmark 1.2%			
TDC AS	Diversified Telecommunication Services	6,000,000	318,481,343
Finland 1.8%			
Stora Enso OYJ, R (EUR/FIM Traded)	Paper & Forest Products	17,000,000	233,781,450
Stora Enso OYJ, R (SEK Traded)	Paper & Forest Products	145,997	2,018,054
UPM-Kymmene Corp.	Paper & Forest Products	12,000,000	239,763,197
			475,562,701
France 3.1%			
Accor SA	Hotels, Restaurants & Leisure	6,100,000	321,626,788
France Telecom SA	Diversified Telecommunication Services	7,000,000	210,742,477
Sanofi-Aventis	Pharmaceuticals	3,130,141	267,150,663
Total SA, B	Oil, Gas & Consumable Fuels	26,062	6,849,793
			806,369,721
Germany 3.4%			
Bayerische Motoren Werke AG	Automobiles	2,502,876	112,363,945
Deutsche Post AG	Air Freight & Logistics	335,080	8,459,654
E.ON AG	Electric Utilities	2,919,990	278,745,962
Muenchener Rueckversicherungs-Gesellschaft	Insurance	222,060	24,854,397
bMuenchener Rueckversicherungs-Gesellschaft, 144A	Insurance	5,417	606,306
Siemens AG	Industrial Conglomerates	5,000,000	380,796,744
Volkswagen AG	Automobiles	1,307,970	68,802,319
			874,629,327
Hong Kong 2.8%			
Cheung Kong Holdings Ltd.	Real Estate	33,999,800	368,799,822
Hong Kong Electric Holdings Ltd.	Electric Utilities	42,000,000	202,929,880
Swire Pacific Ltd., A	Real Estate	9,190,000	87,327,852
Swire Pacific Ltd., B	Real Estate	38,554,500	71,685,231
			730,742,785
Italy 1.5%			
Eni SpA	Oil, Gas & Consumable Fuels	13,400,000	396,645,289

EXAMPLE
STATEMENT OF ASSETS AND LIABILITIES

Statement of Assets and Liabilities, August 31, 2005

Assets:

Investments in securities:

Cost - Unaffiliated issuers	$20,154,201,119
Cost - Non-controlled affiliated issuers	1,081,423,156
Total cost of investments	$21,235,624,275
Value - Unaffiliated issuers	$24,860,164,414
Value - Non-controlled affiliated issuers	1,174,931,123
Total value of investments	26,035,095,537
Cash	4,850
Foreign currency, at value (cost $14,571)	13,389

Receivables:

Investment securities sold	18,966,794
Capital shares sold	50,004,064
Dividends and interest	42,742,083
Total assets	26,146,826,717

Liabilities:

Payables:

Investment securities purchased	115,589,704
Capital shares redeemed	23,122,249
Affiliates	23,497,572
Other liabilities	2,524,582
Total liabilities	164,734,107
Net assets, at value	$25,982,092,610

Net assets consist of:

Paid-in capital	$19,913,029,291
Undistributed net investment income	360,503,840
Net unrealized appreciation (depreciation)	4,799,308,628
Accumulated net realized gain (loss)	909,250,851
Net assets, at value	$25,982,092,610

EXAMPLE
FACT SHEET

GROWTH OF A $10,000 INVESTMENT (WITHOUT SALES CHARGE)
November 29, 1954 to June 30, 2006

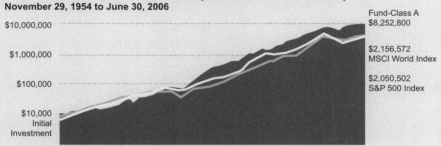

$10,000,000	Fund-Class A
	$8,252,800
$1,000,000	$2,156,572 MSCI World Index
$100,000	$2,050,502 S&P 500 Index
$10,000 Initial Investment	

If the sales charge had been included, the return would have been lower.

AVERAGE ANNUAL TOTAL RETURNS
As of June 30, 2006

		With Maximum Sales Charges[1]				Without Sales Charges			
CLASS	INCEPTION	1-YEAR	5-YEAR	10-YEAR	SINCE INCEPTION	1-YEAR	5-YEAR	10-YEAR	SINCE INCEPTION
A	11/29/54	8.49%	9.10%	9.83%	13.77%	15.13%	10.30%	10.48%	13.90%
B	5/1/95	13.25%	9.57%	9.66%	10.40%	14.25%	9.57%	9.66%	10.40%

GEOGRAPHIC BREAKDOWN[1]

- Europe 41.11%
- North America 40.17%
- Asia 12.62%
- Latin America/Caribbean 0.72%
- Mid-East/Africa 0.57%
- Fixed Income 0.53%
- Cash 4.28%

TOP 10 HOLDINGS[1]

Company A 2.38%	Company F 1.97%
Company B 2.33%	Company G 1.82%
Company C 2.10%	Company H 1.81%
Company D 2.10%	Company I 1.77%
Company E 2.03%	Company J 1.72%

FUND GOAL
The Fund seeks long-term capital growth by investing mainly in the equity securities of companies of any nation, including emerging markets.

Fund Data[1]

Assets .... $30 billion   Beta[2] 0.79
Number of Holdings 98   Dividends .... Annually in Octocber and,
Inception .... 11/29/54   if necessary, December

Symbol

Class A	Class C	Class R	-
ABCDE	FGHIJ	KLMNO	-

MAXIMUM SALES CHARGES
Class A 5.75% initial sales charge   **Class C** 1% contingent deferred sales charge (CDSC) in the first year only

Performance data represent past performance, which does not guarantee future results. Current performance may differ from figures shown. The fund's investment return and principal value will change with market conditions, and you may have a gain or a loss when you sell your shares. The fund may charge a 2% fee on redemptions within seven days.

Not FDIC Insured | May Lose Value | No Bank Guarantee

OPINION
CHOOSING MUTUAL FUNDS

Investors have searched for years for a reliable way to choose mutual funds that are likely to outperform the market. Of the few approaches that have shown promise on paper, most require access to hard-to-find data, or statistical techniques beyond the reach of all but the most sophisticated of quantitative research firms.

A new study has taken a big step forward, suggesting a selection method so easy and direct that investors can only wonder why it hasn't received more attention. The idea is to compare each fund's returns with how it would have performed had it simply held, without trading, the stocks it listed in its most recent public disclosure.

The study was done by three finance professors: Marcin Kacperczyk of the University of British Columbia and Clemens Sialm and Lu Zheng of the University of Michigan. They focused on what they called the "return gap": the difference between a fund's actual returns and what it would have earned had it stuck with its most recently listed holdings. The SEC requires that funds make such disclosures twice a year; the professors report that nearly half of all funds do so at least quarterly.

The study found that, on average, funds with consistently positive

return gaps were much better bets for future performance than those that were consistently negative, regardless of the frequency of portfolio disclosures.

The professors say they believe that their approach works well because it evaluates fund performance more precisely than the customary practice of comparing it with a market benchmark. The benchmark comparisons are fraught with peril, because a fund can look unjustifiably good or bad if it is compared with the wrong index....

The professors' approach sidesteps these problems because each fund is compared only with itself — or what its performance would have been had it not made changes in its portfolio. In this approach, the usual fund pigeonholes don't mean a thing. It doesn't matter whether the fund's manager is more oriented to small- or large-cap stocks, or is more of a value manager than a growth manager, or whether his style falls outside standard categories. With such issues now moot, the professors believe that a fund with a consistently positive return gap should be a particularly good bet....

Source: Mark Hulbert, *New York Times*
January 8, 2006

CASE STUDY: PLAIN ENGLISH FOR INVESTORS

In 1993, Arthur Levitt, Jr., the incoming chairman of the SEC, was shocked by the often-incomprehensible language used in mutual fund prospectuses. When searching for funds to invest in, he found that the language used in these official documents was often "unintelligible." If the chairman of the SEC couldn't understand the jargon, what about the general population?

Levitt spearheaded an initiative to improve investor disclosure by making prospectuses and other documents filed with the SEC more coherent and easily readable. In 1998, the SEC adopted rules requiring mutual funds to use plain English in the cover page, summary, and risk factor sections of all prospectuses. Writers must now use straightforward, clear language while writing, organizing and designing these sections.

The SEC published a handbook called "A Plain English Handbook: How to Create Clear SEC Disclosure Documents" to teach mutual fund companies how to improve their writing. Warren Buffett, known for writing clear letters to Berkshire Hathaway shareholders, wrote an introduction to the manual and stressed the need to write with a specific audience in mind.

"I pretend that I'm writing to my sisters.... Though highly intelligent, they are no experts in accounting or finance. They will understand plain English, but my jargon will puzzle them."

The main problems found in the language used in prospectuses were:

- Long sentences

- Passive voice

- Weak verbs

- Superfluous words

- Legal and financial jargon

- Numerous defined terms

- Abstract words

- Unnecessary details

- Unreadable design and layout

Instead, prospectuses should use everyday words, short sentences, active voice, regular print and personal pronouns that speak directly to the reader. Here's an example of a phrase commonly used in prospectuses that was rewritten in plain English in the SEC handbook:

"No person has been authorized to give any information or make any representation other than those contained or incorporated by reference in this joint proxy statement prospectus, and, if given or made, such information or representation must not be relied upon as having been authorized."

Here is the suggested plain English rewrite:

"You should rely only on the information contained in this document or that we have referred to you. We have not authorized anyone to provide you with information that is different."

Which do you prefer?

Sources: Gremillion Lee, *Mutual Fund Industry Handbook*, John Wiley & Sons, Hoboken, New Jersey: 2005 p.63. *A Plain English Handbook, How to Create Clean SEC Disclosure Document*. US Securities and Exchange Commission, Aug. 1998 http://www.sec.gov/pdf/plain.pdf

 SUMMARY

Mutual funds publish detailed documents to fulfill regulators' disclosure rules. These include the prospectus, shareholder reports, and, in the US, the Statement of Additional Information. They also print fact sheets to provide key shareholder information and to market their funds. Investors should focus on a few key areas of these publications to gather important data necessary for informed investment decision-making.

A prospectus discusses the fund's investment objectives, strategy, risk, management, costs and performance. An investment objective describes the mutual fund's purpose, while the strategy explains how the fund will invest to achieve its goals. The prospectus also explains the risks inherent in investing in specific types of securities. It can also shed light on the fund manager's record and style. A prospectus must clearly include the costs of investing in the fund and how these costs have changed over time. The section on performance will show how the fund rates against benchmarks and similar funds. Details on dividends and trading practices are also found here.

Shareholder reports explain how the fund performed over a specific period and explain the economic and market context for this performance.

They also list the specific securities the fund bought and sold and give reasons for changes in asset allocations. The reports provide the most recent information about the fund's expenses and frequency of trading activity.

The Statement of Additional Information gives details about the board of directors and fund managers and how they are compensated. It also describes how much the fund spends, including payments for marketing and distribution.

The SEC adopted rules in 1998 requiring investment companies to write clearly in these documents and avoid jargon in order to make this information accessible and understandable to average investors.

 QUICK QUIZ

1. You are advising your client about an investment into an emerging markets fund. What are the risks that your client should be aware of and where can you or your client find more information about the risks involved?

2. In the US, the SEC requires that the fund company provide a bar chart that must show the annual total return for the fund for the previous 10 years or since inception. Why do you think they require such a long performance evaluation period?

3. You are studying a fund's financial information and discover that over a 5-year period, the fund's NAV, expense ratio, and turnover ratio have all gone up. Which of these developments give reason for concern?

4. Name five details about a fund's board of directors and fund manager that are found in a Statement of Additional Information.

5. For a quick evaluation of a fund you will often turn to the fund's fact sheet. What information should you expect to find in this document?

ANALYZING PERFORMANCE

4

"Past performance is no guarantee of future performance." In view of this warning printed in every mutual fund prospectus, how then can investors evaluate the vast pool of fund offerings? How can you choose the mutual funds that are most likely to meet your future investment return targets?

There are many charts, data and graphs available for analyzing funds, but there is no standard method for evaluating a fund. The amount of research offered by mutual fund rating companies, websites and brokers can be overwhelming.

So let's stick to the basics: Investors are motivated by both greed and fear. In other words, they want to make the best possible returns while staying in their individual "comfort zone" when it comes to risk. Then, to choose the right fund, they need answers to two key questions:

- Performance: Which figures are key to evaluating a mutual fund's past performance and forecasting future performance?

- Risk: Which characteristics of a fund help determine its degree of risk?

With these tools, you can narrow down the choices and identify the funds that are likely to perform in line with your specific needs. Understanding the methods that fund-rating companies use to rate and categorize funds will also help you make the right decisions.

EVALUATING RETURNS

The first thing investors usually want to know about a fund is: What kind of returns has it made? If they are high, a fund's historical returns are often used in marketing campaigns to attract new investors. While a fund's past returns are not a good indicator of future returns, they do give some indication of whether the fund is worth buying. Before buying into the hype, though, it is important to understand how these returns are generated.

It is not enough simply to look at the change in a mutual fund's price. There are three ways a mutual fund can make money:

- Dividends

- Capital Gains Distributions

- Share price, or NAV increase.

Together these three elements make up a mutual fund's total return.

Dividends

Dividends are the regular income payments received from investments in both stocks and bonds. Many bonds pay dividends in the form of interest payments. Many companies also pay cash dividends quarterly or semi-annually. These payments go into the portfolio of the mutual funds that hold these shares or bonds.

A mutual fund distributes these dividends to its shareholders according to its own schedule. This could be monthly, quarterly, semi-annually or annually. Mutual fund shareholders can often decide whether to receive these payments in cash or receive additional units of the fund.

On the day the mutual fund pays out dividends, its NAV per share drops by an amount equal to the dividend payout, as the size of the fund's assets gets reduced. The day on which the fund makes the dividend payments is called the fund's *ex-dividend date*.

Capital Gains Distributions

Capital gains are the profits a fund makes when the price of its securities rises. This gain is realized when the fund manager sells a security. A realized capital gain is equal to the difference between the sale price and the purchase price of the security. Generally, if funds distribute capital gains to their shareholders, it is done once a year. As with dividends, realized capital gains can be received in cash or they can be reinvested in the fund. The value of the fund drops by the exact amount of the distribution to account for the decrease in the assets it holds.

Increase in Share Price (NAV)

The fund has *unrealized* gains when the fund manager holds onto securities that have risen in price. As a result, the share price, or NAV, of a fund increases. Of course, unrealized losses are also reflected in the NAV if the prices of the securities drop. These gains are only "paper profits" as long as the investor owns the fund. Investors can lock in profits from an increase in NAV due to unrealized gains by selling their units of the fund at a higher price than the price at which they had purchased the units.

Calculating Total Return

Total return is one of the most important elements used to evaluate a fund's performance over several years.

The formula includes: distributions of investment income from dividend and interest payments, distributed realized capital gains, and unrealized capital gains or losses that are factored into the change in the fund's NAV.

$$\text{Total Return} = \frac{\text{NAV2} - \text{NAV1} + \text{CGD} + \text{DIV}}{\text{NAV1}} \times 100 = \%\ \text{Return}$$

NAV2 = the fund's NAV at the end of the measurement period
NAV1 = the fund's NAV at the beginning of the measurement period
CGD = the total capital gains distributed
DIV = the total dividend payments

The various elements of total return carry different levels of importance for different types of mutual funds. For example, with money market funds, all returns come from dividends, while there are no capital gains and usually no share price changes. Longer-term bond and equity-income funds pay high dividends, usually have low capital gains and low to moderate share price changes. On the opposite end of the spectrum, growth equity funds and high-yield junk bond funds typically show greater changes in their NAV due to unrealized capital gains and larger capital gains distributions. Dividend distributions would have less of an impact on these funds' total return.

Annualized Total Return
To reflect the total return of a fund over several years, fund companies provide an *annualized return figure*. This measures the average increase per year during a specific period of time. This calculation includes the compounded returns made on the reinvested dividends and capital gains over the years. Annualized return figures are often used to compare the performance of a fund to similar funds for the same time periods.

Load-Adjusted Total Return
Expenses such as management fees and directors' fees are factored into a fund's NAV every day and do not need to be deducted from the total return. Still, total return figures do not include a fund's sales load or any redemption fees. When these fees are deducted, the calculation is known as a *load-adjusted total return*. Also, sales loads vary depending on the distribution channel. These fees are a one-off charge, making it difficult to include them when a fund is being evaluated over a period of several years.

EVALUATING FUND PERFORMANCE
Once you have calculated a fund's total return, the next step is to put its performance in perspective. This can be achieved by comparing returns with

benchmark indices, other funds, and the market in general. This way you can verify if a fund's return is satisfactory given the context in which it was achieved. Without this context, stand-alone performance numbers have little meaning.

Benchmarks

One useful method of evaluating a fund's performance is comparing it with an appropriate benchmark index. For example, it is unrealistic to expect returns of 15% per year when the benchmark has risen only 5%.

High absolute returns are also not necessarily a reason to stick with a particular fund. Comparing what seems to be an impressive performance to the market trend will show why. If a fund rose 30% in one year, but the index was up 52% that year, then it would have underperformed. When evaluating fund performance, a relative comparison is necessary.

Choosing the right benchmark to use as a comparison is essential. You would not use the performance of a US index as a comparison for a small-cap European fund, and it would make no sense to use it for a bond fund since the index includes only equities.

Investors seek to have their funds match or, better yet, exceed the performance of the benchmark. Some deviation from an index shouldn't be cause for much concern though. Indices are not subject to the costs that a mutual fund must incur to operate. Moreover, the fund manager's research and experience should be factored into considerations about whether the fund has the potential for better performance in future years.

Another way of evaluating a fund's performance is noting the fund's return over the long-term (at least three years) and how it has performed during both bull and bear markets. Comparing the fund's performance during these times to a broader benchmark such as the S&P 500 index is

Figure 4.1 — Major Benchmark Indexes for Different Fund Types

Benchmark Index	Fund Type
Dow Jones Industrial Average	Blue-chip companies
S&P 500	Large-cap, US stocks
Russell 2000	Small-cap, US stocks
Wilshire 5000	Broad US market
Nasdaq Composite Index	Broad US and non-US companies listed on Nasdaq market
Lehman Brothers Aggregate	US government, corporate, mortgage-backed bonds
MSCI World	International stocks in 23 countries
MSCI EAFE	International stocks, excluding US and Canada
MSCI (Europe)	European stocks in 15 countries
MSCI Latin American-Free	Stocks in 7 countries of the Latin-American region
MSCI Emerging Mkts	Emerging markets stocks
MSCI Combined Asia Pacific	Stocks in 13 Asia Pacific countries

useful. When the general market was rising, by what percentage did the fund outperform or under-perform? When the market was falling, did the fund drop in value more than a broad index?

While past performance does not necessarily indicate what returns a fund will produce in the future, these differences in performance will show the fund's volatility compared with general market trends and associated risk. Funds with relatively consistent returns through both bull and bear markets are considered less risky than those that offer 60% increases one year and 30% drops the next. While all investors want top returns, each individual has varying degrees of risk tolerance.

Fund Management Company Changes

Successful investment professionals employed by the fund manager often enjoy celebrity status and are targets for poaching by competing companies.

OPINION
HOW TO CHOOSE FUNDS DURING A BEAR MARKET

Investors can get very emotional during a bear market and sell investments in a panic, fearing further declines. Here are some common tactics investment managers recommend to help ride out the bad times:

- *Don't try to time the market: Stay dedicated to your long-term plan and don't try to predict when the market will rise and fall. Try to balance your portfolio with stocks, bonds and different investment styles.*

- *Diversify: It is important to diversify a portfolio according to types of securities. When large-cap stocks are falling, small-cap funds or real estate funds may be on the rise. By spreading investments over several unrelated market segments, investors can soften the blow of the bear.*

- *Don't track funds too closely: watching your fund's decline on a daily basis will only make you nervous and apt to make rash decisions. Step back and look at the big picture, and compare the fund's performance to the overall market and to your other investments. Mutual funds are long-term investments and returns are not relevant over one week or one month. If your holdings are diversified, some funds will inevitably decline while others are doing well.*

- *Make regular contributions: Because it is difficult to predict peaks and troughs in the market, making regular contributions to a fund will smooth out the fluctuations. This is called dollar-cost averaging, or DCA. Of course, no investment strategy, including dollar-cost averaging, can guarantee a profit or protect against a loss in a declining market. But feeding new money into mutual funds during a bear market buys new shares at lower prices and gives you a lower average purchase price. (For more on DCA see Chapter 6.)*

- *Consider lower-cost funds: In a bull market it is easy to ignore expenses because they are small proportions of the annual return. Still, costs usually do not drop as returns decline and high fees can quickly erode any returns in a bear market.*

- *Add bonds: When equities are tumbling, bonds often rally as investors seek more security. High-quality debt can help balance a portfolio.*

- *Look at international markets: Investing internationally can help diversify a portfolio focused solely on domestic securities. For example, in 2005, the S&P 500 index rose 3% in US dollar terms, while Japan's Nikkei index rose 40% in yen terms.*

Source: Benz, Christine et al., *Morningstar Guide to Mutual Funds,* John Wiley & Sons, Hoboken, New Jersey: 2003 p. 186

When evaluating the likelihood of a fund continuing impressive performance, investors should check if the team running the fund has been reshuffled recently. The current investment advisers may not be the same as the ones responsible for past performance. In this case, the fund's long-term returns may give little indication of how it may perform in the future.

Peer Comparisons

Another way of evaluating fund performance is comparing it to its peers. Fund-rating companies such as Morningstar, Standard & Poor's, Lipper and Value Line provide a ranking to help compare funds with other funds with similar objectives.

Many investors focus on Morningstar's star ratings to help decide among several funds. The ratings assess a fund's risk/reward profile compared with other funds with a similar style. The influence of these ratings should not be underestimated. One study found that almost 90% of the new money invested into stock funds in 1995 went into funds with four-star and five-star ratings from the company.

Morningstar revamped its rating system in 2002 to make it easier to compare funds with specific profiles. The original star rating compared funds within very broad categories. Rather than using four broad peer groups to rate funds (domestic, international, taxable bond, municipal bond), the company's new rating system compares funds with others in 64 different categories. For example, small-cap growth funds are now compared with other small-cap growth funds. These changes allow the fund to be compared against a more appropriate peer group, resulting in a fair comparison. The new rating system was also changed to better represent risk levels. It began using a measure of risk-adjusted returns that penalizes funds for volatility.

As with the previous ranking system, Morningstar's new rating allocates one to five stars and is updated monthly. It takes sales charges into consideration and does not rate funds with less than a three-year track record. The company continues to grade funds on a curve, with 10% of portfolios receiving five stars, 22.5% allocated four stars, 33% getting for three stars, 22.5% given two stars, and 10% getting one star. Morningstar calculates separate ratings for the three-, five- and 10-year periods and then combines the ratings into an aggregate for each fund.

The results of a 2005 study by Morningstar comparing ratings from June 2002 and June 2003 showed the new rating system was more effective in identifying good performers than the original rating system. On average, five-star funds outperform lower-rated funds and tend to be less expensive, less volatile and run by more experienced managers, according to Morningstar.

Still, the system does have its limitations. There are often some potential gems found among the lower-rated funds. There are also future losers among those rated five stars. Fund ratings are also limited by the fact that they can only analyze past performance. They are unable to identify the categories of poor-performing funds that are about to turn around.

"Investing is much too complex for any single measure to sum up the entire merit of a security," says Russel Kinnel, Morningstar's director of mutual fund research. "The star rating is a useful tool, but it's no substitute for doing your homework."

Consistency
One of the most important methods for evaluating a fund is consistency. Investors are advised to choose funds with performance that is consistently ranked above average compared with its peers. This can be more important than high long-term aggregate returns. Funds should be compared with other funds with similar objectives.

INVESTMENT STYLES
A fund manager's investing style helps determine how much risk an investor takes when buying a particular mutual fund. It determines how the manager chooses securities, how these securities are analyzed and when and how often the manager buys and sells. The two major types of investment styles are called *growth* and *value*.

OPINION
STRATEGIES;
HOW FUND RANKINGS CAN CAUSE STOCKS TO GYRATE

Mutual funds are a main cause of the boom-and-bust cycle that so often occurs among individual stocks and industry sectors, a new study has concluded.

Titled "Asset Fire Sales (and Purchases) in Equity Markets," the study was conducted by Joshua D. Coval and Erik Stafford, both associate professors of finance at the Harvard Business School. A version is at http://papers.ssrn. com/sol3/papers.cfm?abstract-id=718201.

In short, the professors conclude that mutual funds regularly make transactions that can set boom-and-bust cycles into motion. One such transaction is a "fire sale," which the researchers define as occurring when a fund must sell a stock very quickly, regardless of price. Another move, called a "forced purchase," is the reverse: it occurs when a fund must buy a stock right away.

Two factors conspire to make such transactions frequent in the fund arena. The first is significant and sudden inflows and outflows. A fund that finishes at or near the bottom of quarterly or yearly performance rankings, for example, will almost certainly receive a large number of redemption requests. In contrast, a fund that comes out near the top of the rankings can expect heavy inflows of new money.

Big outflows and inflows do not necessarily cause fire sales and forced purchases. But they do if a fund manager tries to keep cash balances low at all times, which is the case for a large majority of stock funds.

A fund that receives many redemption requests will have to sell some of its positions to honor them, even when the prices of its stocks are unfavorable. And a fund that receives lots of new cash will feel pressure to put that money to work right away. Usually, the professors say, managers in this situation buy more shares of stocks that their funds already hold.

These fire sales and forced purchases can lead to big changes in the prices of the stocks, according to the researchers. Fire-sale stocks will often be beaten down, while forced-purchase stocks will be bid higher...

Growth Investing

Investment advisers who focus on growth investing choose shares of companies based on expectations of rapid earnings growth. The fund manager believes that the share price will rise if the company's earnings meet or beat analysts' expectations. The period leading up to earnings reports can produce price fluctuations in growth-oriented funds as analysts release reports publishing their expectations. If a company's earnings exceed expectations and growth is expected to continue, its share price is likely to rise, according to growth investors. If earnings decline or are expected to fall below projections, the price will probably decline.

A more conservative style of growth investing is called *growth at a reasonable price,* or *GARP.* Fund managers who follow this philosophy look for reasonably priced stocks of companies that have some characteristic that is likely to spark above-average earnings growth. The share prices of these companies may have declined due to disappointing earnings to make them appear cheap compared with their assets or compared with their peers. Like value investors, GARP investors choose shares of companies they feel are only temporarily down.

Some growth investors are driven by expectations of higher revenue or sales. Shares of newer companies may not have earnings for several years. Instead of focusing on profits, some growth fund managers may buy shares of these companies if they expect their revenue to increase substantially. Many fund managers used this approach for Internet and other technology stocks in the late 1990s and achieved impressive results. The dot-com crash caused many to later change their strategy to reduce exposure to risk.

Within the growth category, *momentum* managers often take the most risk. This type of manager ignores measures of value and selects stocks of companies whose share price he expects will rise rapidly. This style takes into account issues such as "strong buy" recommendations from a majority of analysts that cover the company and significant earnings growth that exceeds market expectations.

Momentum managers choose companies they believe will surprise the market with outstanding earnings. They do not pay attention to the valuation of the stock and may hold securities others deem expensive. These managers typically sell stocks when the company's quarterly earnings growth decelerates, because they consider this an indicator of a future share price decline. The fund manager tries to buy shares just before a major increase in price and attempts to sell before a price decline occurs. This type of strategy is called "timing the market."

Value Investing

Fund managers with a value style of investing are bargain hunters. They search for companies whose market value appears cheap.

Two common measures used are:

- Price-earnings (P/E) ratio

- Price-to-book value (P/B) ratio

Companies that have historically lower ratios, or ratios lower than those of their peers, are often attractive to value investors. Value managers may decide a sudden drop in these companies' stock prices is a result of the market's overreaction to a specific piece of bad news. These moments can be treated as buying opportunities for value investors as they may not have had an impact on the company's fundamentals.

The P/E ratio is calculated by dividing the price of a company's stock by its per-share earnings during the past 12 months. A high P/E indicates that investors are willing to pay more because they expect the company to increase its earnings. A low P/E can mean investors do not believe the company can increase its earnings. It may also be a sign that the company's shares are undervalued compared with its peers and may rise in the future.

P/E ratios are best compared among companies in the same sector. For example, a low P/E of five is not necessarily better than a ratio of 10 for another company in a different industry. Also, a low P/E does not necessarily mean low stock prices. For example, oil companies in 2005 posted returns of more than 50% with P/E ratios of around 10 because earnings soared as oil prices rose.

The P/B ratio is derived by dividing the company's price by the company's *book value* per share. Book value is a company's total assets minus its total liabilities, excluding intangible assets. It represents the amount investors would receive if the company's assets were liquidated.

This ratio shows how the company is valued relative to its assets. A high P/B ratio may show that the price of the stock exceeds the value of the company's net assets and is overpriced. A low P/B ratio may show the stock is selling at a discount to its assets and may be a good buy.

Many value fund managers set specific targets for these ratios that act as buying signals. They sell the stock when the price rises to what they consider its true value, taking into consideration its earnings or book value or some other measure. They may also sell when a company's prospects

"How come Jasper's mutual fund is up twelve per cent and mine's only up eight?"

worsen because of new developments that make it appear that the stock price is unlikely to bounce back.

A value manager will also choose stocks that appear cheap compared with its competitors or if a particular industry appears undeservedly out of favor.

Relative value fund managers compare a company's stock's value to its peers. They compare the company's assets, earnings or sales with similar companies in the same industry. Absolute value fund managers do not compare a stock's value to that of its peers or to the market. Instead, they decide the worth of the company in absolute terms and will buy the shares when they are available at a lower price. To determine the absolute value of a company's stock, these fund managers study the company's assets, balance sheet, opportunities for growth, and especially what private investors have paid for its shares. Value investors are wary of market trends and are often willing to pursue a buy-and-hold strategy for a longer period of time.

Value vs. Growth Investing

Growth investments generally carry more risk of loss compared with value stocks. Growth stocks, which often have high P/E ratios, can fall in price sharply when there is negative news about the industry or the company. If the company does not meet earnings expectations, the share price will fall as investors adjust their forecasts for future earnings. In contrast, value stocks are less influenced by earnings reports and their prices are generally less volatile.

The two investment styles of growth and value have come into and gone out of favor during different market cycles. For example, in the US, value investing did well in the early 1990s as the US economy pulled out of recession. Growth funds had the highest returns during the bull market from 1995 to 1999 as investors focused on the earnings potential of technology stocks due to strong economic growth and technological innovations. After the dot-com crash, growth stocks fell dramatically behind their value counterparts at the beginning of the new century.

Typically, value funds tend to perform better during periods of economic recovery or when investors are concerned about exceedingly high market valuations. Growth strategies tend to do better in the later stages of economic growth or when investors begin to anticipate economic instability.

Some fund managers blend the two strategies to avoid getting hit when one or the other is out of favor. Still, a greater amount of flexibility can make some funds challenging to categorize and sell to investors. Owning these funds makes it difficult to determine whether you are effectively diversified. Because growth and value stocks follow cycles of one style outperforming the other for several years, individual investors can buy some funds that focus on value and some that focus on growth to help lower risk and increase long-term returns.

Style Boxes

Several fund-rating companies have designed matrices that define a fund's investment style.

Morningstar, for example, has created a style box with nine squares to help evaluate a fund. Two factors determine where the fund is categorized within the box: the market capitalization of its holdings and the fund manager's investment style. The rows show the size of the companies in the portfolio by capitalization and the columns indicate the fund manager's investment style.

Figure 4.2 — Morningstar Style Box

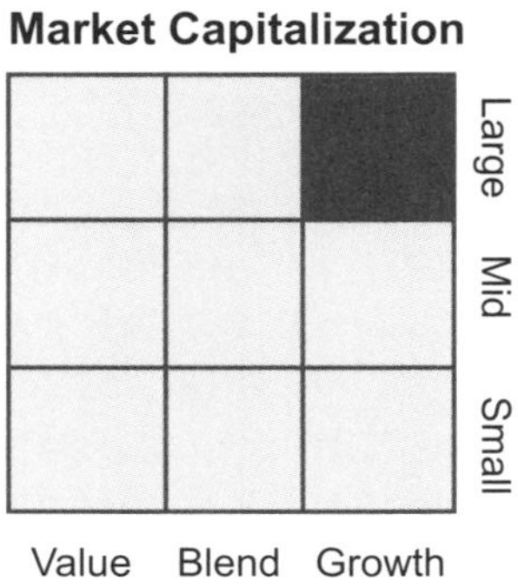

Market Capitalization

Source: Morningstar, Inc.

Funds that, on average, focus on large companies are placed in the top row, funds that buy mid-cap stocks are in the middle, and small-cap funds are found in the bottom row. The fund's style is based on the weighted average of the style scores given to all of its stocks in the portfolio. Each stock receives a growth score and a value score. In Figure 4.2, the red square indicates the fund manager uses a growth investment style and chooses large-cap stocks for the fund's portfolio.

Half of a stock's growth score is based on its long-term projected earnings growth relative to other stocks in the same market-cap range. The rest of the score is based on historical earnings growth, sales growth, cash flow growth, and book value growth relative to other companies in the same market-cap range. Each receives a growth score of zero to 100.

Half of a stock's value score is based on its price-to-projected earnings relative to other stocks in its market-cap range. The rest of the score is based on a mix of price-to-book, price-to-sales, price-to-cash flow and dividend yield relative to the stocks in the same market-cap range. The value score also ranges from zero to 100.

Morningstar sets an investment style score for a stock by subtracting the value score from its growth score. A stock with a high negative score is called a value stock, while one with a high positive score is called a growth stock. Those in between end up in the center of the box, known as the blend column for funds.

Value Line, another fund rating company, uses a similar matrix. But instead of nine boxes, Value Line uses a 16-square matrix. It also uses rows to indicate the market capitalization and columns for investment style. Morningstar, Value Line and other fund rating companies each use their own classification systems for funds rather than the definitions provided by the funds themselves. This standardization allows investors to compare different funds with the same objective or investment style.

Generally, funds placed in the upper left corner of a matrix (large-cap and value) tend to be the least volatile, while those in the lower right (small-cap, growth) often experience the most fluctuations in their returns.

MEASURING RISK

Once you know how to address an investor's greed, it is time to tackle the fear of losing money. All funds carry some element of risk, but each individual has his or her own level of risk tolerance. Investment analysts have developed a range of tools and classifications to measure the risk of different mutual funds.

Investors themselves are often less specific than industry analysts in their definitions of risk. In 1997 the Investment Company Institute (ICI) released the results of a survey on what investors thought about risk.

Most of the survey participants included more than one concept of risk in their definition. The concepts included in shareholders' definitions of mutual fund risk included:

- Losing some of an original investment (49% of the respondents picked this definition)

- An investment fluctuating in value (46%)

- Not having enough money to achieve investment goals (41%)

- Investment not keeping pace with inflation (40%)

- Decline in income distributed by the fund (33%)

Most of the shareholders surveyed assessed the risk of a prospective fund investment according to an intermediate-term or long-term time horizon. More than 60% said they consider fund risk according to a 1-5 year period, while 28% looked at a period of more than five years.

Investors wanted both a narrative description of a fund's risk as well as a bar graph showing the fund's return over a specific period. The SEC requires both of these types of descriptions in a fund's prospectus.

Analysts develop many statistical methods to measure risk, which is often defined as the level of variation in returns. The greater the fluctuation in returns, the more difficult it will be for an investor to liquidate an investment at a favorable price at any given time.

Past volatility is seen as an indication of the degree of future risk. Big swings in prices usually indicate there will be a wild ride ahead. *Standard deviation* is a common measure of a fund's volatility. It represents the degree to which a fund's returns have varied from its average return during a specific period.

Funds with lower risk generally offer steady returns over the long term, which are fairly predictable through both bull and bear markets. With two funds in the same category, the one with a standard deviation of 30 is likely to tumble much further than one with a standard deviation of 17 when the sector is out of favor. Fund rating companies such as Morningstar provide these statistics.

Still, standard deviation does not indicate whether the fluctuations are gains or losses, an important difference for investors. Morningstar's risk rating, which accounts for one half of its star rating, looks at a fund's losses compared with its category peers as well as variations in returns such as standard deviation. These risk measures are assigned according to the specific fund category to allow investors to compare funds that invest in the same way.

Fund analysis companies also describe a mutual fund's risk using three concepts from modern portfolio theory: *alpha, beta* and *R-squared*.

Alpha: Alpha is a measure of a fund's excess return relative to a market index. A positive alpha means the fund manager produced a higher return than the benchmark, while a negative alpha shows the fund did not get enough reward for the amount of risk it took.

OPINION
STRATEGIES; PAID FOR PERFORMANCE, AND FREED FROM THE HERD

Evidence is mounting that mutual fund managers are more likely to think for themselves when their pay is closely linked to their fund's performance...

In a recent study, Massimo Massa, a finance professor at INSEAD, a the French business school, and two Ph.D. students there, Nishant Dass and Rajdeep Patgiri, found that performance incentives have had a significant and salutary influence on the buying and selling decisions of fund managers.

The study, "Mutual Funds and Bubbles: The Surprising Role of Contractual Incentives," has circulated in academic circles since July.

(A version is at http://papers.ssrn. com/sol3/papers.cfm?abstract-id=759365.)

Funds compensate their managers in a variety of ways — and some methods, of course, offer more performance incentives than others. The managers who have the least incentive for good performance, according to the researchers, are those who are paid a declining percentage of assets under management as those assets grow. At the other end of the spectrum are managers, whose compensation is significantly greater if certain performance hurdles are met. In the middle

are those whose compensation is a flat percentage of assets under management....

The researchers say they believe that compensation incentives affect a manager's willingness to buy and sell the same stocks that others are trading. They theorize that managers who are the least rewarded for good performance tend to be most worried about ending up at the bottom of the rankings — and are not very motivated to take a risk and try to finish at the top. This means that they will be more likely to mimic other funds' portfolios, something that the researchers call herding behavior....

The new research has major public policy implications. Securities regulators typically have taken a jaundiced view of pay-for-performance among mutual funds, based on the idea that such compensation may encourage fund managers to incur too much risk. But the researchers believe that mutual funds whose managers are poorly compensated for performance may unwittingly be contributing to the market's boom-and-bust cycle. Funds with stronger performance incentives "may provide a useful counterweight" to offset future bubbles, they said....

Source: Mark Hulbert, *New York Times*
October 23, 2005

Beta: Beta measures the sensitivity of a fund's returns to the returns of a market index. A beta coefficient of more than 1.0 shows the fund's returns are more volatile than the benchmark index, which is assigned a baseline beta of 1.0. A beta of between zero and 1.0 shows the fund is less volatile. A fund with a beta of 1.0 tracks the benchmark.

For example, a fund with a beta of 1.3 is 30% more volatile than the index. It will, on average, rise 30% more when the market is increasing and tumble 30% more when the market is declining. A beta of 0.8 is less volatile than the market. The fund will give a return 20% lower than the market when the market is rising and decline 20% less when it is falling.

R-Squared: R-squared measures whether the fund's price movements are correlated to the benchmark index on a scale from one to 100. A fund that mirrors the movements of the S&P 500 index, for example, would have an R-squared of 100, because 100% of its fluctuations are determined by the S&P. A low R-squared number means the fund's movements are independent of the index.

Beta figures are only useful if the R-squared is high, meaning the fund is being compared with an appropriate index.

Turnover Rate

Another possible indicator of risk is a mutual fund's turnover rate. This measures how often a fund manager trades securities. It shows the percentage of the portfolio that is bought and sold over a year. A turnover rate of 100% indicates that the manager changes the entire portfolio within a year. A rate of 50% means half of the securities are changed, while a rate of 200% shows the securities are traded twice within the year.

A low turnover rate of less than 30% indicates the fund manager holds the securities for a longer period. Some fund managers have a high turnover rate of more than 100% because they actively trade their portfolio. These funds may follow a momentum style of investing, buying when stocks are rising and selling when the market slows down. These types of funds may have a turnover rate of more than 300%.

High turnover rates result in more transaction costs from commissions and other fees that may eat away at the fund's returns. Turnover costs are not included in the fund's expense ratio and must be considered in addition to these costs.

To be sure, high turnover is not necessarily a negative feature. Sometimes active trading is necessary to achieve short-term profits when dealing with certain securities focused on emerging markets, small-cap stocks and high-yield bonds. If the fund manager has good timing, this may result in high returns. However, warning lights start flashing when a fund manager has poor returns and a high turnover rate. High turnover is a particular concern during bear markets, when it erodes already low or negative returns.

Taxes

Another major risk associated with a high turnover rate is that more capital gains and losses are realized as a result. These gains are often subject to capital gains tax. Actively traded funds create high capital gains distributions and shareholders often must then pay high taxes.

Owners of funds that are performing poorly may still have to pay tax. The managers of these funds may sell off some of their most profitable securities and create taxable gains. In the most negative cases, shareholders may have to pay capital gains taxes that more than offset any increase in returns. Many fund managers do not pay attention to these additional costs because they are focused on achieving stellar annual returns.

Risks Associated with Specific Fund Categories

Certain types of securities and categories of funds have specific inherent risks associated with them. These must be taken into account when choosing funds for an investor's portfolio.

Foreign and Global Equity Funds: Currency Risk and Country Risk

Foreign and global mutual funds give investors an opportunity to access new markets much more easily than buying individual stocks in those countries. Still, there are unique risks associated with investing in these types of funds. Many of these investments are denominated in foreign currency.

If the investor's main currency is the US dollar, then the value of the investment will fluctuate as the dollar's value changes against other currencies. If the dollar strengthens against the foreign currency, the investment will be worth less when converted into dollars. If the US dollar weakens against the foreign currency, any returns from the foreign fund will be worth more when converted into US dollars. Changes in currency values will add to the volatility of an international or global fund.

Another consideration is the risk of concentrating too much money in the stocks of a particular country, which increases exposure to a particular currency and political risk. Foreign and global equity funds state in their prospectuses the percentage of assets invested in a particular country. These allocations change throughout the year, however, and may be difficult to track. As a result, the level of risk associated with these types of funds may change over time.

Bond Funds: Quality and Interest Rate Risk

Bonds are generally stereotyped as a "safe" investments. Investors are advised to switch to bonds or bond funds as they near retirement age, become less tolerant of risk, and require a steady income from their investments. What is less known, however, is that bonds vary significantly in terms of risk and many are more speculative plays than equities.

Unlike individual investors, who generally buy bonds and hold them until maturity, bond fund managers trade bonds with the same frequency as stocks. When bond prices rise, the fund manager can sell to realize the gain. When it drops in value, the manager may do the same and realize a loss. Bond funds are not required to hold the bond to maturity to receive the face value.

The quality of a bond is another factor that contributes to risk. Credit rating companies such as Fitch, Moody's, and Standard & Poor's assign ratings to bonds to define their credit risk or the risk the issuer will default on the bond. The safest bonds are called "investment grade." These bonds produce the lowest yield and include many types of government bonds. A high-yield, or junk, bond fund includes low-quality debt instruments issued by companies or governments of emerging economies. These bonds experience larger price fluctuations and pay the highest yields.

The prices of bonds are negatively correlated to interest rates, meaning when interest rates rise, bond prices will drop, and vice versa. The amount of the price change depends on the length of the bond's maturity. Short-term bonds will see smaller price changes when interest rates change than longer-term bonds. The safest bonds are those with high creditworthiness ratings and short-term maturities.

OPINION
THE CHILL OF THE CHASE: BUYING TOP-PERFORMING FUNDS OFTEN LEADS TO DISAPPOINTMENT

BOSTON (MarketWatch) — Most investors buy into mutual funds based largely on good past performance and then sell those funds due mostly to disappointing results. It's a sad pattern bound to repeat itself if performance alone is your driving factor in fund selection.

According to the latest Standard & Poor's Mutual Fund Performance Persistence Scorecard, you have

little reason to believe that a fund that is a top performer today will maintain its edge tomorrow. That's hardly new information, as researchers have known for years that funds tend to lead the pack when the asset classes they own are hot but fall back as the market cycle turns.

The S&P study focused on domestic equity funds and not more volatile offerings like sector and international funds. And it clearly points investors away from chasing the best recent performers because they're not likely to be kings of the hill for long.

According to the study, just 15.5% of large cap funds were able to maintain a spot in the top 25% of their peer group over three consecutive years. The numbers get worse when you look at midcap funds (10.2%) and small-cap funds (9.8%).

Over five years, just 1.9% of funds buying large-company stocks were able to maintain a top-quartile ranking, compared with 3.1% of small-cap funds and no midcap funds whatsoever.

One interesting side note to the performance measurement is that funds that are among the very worst performers tend to stay there, frequently burdened by *heavy costs and poor management. So while picking from the top of the fund pool is not necessarily going to deliver a long-term winner, it's a better bet than taking the contrarian approach, selecting a dog and hoping it becomes a big winner.*

What the S&P study shows is that the funds that are capable of remaining at the top of their peer group have a few elements in common, most notably low costs, long-tenured managers and the ability to minimize losses when the market turns sour.

In short, with past performance as the primary guide, you're likely to be disappointed in the results the fund achieves for you.

Source: Chuck Jaffe, *MarketWatch Last Update: 12:01 AM ET,* Feb 19, 2006 (excerpt)

SUMMARY

To choose among the vast array of mutual fund offerings, investors must understand how to evaluate past performance and identify the degree of risk associated with a particular fund. The total return of a fund includes dividends, capital gains distributions, and the increase in the net asset value of the fund. Each element of total return has greater weight depending on the type of securities included in a fund.

Fund performance must be put into perspective by analyzing the context in which it was achieved. To get a clearer picture of the fund's returns, they must be compared with an appropriate benchmark index, the returns of other similar companies and the general market. Studying performance over a longer period, during both bull and bear markets, gives a clue as to how the fund may perform in the future. Fund rating companies provide rating systems and tools to compare the performance of funds with other funds with similar objectives. The most important aspect of fund performance is consistency. Investors are advised to choose funds with returns that are ranked above average compared with their peers the majority of the time.

Each individual investor has a particular level of risk tolerance. The amount of risk a fund takes can be evaluated by studying the fund manager's investment style. A growth style of investing focuses on expectations of rapid earnings growth and pays less heed to price valuations. Value investors search for cheap prices relative to a company's assets, earnings, or the prices of other similar companies.

Other measures of risk include the fund's standard deviation, elements of modern portfolio theory (alpha, beta, R-squared) and turnover rates. Particular types of funds and securities also carry a specific set of risks. With foreign and global funds, investors must take currency and country risk into consideration. Bond funds usually carry interest rate and credit-quality risk.

 QUICK QUIZ

1. Joe bought 1,000 units in fund XYZ on January 17, 2005 at a NAV of $25.44/unit. His entry fee was 2.5%. On January 16, 2006 he sold all his holdings at a price of $28.37. During the year he received four dividend payments of $0.40/unit, $0.60/unit, $0.30/unit, and $0.74/unit. What was his total return for the year he held the fund?

2. You are creating a balanced mutual fund portfolio for a client. The portfolio consists of bond and equity funds that invest in US securities. Your client would like to benchmark the performance of your portfolio to the performance of the S&P 500 index. What is wrong with this idea and what would you suggest as an alternative?

3. Why is it that a typical index tracker fund almost always underperforms the index it is tracking?

4. Two fund managers — a "value" investor and a "growth" investor – are analyzing two companies, Google and Exxon Mobil. Google has a P/E ratio of 65 and Exxon Mobil a P/E ratio of 10. How is each investor likely to evaluate each of the two stocks?

5. In a Morningstar style box, what do the rows indicate? What do the columns indicate?

6. You are evaluating two funds for a client who considers himself a conservative investor. The first fund has an average annual return over the past five years of 8% with a volatility of 15%. The second fund has an average annual return over the same period of 12% with a volatility of 7%. Which of the two funds would you recommend and why?

MUTUAL FUND COSTS

5

Mutual funds provide a wide variety of services that help make investing affordable, easy, and accessible. Just like with any service, these benefits have a cost.

Sales and service personnel must be paid to inform investors about the fund and to answer their questions both before and after they purchase it. When the fund is purchased, money must be transferred, credited, recorded and checked to meet various legal standards such as money laundering regulations.

After the sale is completed, a transfer agency must be paid for transferring various payments such as dividends, and a custodian bank must be paid to ensure that the fund assets are physically safe, very often in different parts of the world. Call center staff must be paid to answer investors' questions regarding the fund, and a number of other services accrue costs.

Any mutual fund investor should be aware of the various charges that must be paid when owning funds. Fortunately, there are many options available for paying these costs, such as different share classes with their own payment structures.

The fees paid for owning mutual funds can affect returns over time. It is important to note that fund returns are always stated after expenses. Higher expenses do not guarantee better performance and neither do they guarantee worse performance. Of course, a high-cost fund should perform better or provide service levels that are superior to low-cost funds.

Before investing, it is necessary to make an informed decision about whether these fees are acceptable considering the services and benefits received.

While people usually have a clear idea of their regular expenses such as heating, transportation, and food, many investors do not know the exact amounts paid for the various financial services they use. Fortunately, the mutual fund industry has become increasingly transparent, and mutual fund providers explain fund expenses in the prospectus and annual reports of their funds. Standardized tables and plain-English descriptions provide the tools for making informed decisions.

OPINION
11TH ANNUAL DIRECTORS' CONFERENCE

For long-term investors, cost is one important consideration among many others. There are, of course, a lot of contending views about mutual fund fees. There are an awful lot of numbers thrown about. Sometimes it seems that mutual funds have replaced baseball as the leading cause of statistics. It is easy to lose sight of the most basic facts, so let me cite just two that everyone discussing mutual fund fees ought to bear in mind.

First, what is the long-term trend? ICI has examined how the cost of owning mutual funds has changed since 1980, taking into account sales charges, 12b-1 fees, management fees and all other operating expenses. Over this period, the cost of owning funds has declined by nearly half, even as the services shareholders receive have greatly expanded.

Second, what explains this trend? Put simply, competition. It turns out that the SEC is not the only regulator of our industry. Market forces are at least as tough.

A number of specific factors underlie the dramatic decline in the costs shareholders incur. These include the wide availability of information on fees, the increased focus of shareholders on good performance and low expense ratios, the wide range of funds available, the emergence of no-load funds and fund supermarkets, the role of the Internet in fostering increased competition and easier price comparisons, and other factors.

For example, the median front-end load on equity funds dropped from 8.5% in 1980 to 5.5% in 2004. Load waivers have also become commonplace. And economies of scale have helped reduce the expense ratios of many individual funds as they have grown.

Source: *Stevens, Paul Schott. "Fund Fees and Expenses," 11th Annual Directors Conference,* Washington, DC: November 4, 2005. Reprinted with permission from the Investment Company Institute (www.ici.org).

While fees are a major factor to evaluate when choosing among funds, they should not scare investors away from investing in mutual funds at all. Low transaction costs are one of the main advantages of mutual funds, compared with the commissions most investors pay when buying and selling individual stocks and bonds. It is better to play the game armed with information than to sit on the sidelines.

FEE TABLES

The first step to understanding mutual fund costs is the fee table located at the beginning of a registered fund's prospectus. It should list all the costs related to investing in a specific fund and helps investors compare the costs of one fund with those of another.

Fee tables are usually divided into two sections, "shareholder fees" and "annual fund operating expenses." The first describes any sales commissions or transaction fees incurred when an investor purchases, redeems or exchanges shares. The second section details the ongoing fees paid each year.

The fee table may also include a hypothetical example that describes how much an investor must pay on say a $10,000 investment based on a 5% return. This calculation would include shareholder fees and operating expenses.

Some websites can help estimate how much an investor would pay in fees given the dollar amount invested, time frame, and expected annual return. One cost calculator can be found at the US Securities and Exchange Commission's website (www.sec.gov/mfcc/mfcc-int.htm). It allows investors to compare the costs of several funds.

Consider the following examples of hypothetical mutual fund fee tables for a global equity fund (Figure 5.1) and a US bond fund (Figure 5.2), outlining all of the fees a mutual fund may charge. Note that not all funds charge all of the fees listed.

Figure 5.1 — Sample Mutual Fund Fee Table for a Global Equity Fund

ABC Global Equity Fund	
Shareholder Fees	
A. Maximum Sales Charge (Load) Imposed on Purchases (percentage of offering price)	4.5%
B. Maximum Deferred Sales Charge (Load)	None
C. Maximum Sales Charge (Load) on Reinvested Dividends	None
D. Redemption Fee	None
E. Exchange Fee	None
F. Annual Account Maintenance Fee	None
Annual Fund Operating Expenses	
G. Management Fee	0.72%
H. Distribution (12b-1) Fee	0.25%
I. Other Expenses	0.20%
J. Total Annual Fund Operating Expenses (Expense Ratio)	1.17%

Figure 5.2 — Sample Mutual Fund Fee Table for a US Bond Fund

XYZ US Bond Fund	
Shareholder Fees	
A. Maximum Sales Charge (Load) Imposed on Purchases (percentage of offering price)	None
B. Maximum Deferred Sales Charge (Load)	None
C. Maximum Sales Charge (Load) on Reinvested Dividends	None
D. Redemption Fee	None
E. Exchange Fee	None
F. Annual Account Maintenance Fee	None
Annual Fund Operating Expenses	
G. Management Fee	0.35%
H. Distribution (12b-1) Fee	None
I. Other Expenses	0.21%
J. Total Annual Fund Operating Expenses (Expense Ratio)	0.56%

TYPES OF EXPENSES

There are two major types of expenses related to a mutual fund: those related to operating the fund and those related to selling the fund. Operating expenses are ongoing costs that pay for the daily operations of a fund. Sales expenses are used to compensate brokers and financial advisers who sell the funds on behalf of the fund management company.

Operating Expenses

Operating expenses are the annual, ongoing costs of running a mutual fund. Every fund must charge fees to pay for its day-to-day operating costs. Operating expenses are incurred for paying the fund manager and research analysts, maintaining customer hotlines and websites, as well as for printing and mailing documents.

Operating expenses are presented in the prospectus as a percentage of fund assets or value. They can be found in the expenses section of the prospectus under "Total Fund Operating Expenses." A portion of these fees is deducted daily from the fund's net asset value (NAV).

There are many factors to consider before deciding whether a fund's operating costs are low or high. Some frugal bond-fund investors believe they can get better returns by staying away from funds that charge more than, say, 0.5% per year in operating expenses. But that can be "penny wise and pound foolish," since the lower expense fund may not perform as well as a fund charging more. Also, the fund with the lower expenses could have much poorer customer service, leaving the investor in the lurch when he has an urgent question about his fund.

To be sure, funds that charge significantly more than their peers may be doing so because they have few assets under management and do not benefit from economies of scale. As a result, a smaller group of investors covers the

Figure 5.3 — Types of Mutual Fund Costs

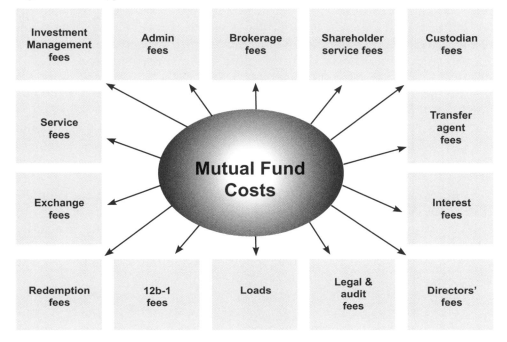

expenses of running the fund, making each individual's expenses higher. Another reason may simply be inefficient or inexperienced management of the fund's operations. The managers of these funds may then need to take more risk in an attempt to raise their returns to compensate for the extra costs.

Certain mutual funds may waive some expenses to help attract investors. Still, when this grace period is over, the investor must pay these ongoing annual fees.

Let's take a closer look at the types of fees that make up a fund's operating expenses.

Management Fees
One of the most important operating expenses is a mutual fund's *management fee*. This is an ongoing annual fee charged by the investment advisory company for researching and choosing securities to include in the fund's portfolio. This type of expertise is one of the main benefits of investing in mutual funds and it does not come cheap. Management fees are usually the largest single operating expense of the fund.

These fees are deducted when the fund calculates its daily NAV. As with other operating expenses, it is stated as an annual percentage of the fund's average daily net assets.

Some mutual funds gradually reduce their management fees to pre-set amounts as their average daily net assets increase. Because high management fees can be a significant drag on the performance of a new fund, some fund advisory companies may even waive their fee in the first few years of the fund's operations. The new fund then benefits from a higher total return, which then attracts more investors. Investors should be aware that the management fee will be reinstated once the fund has a sufficient track record. The terms of the agreement must be disclosed in the fund's prospectus.

Consider the effects that two different management fees have on returns. If Fund A has a management fee of 1.4%, an investor must pay $140 dollars out of every $10,000 invested in a fund ($10,000 x 0.014). For Fund B, if the fee is 0.8%, the investor pays $80 in management fees.

If we assume both funds have a gross annual return of 10%, this would be about $1,000 ($10,000 x 0.10). After deducting the management fee, Fund A would have a return of $860, while Fund B would have a return of $920.

But what constitutes a high management fee? The answer isn't simple. It depends on what types of securities a fund owns.

Funds that focus on international markets or specific industries often have higher management fees because of the greater use and costs of research. Domestic bond and money market funds normally have the lowest fees.

Fees are particularly important for money market and bond mutual funds because these types of securities are priced more efficiently in the markets. As a result, slight variations in management fees can have a significant impact on returns.

Administration Fees

Administration fees are expenses other than management fees that may not be broken out as a separate line item. These fees pay for employees, rent, benefits, equipment, and other aspects of running the fund. They are often grouped as "other expenses" in a prospectus. Like other operating fees, a portion of these fees is deducted daily when the NAV is calculated.

Like management fees, administration fees are stated as an annualized rate based on average daily net assets. They may be scheduled to decline as a fund's assets increase or they may be waived temporarily to attract new investors. The terms of these fee agreements are disclosed in a fund's prospectus.

Brokerage Fees

Among the fees that are not as easy to track are *brokerage fees,* also known as *turnover costs* or *portfolio transaction fees.* These fees cover the costs of buying and selling securities for the fund. They are not listed in the annual operating expense figures reported by a fund. Instead, US funds itemize them in the fund's Statement of Additional Information (SAI).

Brokerage fees increase the more often a fund manager trades securities. High levels of trading can, in some cases, erode returns. The turnover rate can give an insight into the investment style of a mutual fund. Some types of more speculative funds, such as growth funds, typically trade more frequently than less speculative funds, such as index or income-focused funds.

Shareholder Service Fees

These fees are charged for all the customer services provided to shareholders. This includes providing information to shareholders via a customer service hotline, mailing documents to potential investors, maintaining a website, and printing and mailing out semiannual and annual reports as well as other documents.

These fees are stated as an annual percentage rate based on the daily net assets of the fund. They are paid to the shareholder-servicing agent, which may be an outside company or a division of the fund company.

Custodian Fees

Custodian fees are paid to the custodian bank, which is hired to hold the fund's assets. Custodian banks are contracted to protect the shareholder in the event that the management company does not fulfill its agreed management duties or attempts to defraud investors. These custodians also often hold assets for other types of clients such as pension funds and trusts.

Mutual funds that hold securities that are issued and traded in foreign markets often must use sub-custodians who can participate in the local markets, interact with the local clearing agencies and hold accounts in the local depositories. The fund can designate a global custodian, usually a large bank, to manage a network of sub-custodians.

Transfer Agent Fees

Transfer fees are paid to the transfer agent for maintaining shareholder records. These fees are often based on the number of shareholder accounts managed by the agent. Many large fund families fulfill these functions internally and collect money from specific funds within the family for the services. Because these functions require significant resources to keep track of a large number of accounts, some fund companies have outsourced these functions to third-party transfer agents who service many fund families.

Interest Fees

Mutual funds can sometimes borrow money to maintain the cash flow when market conditions fluctuate. These loans often help pay shareholder redemptions during a run on investments in a bear market. With a loan, the mutual fund is protected from having to sell its assets at unfavorable prices to redeem shares.

Interest on these loans and the fees charged for maintaining credit lines at banks are considered part of a mutual fund's operating expenses. They are listed as a line item in a US-registered fund's SAI.

Directors' Fees

Directors' fees are paid to the members of the fund's board of directors. This is compensation for supervising the mutual fund's adviser and covers all of the expenses of board meetings.

Legal and Audit Fees
Independent legal and accounting firms charge mutual funds to prepare filings and financial statements for regulators. These costs are also often listed in the annual report as registration and filing fees.

Miscellaneous Expenses
Operating expenses can include a variety of so-called miscellaneous expenses, depending on the needs of specific mutual funds. Details are often listed in the footnotes of financial documents published by the mutual fund.

Sales Fees
Since commissions for brokers and financial advisers were deregulated by the SEC in 1975, a myriad of fund categories, known as share classes, have been designed based on the types of sales fees they charge. In the early days, most of the funds sold were known as "load" funds, meaning they charged a sales commission. Today, some mutual fund companies are selling funds to investors directly, without charging sales fees. These funds are called "no-load funds."

According to the Investment Company Institute (ICI), in 1970, 90% of fund assets were purchased through advisers and 10% were purchased directly from mutual fund companies. By 2003, 58% of fund assets were invested through a professional financial adviser, 15% were purchased directly from the fund company and 7% were purchased from a discount broker or mutual fund supermarket. The remainder was purchased via defined contribution retirement plans.

On the surface, no-load funds may appear to be the cheapest option available to investors. But a deeper look is necessary to come to that conclusion. Other, less obvious costs must be taken into consideration, such as brokerage fees charged when the investor leaves the fund.

Different cost structures have particular advantages and disadvantages for the investor. These depend on the annual expenses, the size of the load, and how long the investor plans to hold the fund.

Front-end Loads
A *front-end* load is a sales charge that is included in a mutual fund's public offering price, the price at which fund shares are bought by investors. The front-end load is paid when an investor buys the fund. As a result, the public offering price for these types of funds is higher than the fund's net asset value (NAV).

All new money invested into a fund is subject to this sales charge. In recent years, increased competition, intensified by online fund supermarkets, has brought down the level of the front-end load.

Breakpoints
Front-end loads offer investors *breakpoints*. These are discounts on the load that are given at specific set investment levels. The more an investor puts

into a fund, the lower the sales charges he pays.

Each mutual fund sets its own breakpoint schedule (see Figure 5.4). Some reduce their sales loads for investors that make large lump-sum investments. Other load funds give discounts if the total amount of purchases or the total market value of shares a mutual fund investor buys reaches a set level. Any subsequent purchases of mutual funds would then receive a discount on the sales charge. This arrangement is called the *right of accumulation.*

Funds are not required to offer breakpoints, but if they do exist, the fund must disclose them. In the US, members of the National Association of Securities Dealers (NASD) are not permitted to sell shares of a fund in an amount that is "just below" the fund's sales load breakpoint just to earn a higher commission.

Investors are also offered discounts when buying several funds within the same fund family. If the total amount of investments within a family of funds reaches a specific target, the investor will pay a lower sales charge on any further investments in that fund family. These types of fee structures encourage investor loyalty to a large fund family. Large families of funds also sometimes offer the option of switching the money invested in a particular load fund into another fund within the family without paying an extra charge.

Figure 5.4 — Sample Breakpoint Table

Sales Charge	Purchase Range		
5.75%	$0.00	—	$49,999.00
4.50%	$50,000.00	—	$99,999.00
3.50%	$100,000.00	—	$249,999.00
2.50%	$250,000.00	—	$499,999.00
2.00%	$500,000.00	—	$999,999.00
0.00%	$1,000,000.00 +		

Back-end Loads

Loads that are charged when investors sell a fund, usually within a relatively short period of time, are called *back-end loads.* They are also sometimes called *contingent deferred sales charges.* A mutual fund company may phase out the back-end load if an investor holds the fund for a number of years without selling. This structure is designed to encourage investors to buy mutual funds and hold them for longer periods of time. Figure 5.5 provides an example of a back-end load schedule.

Figure 5.5 — Back-end Load Schedule

Redemption In	Back-end Load
First Year	5%
Second Year	4%
Third Year	3%
Fourth or Fifth Year	2%
Sixth Year	1%
Seventh Year onwards	no load

To keep the back-end load at a minimum, mutual funds first redeem shares in an investor's account that are not subject to the charge. These shares may have been held for a long period or were bought through a dividend investment plan. The fund will next redeem the shares that qualify for the lowest load charge.

12b-1 Fees

The US Securities and Exchange Commission introduced a rule in 1980 allowing fund companies to charge a new fee, called a *12b-1 fee*, to cover the costs of marketing and distributing their funds and attracting new investors. The fee includes the costs of advertising a mutual fund or annual payments made to brokers who sell the fund.

The 12b-1 fees are deducted annually from the fund's assets. As investor resistance to loads increased in the 1980s, mutual fund companies started using these fees as a way to collect payments for broker commissions without

"And before you know it you're looking at everyone as a commission."

charging a front-end load. These different payment structures resulted in the creation of new share classes.

The 12b-1 fees are ongoing costs that never disappear. They are unrelated to specific transactions. Unlike loads, 12b-1 fees are included in expense ratios and are one of the factors affecting the differences in expense ratios among mutual funds.

In the US, 12b-1 fees used to pay marketing and distribution expenses cannot legally exceed 0.75% of the fund's average net assets per year. There is also a lifetime cap based on the fund's overall sales. A fund may also pay a service fee up to 0.25% of average net assets each year to pay sales professionals for ongoing services.

Redemption Fee

Some mutual funds charge a flat fee when investors redeem part or all of their shares. This fee is often confused with a back-end load. In contrast to back-end loads, the redemption fee does not decline when an investor holds mutual fund shares for a long period. Companies that impose redemption fees are often using them to try to discourage investors from trading mutual funds as frequently as speculative stocks.

Exchange Fee

Mutual funds can impose a fee on shareholders if they exchange or transfer their assets to another fund within the same fund group or family of funds. Many mutual funds waive this fee to develop investor loyalty to the group of funds.

Service Fee

Service fees are ongoing payments to the bank, broker or mutual fund supermarket that services the mutual fund investors' accounts. Part of the service fee may also be paid to the financial advisers that recommend the fund to investors. They are sometimes lumped together in expense tables under the category of 12b-1 fees.

Share Classes

Compared with the 1980s, investors now have much more choice in terms of mutual fund cost structures. Instead of one type of mutual fund share, they may be faced with a choice of three or more. Each offers a different way to pay for the services of a mutual fund.

The benefit of having more classes of shares is that mutual fund companies can market the same fund to investors with different time horizons, amounts to invest, and perspectives on costs. To be sure, some analysts do not see this as a positive development, claiming that the different fee structures simply confuse investors.

Different mutual fund shares are categorized into classes according to their various load structures. However, regardless of whether they are Class A, B, or C shares, all the share classes of a particular mutual fund are backed by the same portfolio of securities.

The main difference is how the front-end load, back-end load, 12b-1 fee and service fees are structured (see Figure 5.6).

Figure 5.6 — Mutual Fund Class Comparison

	Class A	Class B	Class C
Front-end Load	Yes (can be reduced with breakpoints)	None	None
Back-end Load	None	Declines over several years	Lower than Class B
12b-1 Fees	Lower than B or C shares	Higher than A shares	Higher than A shares
Converts to Class A Shares	N/A	Yes after several years, cutting costs	No

- **Class A** shares typically have front-end loads. The sales charge is taken by the mutual fund company upfront from the initial investment. Front-end loads may typically range from 3% to 5.75%. Because they do not have high ongoing costs, Class A shares can be the best option for long-term investors buying mutual funds through a broker or financial adviser. Some reduce the front-end load as the size of the investment increases. About 82% of all Class A shares have 12b-1 fees of less than 0.30%, according to the Investment Comapany Institute (ICI).

- **Class B** shares charge back-end loads, which are paid by investors when they sell a fund. These charges decrease the longer an investor owns the fund. This is often the first choice of many investors because of the attractiveness of there being no initial cost. All of the investor's money is immediately put to work.

  But holding these types of shares for a long period has its disadvantages since B shares normally include higher 12b-1 fees, which are ongoing annual fees. Over time these costs will lower the return and may also exceed the initial sales charges the investor was trying to escape.

  Ongoing expenses can be much more painful for investors than one-time costs. Therefore, perhaps the best options are Class B shares that can be converted into Class A shares after a certain number of years. Since Class A shares typically have much lower 12b-1 fees, investors will have lower ongoing expenses once the Class B shares are converted.

- **Class C** shares usually have lower back-end loads than B shares that are charged for a shorter period, such as a year. These shares often have higher annual costs because they charge an annual fee to pay the broker who sold the fund. They also generally do not convert to another class. C shares are often not a good choice for long-term investors.

B and C share classes rely most on 12b-1 fees to compensate financial advisers. Both B and C shares charge 12b-1 fees of between 0.75% and 1.00% of assets. B shares make up just 6% of mutual fund assets and C shares make up 2%, but together they account for more than half of all the 12b-1 fees collected, according to the ICI.

- **Class D** shares are usually pure no-load shares sold only to institutions or bought through an employer-sponsored retirement plan that purchases very large amounts.

No-load Funds

"Do-it-yourself" investors can analyze and choose no-load funds using information provided over the Internet or directly from fund companies without intermediaries such as brokers or financial advisers.

These types of funds have no front-end or back-end fee. They are purchased directly by mail, over the phone or via the Internet by investors who prefer to do their own research.

The Internet has become an important tool for research for these types of investors. A 2000 ICI study found that more shareholders owning "direct marketed" funds visited fund websites than did shareholders owning "sales-force-marketed" funds or funds from employer-sponsored retirement plans.

Investors should be aware, though, that "no load" does not usually mean there are no costs involved. No-load funds typically charge 12b-1 fees of as much as 25 basis points (0.25%). This is especially true of mutual funds sold through fund supermarkets. After all, discount brokers do not work for free!

No-load funds can also charge purchase fees, redemption fees, exchange fees and account fees. No-load funds also have ongoing operating expenses like all other funds.

Another variation on a no-load fund is called a "pure no-load fund." These funds do not charge front-end or back-end loads, 12b-1 fees, or service fees. Still, they can have high expenses because of high management fees.

Performance Fees

Advisory fees of some funds are also adjusted based on the fund's performance. The rate is higher when the fund's return exceeds a specific benchmark during a certain time period. The fee rate is reduced when the

*"I'll be honest with you, Jeannette,
I'm looking for a no-load relationship."*

fund's performance underperforms the benchmark. The fee increases or decreases proportionately with the investment performance for the fund compared with the benchmark.

When Paying Loads Makes Sense

If there are no-load funds available, then when does it make sense to pay a load?

Loads do not necessarily buy better analysts or fund managers since the loads are used to pay brokers and financial advisers who promote and sell the fund. In 1995, Morningstar studied the differences between load and no-load funds and found that no-load funds outperformed in the short run when the load-fund performance was adjusted to account for loads. However, the two groups had similar performance after 10 years.

This indicates that over the long term, loads are not necessarily a significant factor and, for the long-term investor, should not be the primary consideration when selecting a fund.

Some investors choose to do their own research and avoid the load. Still, more than two-thirds of the individuals who invest outside of retirement plans choose to rely on the advice of a financial professional such as a broker, financial planner or adviser to help choose funds or create a long-term investment plan. Even if you do your own research, there are other cases where buying a load fund merits serious consideration.

Some of the top fund managers only work for load funds. In this case, investors may be willing to pay extra to gain access to the expertise. Another reason to buy a load fund is to invest in a particular industry or geographical area that is inaccessible through no-load funds. This could be a very specialized fund that is focused on semiconductors, emerging markets or small-cap growth stocks.

Some fund houses sell certain specialized funds directly to investors. Nevertheless, the company charges loads that go to the fund house rather than to a financial adviser. Some investors will pay the load to gain access to these specialized funds.

EXPENSE RATIO

The expense ratio is often seen as the most important measure for understanding how efficiently a fund is managed.

The annual expense ratio equals total operating expenses divided by total net assets. Operating expenses include: investment management fees, administrative service fees, custodian and transfer fees, shareholder service fees, directors' fees, legal and audit fees, interest costs, and 12b-1 fees. The investment management fee is often the biggest part of the expense ratio.

Operating costs exclude brokerage costs, because the amount of brokerage costs depends on the frequency of trading by the fund manager. Operating costs also exclude front-end and back-end loads, because they vary according to the breakpoint schedule and the length of time an investor holds on to the mutual fund shares.

The expense ratio is stated in the fund's prospectus and published regularly in newspapers and other publications. In the US, the SEC requires a summary of all expenses and fees. It includes an example of costs using a hypothetical $10,000 investment. This type of example shows how much the expenses would total if the money were held in a fund for one year, three years, five years, and 10 years. Mutual funds disclose reasons for high expense ratios at any given time in the SAI.

The lower the expense ratio, the higher the amount of return that will be paid to shareholders. The higher the ratio, the lower the return received by investors.

For example, if your fund has an expense ratio of 1.5% and has a gross annual return of 20%, the net return will be 18.5% (20% — 1.5%). On the other hand, if the fund only has a gross annual return of 10%, then the net return will be 8.5%. In the first example, the expense ratio makes up 7.5% of gross return (1.5/20). In the second case, it makes up 15% (1.5/10). This shows that the effect of the expense ratio on returns increases as fund performance drops.

Expense ratios vary depending on the investment style of a fund and the type of securities it owns. Most bond and money market funds in the US have expense ratios of less than 1.5%, while slightly less than half of all equity funds have annual expenses at or below this level, according to the ICI.

Among bond and money market funds, those that invest in US government and agency securities may have the lowest expense ratios. Among equity funds, those that invest in international markets tend to have higher research costs than similar domestic equity funds. For domestic funds, sector funds and small-cap funds are also more expensive to operate because of higher research costs.

It is noteworthy, though, that while equity funds typically cost more than bond and money market funds, equity funds historically have provided a higher long-term return, even after expenses are deducted. Different types of stock funds, US or global, also vary in costs.

Expense Ratio Trends

Investors often use expense ratios to compare funds. But certain particularities about this measure must be noted when using it to evaluate fund costs.

One important trend is the increasing use of ongoing costs, such as 12b-1 fees. While many expect economies of scale to take effect as a fund's assets grow, in reality the expense ratio does not usually drop proportionately with a fund's increase in assets. This is partly due to the increasing use of ongoing fees to compensate brokers and financial advisers selling the funds.

Americans paid about $55 billion in mutual fund expenses in 2004, compared with $5 billion in 1989, because the industry has seen tremendous growth. Assets grew at about the same pace as the growth of costs, indicating that few of the economies of scale of the industry's significant growth trickled down to the average investor. As assets grow, economies of scale should come from the relatively fixed costs of running funds, such as accounting and legal expenses. However, there are a number of reasons why larger asset amounts have not resulted in lower expense ratios.

With the development of new share classes, 12b-1 fees used to pay brokers and advisers became to be included in expense ratios preventing expense ratios from significant declines.

Another reason for the slow drop in expense ratios is the shift in demand toward investment styles that are more expensive. In 1980, 6% of US equity funds were more expensive international or sector funds, compared with 30% in 2002, according to the ICI. A total of 3% of US equity fund assets were in international or sector funds, compared with 18% in 2002. Also, there has been a shift by investors to higher-fee equity funds.

A third reason is that there has been an explosive growth in the number of mutual funds. Many of the new funds have remained small and have not benefited from economies of scale, according to the ICI.

Newer funds have tended to stay smaller than those that have a longer track record (see Figure 5.7). For example, US equity funds created before 1991 had average net assets of $1.9 billion in December 2002, while the average for those created after 1990 was smaller. Funds created in 1991 had an average size of $802 million, while the average for those created in 2002 was $45 million, the ICI says.

The increase in the number of shareholder accounts has also driven up operational costs for some mutual funds. There has been about a 20-fold increase in the number of fund shareholders since 1980. In 1980, there were five million shareholders, and mutual funds managed 12 million accounts, according to the ICI. This rose to 95 million shareholders by 2002, when mutual funds managed 250 million accounts.

Improvements in customer service since 1980 have also added to costs. Shareholders can now access information about their accounts via

Figure 5.7 — Average Equity Fund Size ($ millions) at Year-End 2002 by Year of Inception

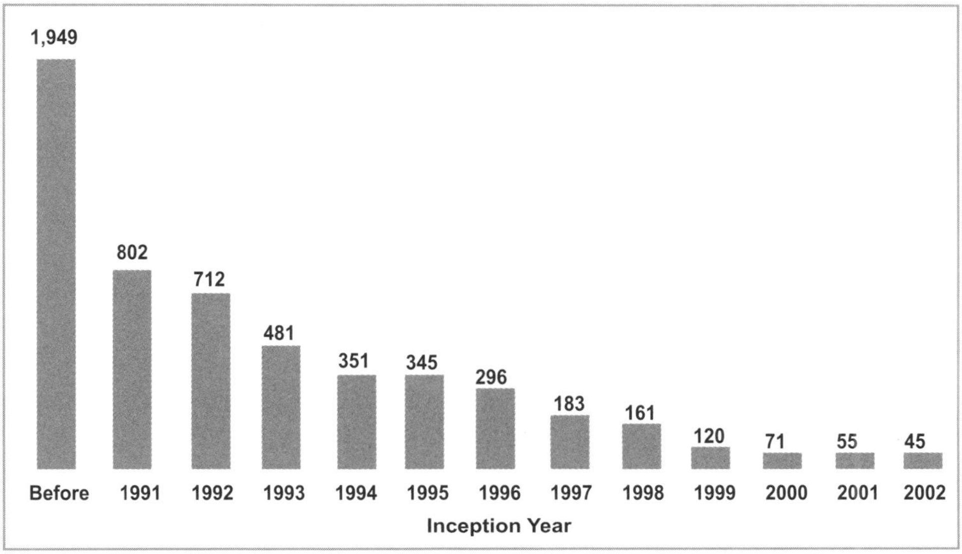

*Equity funds include hybrid funds

Source: Fundamentals, Vol. 13, No. 1, Copyright © 2004 by the Investment Company Institute (www.ici.org). Reprinted with permission.

the Internet at any time of day and fund companies provide many of their documents on the Internet. They have developed more intricate record-keeping services, and many bond and money market funds provide check-writing services.

Cost Trends

Rather than examine expense ratios on their own, it may be more useful to look at broader measures of fees and expenses that factor in the cost of loads to understand the latest cost trends affecting investors. When looking at costs in this way, it is clear that the total costs incurred by mutual fund investors have declined significantly as sales loads have shrunk and industry competition has grown.

On average, the combined loads and expense ratios paid by fund shareholders for buying an equity fund in 2002 were 1.25% of the value of the shares purchased. This is a decline of 45% from 2.26% in 1980, an ICI study showed. For bond funds, the decline over the same period was 42%, and for money market funds it was 38%.

This is largely due to the significant decline in load costs since 1980. The average maximum front-end load declined 40% during this time period. Almost all funds with front-end loads charged a maximum load of less than

6% in 2002. In 1980 the average was 7.4%, and 60% of the funds charged 8.0% or more, the ICI says.

Another reason for the decline is that a larger proportion of loads is now waived than in the early 1980s. This is because shares with front-end loads are now often sold through 401(k) and other retirement plans with their loads waived.

Generally, investors are holding most of their stock and bond fund assets in funds charging below-average operational and management expenses, according to the ICI. About 90% of the net "new cash" flowing into stock funds from 2003 to 2005 went to funds with costs lower than the median fund, compared with 75% of the flows to funds below the median in the mid-1990s.

The use of fee waivers to retain and attract clients is another example of increased fund competition based on cost. While small funds tend to have higher operational costs as a percentage of assets than larger funds (because of the lack of economies of scale), many still waive a portion of their fees to compete with the larger funds. Without the intense competition, these small funds would not normally waive the fees they need to provide a profit to the fund sponsor.

FEES AND RETURNS

At the end of the day, what matters is the return you get on your mutual fund investment. There are many good reasons to choose cheap funds to keep costs down and increase chances of a higher return. But there are also good reasons to pay higher fees if these are justified by higher returns, better customer service, freely available research, and a large pool of funds to choose from within the same fund family or supermarket. The most important thing is to be aware of the different types of fees and the basis on which they are charged.

The fund industry is hugely competitive and there is no better form of advertising than past performance. This will help keep costs down. It is not in the fund manager's interest to charge excessively high fees that negatively affect performance.

SUMMARY

Costs associated with investing in mutual funds may have an influence on the size of returns. All funds charge them, but costs vary among different funds. There is often no correlation between high fees and good fund performance.

Operating expenses are the ongoing costs of running a mutual fund. They are used to pay for fund managers, analysts, customer service and publishing documents. A portion is deducted daily from the fund's net asset value. Management fees usually make up the biggest percentage of operating expenses. They are charged by fund managers for researching and choosing securities for a fund. Other operating expenses include administrative fees, brokerage fees, custodian and transfer agent fees, directors' fees, interest fees, legal and audit fees, and shareholder service fees.

Loads are charges paid to brokers or financial advisers as a sales commission. Front-end loads are paid when an investor buys the fund. Mutual funds offer breakpoints to investors on front-end loads. These are discounts given when the size of an individual's investment reaches certain predetermined levels. Back-end loads are sales charges paid when investors sell a fund.

12b-1 fees cover the costs of marketing and distributing funds and attracting new investors. These are ongoing fees and are often used to compensate brokers when investors pay no loads or low loads.

Mutual funds offer different classes of shares to investors with different time horizons and views on costs. Class A shares usually have front-end loads and a low 12b-1 fee. Class B shares charge back-end loads and higher 12b-1 fees. They may be converted to Class A shares over time. Class C shares charge lower loads, but they have higher annual fees. Class D shares are usually pure no-load funds.

No-load funds are geared towards investors who choose their investments independently, without a broker. These funds usually do not have front-end or back-end loads, but they still charge 12b-1 fees and could have high management fees.

Expense ratios measure how efficiently a fund is managed. This ratio equals total operating expenses divided by total net assets. Expense ratios exclude loads and brokerage costs. The higher the expense ratio, the lower the returns received by the investor. Expense ratios have not declined significantly with the growth of the mutual fund industry because of the increase in the costs of managing many accounts, the increasing popularity of funds that are more expensive to run, and the increased use of ongoing 12b-1 fees to compensate financial advisers. Still, the size of load costs has declined significantly in the past two decades, reducing total expenses for investors.

QUICK QUIZ

1. You are studying two funds for investment. The first is an index tracker fund, the other a global emerging markets equity fund. What would your expectations be in terms of management fees for the two funds?

2. An investor is looking at buying a mutual fund that has different share classes. Class A has a 5% sales charge and an annual management fee of 1.5%. Class B has no sales charge but charges an exit fee based on the fund's NAV of 5% in the first year, 4% in the second year, 3% in the third year, 2% in the fourth year, and 1% in the fifth year. The annual management fee is 2.5% per year. The investor plans to hold the fund for four years and expects a 10% return per year. Which share class would be cheapest to buy?

3. Despite the significant growth in the mutual fund industry over the past 20 years, expense ratios have not fallen much. Discuss some of the reasons for this.

4. You are evaluating two mutual funds for a client. The two funds have a similar investment objective and invest in the same geographical area. One fund has returned 10% p.a. over the past five years with an annual total expense ratio of 2.5%. The other fund has returned 9% p.a. over the same period with an annual total expense ratio of 1.5%. Discuss your considerations when choosing between the two funds.

5. Explain the main differences between A, B, and C shares. Which share class would you recommend to an investor planning to hold a fund for 10 years?

6

BUYING AND SELLING MUTUAL FUND SHARES

When the TV news reports a market crash, mutual fund investors may start to worry. Should they call their financial adviser or broker in the middle of the day and sell? Are their retirement savings at risk? Or is this a major buying opportunity? Should they add to their portfolio before the market bounces back?

Before making any impulsive decisions, investors must understand that buying and selling mutual fund shares is very different from trading individual securities such as equities.

First, mutual fund shares are not traded like stocks (unless they are closed-end funds). They can only be purchased from or redeemed by the mutual fund company. Second, mutual fund prices are determined just once a day, while equity prices fluctuate throughout the day. Daily changes in the markets should not be a concern because mutual funds are meant as investment vehicles for long-term planning.

HOW TO BUY MUTUAL FUND SHARES
Fund Pricing
Mutual fund shares are structured as very liquid investments because investors have the right to redeem their shares on a daily basis. Most mutual funds also offer shares to new investors on an ongoing basis and allow investors to transfer their money from one fund to another within the same fund family.

One of the major differences between mutual fund shares and equities is the way in which their prices are determined.

Mutual fund purchase and sale prices are set through a system called *forward pricing*. Mutual funds calculate and report the net asset value of their shares after the stock markets close every day. The net asset value is the current market value of all of the fund's assets, minus liabilities, divided by the outstanding number of shares.

Unlike company shares, mutual fund shares have no intra-day prices. The price at which investors buy shares is set at the end of each day, regardless of the time of day the purchase order was received. For example, when checking mutual fund prices at midday, investors are quoted the price set after markets closed the previous day. Fund prices are set only once a day because the prices of the securities in the fund's portfolio are constantly changing throughout the day. The number of outstanding shares is also always fluctuating because of new purchase orders and requests for redemptions.

Once markets close, each fund "marks to market" its portfolio by calculating the total value of securities and cash equivalents held in its portfolio based on their closing prices. The fund then subtracts any expenses, fees or trading costs. It divides the net amount by the number of fund shares outstanding at the end of the day after all of the buy and sell orders are processed.

Orders received before the close of trading get the price calculated at the end of trading on that day. Orders received after trading closes receive the price determined after the close of trading the next business day.

Mutual funds are priced during a short timeframe. When markets close in New York at 16:00, a US mutual fund usually receives the prices for securities it holds from a pricing service. Fund accountants then validate the prices and each fund in the US must report its value by 17:55 Eastern Time for the fund price to make it into the next day's morning newspapers. The prices are also automatically sent directly to the public via different newswire services and the Internet. Fund prices may also be available through the fund's toll-free telephone service and website.

Investors can determine the profitability of their holdings by comparing the published net asset value with the price at which they bought the shares. The difference is the investor's unrealized gain or loss. The net asset value is also the approximate value an investor would receive if he liquidated his shares, excluding any back-end load or other fees.

Funds are purchased at their public offering price. If they are no-load funds, the public offering price equals the net asset value. If there is a front-end sales charge, the public offering price will exceed the NAV. The public offering price is not published because it can vary among investors buying the same shares, as different investors are eligible for different breakpoints.

As we have mentioned, most mutual funds with front-end loads offer breakpoints, i.e. discounts on the sales load if the amount invested is large. Many mutual funds will allow you to qualify for the discount even if you are just approaching the asset level required. This is because it is usually illegal for the fund to sell you an amount of shares that is just under the breakpoint level in order to earn a higher sales fee. This is made possible with a letter of intent, basically a promise that an investor's purchases will meet or surpass the amount set in the breakpoint schedule by a certain deadline.

For example, an investor plans to put $3,000 in a front-end load mutual fund initially and plans to invest an additional $50,000 over the next year. The front-end load on the initial purchase may be 4.5%. However, the fund may offer a breakpoint of 3% at the $50,000 level. The client is eligible to sign a letter of intent with the mutual fund company to receive the lower sales charge of 3% on all fund purchases over a specific period of time, usually a maximum of 13 months. If the terms of the agreement are not met by the designated date, the applicable higher sales charge will be deducted from the client's account.

Many mutual funds impose redemption fees to discourage frequent trading by market timers that could increase fund administration costs that are borne by all fund shareholders.

BUYING STRATEGIES
Pay Yourself First: Dollar-Cost Averaging
When Mr. X gets his salary, he pays for his rent, makes car payments, and settles heating bills; however, without a clear investment strategy in place, he often neglects to pay himself first, i.e. make an investment for his future. To make sure savings grow, one important method is to invest money in funds regularly.

One approach for creating a steady investment plan and meeting financial goals is buying mutual funds using *dollar-cost averaging* (DCA). Simply put, this means investing money in equal amounts on a regular basis, such as once a month or once per quarter.

Mutual fund companies often offer automatic investment plans that allow money to be regularly debited from a savings or checking account on a set date for immediate investment into a particular fund. Arranging to have money electronically transferred allows you to just invest once. Once the system is in place, the automatic investment plan will take care of ongoing contributions. The contributions do not need to be significant. Many mutual funds offer these automatic plans for as little as $50 a month, a quarter or annually.

The benefit of this strategy is that an investor can buy cheaper shares on average by spreading out investments during different market cycles. The shares are purchased automatically, at regular intervals, without considering the offer price on the day of the purchase when you use DCA.

With dollar-cost averaging, there is no agonizing about whether it is "the right time to invest." If the share price has dropped on the investment date, you are able to buy more shares for the fixed amount invested during that particular period. If the fund's price has risen, you would buy fewer shares for that amount. Over the long term, the cost of each share is typically lower than the average price during the same period when you use DCA.

Why is that? See Figure 6.1. Say an investor commits to investing $500 in a particular fund on the first of every month. When the share price falls as low as $8.00 in March, he is able to buy 62.5 shares. When the share price rises to a high of $12.25 in May, he buys 40.8 shares. The average price over the six months is about $10. But the average cost of the shares for the investor is just $9.77.

Of course, no investment strategy, including dollar-cost averaging, can guarantee a profit or protect against a loss in a declining market. But dollar-cost averaging does have many benefits.

First, it can ease the anxiety of investing in a riskier fund all at once.

Figure 6.1 — Average Cost of Shares

Month	Monthly Investment Amount	Share Price	No. of shares Purchased Each Month
January	$500	$9.00	55.6
February	$500	$10.00	50.0
March	$500	$8.00	62.5
April	$500	$11.75	42.6
May	$500	$12.25	40.8
June	$500	$9.00	55.6
TOTAL	$3,000		307.1
Average Share Cost: $9.77 ($3,000 ÷ 307.1 shares)			

Establishing a systematic investment plan can create a long-term outlook that can ease the stress of market fluctuations.

With a regular investment schedule, in the end, an investor may actually invest more than when allocating a lump sum. If the price of the fund falls, it is possible to buy more shares at a lower price. Investors may regret investing all the money at once in a lump sum if the price declines and reduces the value of the investment.

On the other hand, if the investment increases in value, an investor may have preferred to put all the money to work at once. Unfortunately, most of us do not have a crystal ball to set this kind of timing in advance.

Of course, one risk of DCA is that an investor may stop the regular payments if he gets nervous when he sees the fund's value is declining. The strategy is only effective if nerves do not get in the way of regular investing.

To be sure, studies have shown that dollar-cost averaging may not be the best way to invest a sudden inheritance or windfall. One study by professors at Wright State University showed that investing such a lump sum as soon as it is received brings greater returns than dollar-cost averaging, although at a higher risk.

The study tracked lump-sum versus regular investments over 780 different 12-month periods from 1926 through 1991. The study indicated that an investor would have received higher returns 64.5% of the time by investing his money in a lump sum.

Still, adopting a dollar-cost averaging system as a long-term strategy may help investors feel more comfortable during market downturns, as it lowers the average cost per share.

To make the strategy work, investors must follow three golden rules for dollar-cost averaging:

- Begin investing now: Instead of waiting for the right time to invest, it may be the best strategy to just start right away. Over the long term, it makes relatively little difference whether the market was up or down at the beginning of a period of regular investing.

- Focus on the number of shares, not on share prices: A declining share price is not a welcome event for someone planning to sell. But if you are accumulating shares, it can be a good thing. Lower prices mean the chance to buy more shares at a lower price. These shares have the potential to grow in value if the market rises again.

- Prepare to ride out market declines: Remember that dollar-cost averaging works best over longer periods of time. You must be ready to commit to regular investments on a set schedule *no matter what*. This is especially important during a market decline.

Timing the Market

The opposite style of investing to dollar-cost averaging is timing the market. Some investors prefer to try to identify the best time to purchase and sell their securities to try to maximize their returns and reduce losses. This style of investing in mutual funds follows the old maxim: "buy low, sell high." It relies on forecasts and market analysis and is used by many brokers, financial analysts and mutual fund managers. Some market timers use technical analysis to look for trends or patterns in market fluctuations to determine when the next dip or peak will occur.

Advocates of these strategies say that forecasting the highs and lows of the market can bring higher returns. There are two forms of market timing, known as *pure market timing* and *dynamic asset allocation*.

Pure market timing strategists choose when to be 100% invested in one of three asset types: equities, bonds and money markets. Dynamic asset allocators shift the weighting of their assets in all of these types of securities based on market fluctuations and the probability of return compared with risk in each of these asset classes.

Still, market timing is not as simple as it sounds. Investors who try to time the market often find their investments perform worse than those that simply buy and hold securities because they often badly time their purchases and sales. An investor who believes the market will go down may take his money out of equities and then miss on the best performing months of the year. Short-term market fluctuations are usually unpredictable and sudden. Pinpointing a low or a high in the market is usually only possible when looking at past performance.

Buy and Hold

Rather than trying to time the market, investors who hold securities for a longer period of time ride out the bad times and tend to end up on top. This is known as a "buy and hold" strategy. In general, the equities markets have produced superior returns year after year. While some years are better and some are worse, the general trend is up.

One study published in the *Financial Analysts' Journal*, February 2001 issue, compared buy-and-hold strategies with market timing tactics from 1926 through 1999. The study showed how difficult it is to time the market. It compared the results of a buy-and-hold strategy with all the possible market-timing strategies in the time period to determine what percentage of the timing strategies produced a greater return. To do this, the authors determined all the possible market-timing combinations during the period, with different switching frequencies. They assumed that in any given month, an investor could be in either Treasury bills or in equities. They determined all the possible returns that could have come from the various switches. In the end, *only about a third* of all possible monthly market-timing combinations had better returns than the buy-and-hold strategy. Annual switches had even worse results.

The debate about the benefits of a buy-and-hold strategy relative to market timing is bound to continue. What's clear is that in order to be successful, the forecasting of market fluctuations requires the type of expertise and information investment professionals have access to on a daily basis. Most importantly, it requires a great deal of discipline.

Individual investors are usually advised to stick to the tried and true, but perhaps less exciting, strategy of investing for the long term. By using a buy-and-hold strategy, individual investors can benefit from *compounding*, the ability of your investments to make money. Over time your level of risk will decline because as your investment grows, the chance of losing the original principal drops.

Reinvesting Dividends and Capital Gains

For many funds, it is not just fund price growth, but also the reinvestment of earnings that fuels returns. Dividends come from the regular payments made by companies to shareholders and the interest paid on bonds and money market funds. Funds also make capital gains and losses when a manager sells securities in the portfolio.

Unless the investor is retired and relies on the regular income from these payments for a living, there may be no need to collect these periodic payments in cash. Many investors opt to have them automatically reinvested in the fund. This increases the number of shares that can be purchased without investing new money. It gives the investor the chance to make even more money due to compounding. Each year he earns returns on the returns he made the previous year plus distributions, as well as on the initial investment.

Mutual funds usually do not charge any front-end or back-end load on shares bought through a dividend reinvestment arrangement. Still, these dividend payments are often subject to taxes.

This straightforward system of reinvesting these payouts is a benefit of investing in mutual funds compared with individual stocks. When investing in stocks, the dividend may be paid in cash or put in a money market account at a brokerage. Some brokerages reinvest these payouts but charge a fee.

"My summer vacation: How I made money in a bear market."

Others offer a dividend reinvestment plan, called a DRIP, which allows you to buy stocks and have all the dividends automatically reinvested.

Reinvesting dividends and capital gains is often essential to good returns. A total-return index, such as the S&P 500 index, assumes that all dividends and distributions are reinvested.

Buying on Margin

When investing with a brokerage, one interesting option is the ability to buy on margin. The brokerage firm gives a loan backed by your mutual funds and other securities, which are used as collateral. The loan can be used to buy additional shares in mutual funds.

In a bull market, buying on margin can enhance returns, but when the market heads south, investors are often advised to quickly pay back the loan to avoid mounting losses.

Consider the following example. In a bull market, an investor invests $100,000 plus a $50,000 loan in a fund with a 10% return. The return on the total investment is $15,000. After subtracting 5% of the margin investment, or $2,500, for financing costs, the net return is $12,500. That's a 12.5% increase from the initial investment.

In a bear market, an investor makes the same investment, $100,000 plus a $50,000 loan. This time the market falls by 10%. The loss incurred is $15,000 plus $2,500 for financing costs. As a result, the net loss is $17,500 or a 17.5% loss of the initial investment.

WHERE TO BUY MUTUAL FUND SHARES

Investors can buy mutual funds in many different ways, either directly from

NEWS CLIP
STRATEGIES; BLAME THE FUND MANAGER, OR THE FACE IN THE MIRROR?

Most mutual fund investors have only themselves to blame if their portfolios seriously lag behind the market. That is the conclusion of a new study that says the typical investor has an atrocious sense of timing.

People tend to dump mutual funds just before the funds enter several-year periods of above-average performance, and to buy funds that are about to sag. In fact, the study found that the performance of most fund portfolios would improve markedly if the owners just left well enough alone.

The study, "Dumb Money: Mutual Fund Flows and the Cross-Section of Stock Returns," was conducted by two finance professors, Andrea Frazzini of the University of Chicago and Owen A. Lamont of Yale.

Investors tend to blame fund managers for poor returns, but the professors argue that this is not entirely fair. By focusing on the decisions that investors make in shifting money into and out of various funds, the professors found that managers were more victims than perpetrators...

Just by sticking with the funds you own or by investing in an index fund that mirrors the market, you can resist the temptation to buy the flavor of the month and dump a short-term loser. That alone would improve returns for the average fund investor, according to the professors.

Bold investors may want to go a step further, by using an active reallocation strategy that is contrary to what most people are doing. That means shifting money away from funds that are receiving the most inflows and into funds that are suffering the most outflows.

This idea, however, is not for the weak of heart.... It takes rare courage to stick with a contrarian strategy at such a time. Consider all the investors in the late 1990's who couldn't stick with value funds in the face of growth funds' stunning gains.

But, as was so amply illustrated after the Internet bubble burst, the rewards of avoiding the most popular funds can be enormous.

Source: Mark Hulbert, *New York Times,* February 26, 2006

the fund company, through a discount broker, or through a financial adviser. Where to buy funds is a personal preference and depends on an investor's individual needs and desire for additional services.

Buying Direct

The no-frills option is to buy funds directly from the fund companies. Buying direct has some advantages for cost-conscious investors. By buying direct from a no-load fund company, an investor may avoid brokerage transaction costs and sales loads.

Investors with a small amount to invest may opt for direct investing to avoid broker transaction fees. These may not be an issue when buying funds from the fund company itself.

However, many fund companies rely on intermediaries such as brokers and financial advisers to sell their funds. Since they do not want to compete with these people, they add the nominal charges or commissions so the customers will not get an advantage from buying direct.

Choosing to stick with a specific fund family with a broad array of fund choices may be another reason to buy funds directly. This is another way of reducing fees. There are many fund companies that offer enough choice to allocate money to funds with different investment styles and risk profiles.

Discount Brokers and Mutual Fund Supermarkets

Initially no-load mutual funds were only available for sale directly from the fund companies themselves. Switching assets between funds required filling out new applications, mailing checks or arranging wire transfers, etc. In 1984, the process was simplified with the creation of the first mutual fund supermarket, established by a brokerage firm. Since then, many more supermarkets have sprung up on the Internet, offering a one-stop shopping experience for mutual funds.

The main advantage of using discount fund supermarkets is the reduction of paperwork needed to buy and sell mutual funds. Just one application form is needed to start investing in a wide variety of funds. Instead of receiving account statements from many different fund companies, the supermarket sends investors one statement that consolidates all mutual fund transactions and records. Switching assets among different funds is easy with a fund supermarket.

Buying from a fund supermarket gives access to a large selection of funds from different fund companies. Usually individual fund companies specialize in certain types of investments. Using a supermarket allows access to specialists in many different types of funds without needing to approach each company individually.

Some discount brokerages also offer additional perks such as check-writing and debit cards that provide easy access to money.

Of course all of these additional services come with a price tag. Discount brokers charge transaction fees for buying and selling some of the funds, while others charge a flat fee for their services.

In what some see as the best of both worlds, some of the major fund companies have created discount brokerage divisions that offer mutual funds from other companies. This gives the option of buying funds from the main company without transaction fees and the choice of funds from other fund companies.

This option makes sense if an investor plans to invest most of his assets with the mutual fund company running the discount brokerage and wants to put a smaller percentage of his assets with other funds offered by the company's discount brokerage division. This type of supermarket charges brokerage transaction fees on the funds offered by other fund companies.

As indicated in Figure 6.2, there has been a shift among investors towards investing in defined contribution retirement plans and an increase in the use of discount brokers and mutual fund supermarkets.

Figure 6.2 — % of Mutual Fund Assets by Purchase Source, Selected Years

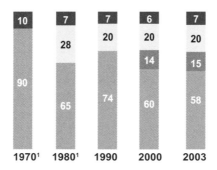

■ Discount broker/mutual fund supermarket
  Defined contribution retirement plan
■ Directly from mutual fund company
▨ Professional financial adviser

[1]Based on holdings of stock, bond, and hybrid mutual funds.
Note: Components may not add to 100% because of rounding.

Source: Fundamentals, Vol. 14, No. 3, Copyright © 2005 by the Investment Company Institute (www.ici.org). Reprinted with permission.

Financial Advisers
There are many reasons to consider hiring a financial adviser. Some new investors may be intimidated by the vast array of choices offered through discount brokerages or lack the confidence to choose funds directly from a fund company. Others simply dislike investing or are too busy to take care of it themselves. Some seek guidance for creating a long-term plan to meet specific financial goals.

The use of financial advisers to help choose mutual funds is widespread. About two-thirds of all mutual fund shareholders in the US own funds outside defined contribution retirement plans. Among these investors, more than 80% own fund shares through professional financial advisers, according to a 2004 survey by the ICI. About half own funds solely through advisers, while one-third own funds bought from advisers as well as directly through fund companies, discount brokers or fund supermarkets.

A majority of fund investors across different categories — such as age, education, year of initial fund purchase, and household mutual fund assets — buy most of their funds through advisers. Some types of investors are more likely to use financial advisers exclusively than others.

The biggest difference is in terms of education. While 90% of fund shareholders with a high school education or less bought funds through advisers, 77% with graduate degrees used advisers, according to the ICI.

Shareholders aged 55 to 64 are also most likely to use only advisers as they approach retirement and may need assistance with planning. Among investors who use advisers, 44% use at least two types of advisers, such as full-service brokers and independent financial planners.

Hiring the right adviser can be a challenge. The first thing to consider is how they are paid and whether there are any conflicts of interest. Financial advisers are compensated either through: (1) a sales commission; (2) a fee based on the amount of assets invested; or (3) an hourly consulting charge.

There are some disadvantages to the commission-based system. For example, advisers who make high commissions on certain funds may recommend them even if they are not appropriate for a particular investor. Also, commissions come out of the money earmarked for investments, which means less money is put to work initially. Commissions also create incentives for advisers to encourage clients to trade often since the advisers make a commission every time a client buys or sells a fund.

Employer-based Retirement Accounts

Another popular source of mutual fund investments is company-sponsored retirement funds. These plans have been a major driver for the growth of the industry. Companies often offer retirement accounts that provide large tax breaks. The most common in the US are called 401(k) plans, which are typically offered by larger companies. They allow investors to save a certain amount per year, which is excluded from reported income and free from US federal and state income taxes. The money is taken out of an employee's salary before the salary is subject to tax.

An added benefit of these plans is that employers often will match a portion of an investor's contributions. For example, an employer may offer to contribute 50 cents for every dollar invested up to a certain percentage of the salary. If an employee contributes $5,000, he would receive an additional bonus of $2,500. Some of these plans also allow loans, which are then repaid with withdrawals from the salary.

These plans allow investors to take advantage of a dollar-cost averaging

"My broker says don't panic, I'm still young enough to recoup my losses."

strategy because they make contributions regularly from their paychecks. This may give them the opportunity to invest in more volatile funds that they would normally exclude from the rest of their portfolio.

SELLING MUTUAL FUND SHARES
Deciding When to Sell Fund Shares
Mutual funds sometimes change, or the needs of an investor change, prompting the investor to re-evaluate current holdings. Knowing when to sell can be more difficult than deciding when to buy. Investors are often afraid to forgo potential earnings if they sell at the wrong times. Still, some instances are red flags and may be good reasons to redeem shares in a fund.

- **Rebalancing a Portfolio**
  Frequent reviews are necessary to determine if your asset allocation has not changed given your investment goals. For example, if a particular large-cap equity fund did particularly well in a certain year, it may be time to sell some shares to bring the allocation of assets back in line.

- **Style Changes**
  If a fund manager of a small-cap growth fund has started buying mid-cap growth funds as the assets of the fund expand, it may be time to shop around for a different small-cap fund to rebalance the styles you invest in. An investor may mistakenly buy a fund under the impression that it is a conservative, blue-chip fund and later discover that the fund manager takes more risk than he expected. It is better to switch money to a fund that makes the investor comfortable than hold on to a mistake.

Checkout Receipt

Cupertino Library
04/05/14 03:02PM

Use our CATALOG at
www.sccl.org/catalog/
or TELECIRC at 800-471-0991 to:

Renew titles
List titles checked out to you
Learn the total of fines owed
Review titles being held for you

Requires
Valid library card and PIN
(Personal Identification Number)

Library Catalog and Telecirc
are available daily

****

PATRON: 729035

The informed investor : a hype-free guid
33305201975764   Due: 04/26/14

Mutual funds : an introduction to the co
33305220772572   Due: 04/26/14

TOTAL: 2

- **Manager Changes**

  When a fund manager is replaced, investors need to assess the skills of the new fund manager before deciding to sell. In a passively managed fund, such as an index fund, the change in management may not make a big difference. If the new fund manager has a long-term record at a different fund, it is relatively easy to determine if he is a good substitute for his predecessor. Investors should also look at how well the fund company has handled previous changes.

- **Changing Investment Goals**

  A sudden inheritance received by a young professional saving for a first home may bring a need for asset reallocation. The investor may now be able to afford the house and may change his time horizon to refocus his investments on retirement savings instead. Now he can buy funds that take more risk, switching from a balanced fund to equities, for example.

- **Poor Performance**

  A couple of years of underperformance may not make a difference in the long run, but several years of returns that lag its peers make a fund a candidate for a sale. Before selling the fund, make sure its performance is being compared with an appropriate benchmark.

Deciding Which Fund Shares to Sell

The sale of shares can be subject to tax, so it is necessary to choose which fund shares to sell when you begin redeeming your holdings. There are several ways of deciding which to sell.

- **Specific Shares**

  When redeeming shares, an investor can tell the fund company which specific shares to redeem based on their cost. For example, an investor bought 100 shares in Fund A two years ago at $20 a share and another 100 shares at $40 a share one year ago. Today the fund is worth $60 a share. He can decide to sell the more recent shares purchased or the first ones purchased or a combination of the shares. For the purpose of the transaction, the shares can be identified by the date of purchase or the cost at which they were bought.

- **First-In-First-Out**

  Another method of accounting for the shares being sold is called the *first-in-first-out* method. This simply means that the first shares that are sold are the first shares that were purchased. This could lead to paying higher taxes if the equity fund has appreciated over time.

OPINION
THE EMOTIONAL SIDE OF INVESTING

It is easy to get emotionally involved in investing. Feelings of frustration or excitement can get in the way of clear thinking. The markets can play havoc on your peace of mind as they fluctuate like a roller coaster.

Would our decisions about buying and selling mutual funds or other investments improve if we were devoid of emotion? One recent study by Stanford University marketing professor Baba Shiv says yes. In his experiment, people with certain kinds of brain injuries earned more money investing than a comparison group.

The study, published in June 2005 in Psychological Science, analyzed investment decisions by people with brain lesions that made them unable to feel emotions. Their other brain functions were normal. All participants received $20 at the beginning of a 20-round coin toss game. Each had a choice whether to risk $1 on a coin toss. If they didn't participate, they kept their money. If they won, they earned $2.50. They gave away $1 if they lost.

Financially, it made the most sense to play each round because the potential return was much more significant than the potential loss. With a 50-50 chance of winning, the value of playing each round

was $1.25, while the value of not participating was $1.

Participants with brain damage, which affected their ability to feel emotion, took the most profitable strategy. They invested in 84% of the rounds, earning an average of $25.70. The other participants invested in just 58% of the rounds, earning an average of $22.80. Over time the normal participants became more conservative and risk-averse after they lost money in a few rounds.

One of the co-authors of the study, Antoine Bechara, theorized that successful investors could sometimes be called "functional psychopaths." They are probably better able to control their emotions or feel emotions less intensely than others.

What does this teach normal investors? While we cannot turn into investing automatons, we can try to look at our portfolios objectively. Do not get angry, frustrated or too excited. Schedule regular invest-ment checkups and steady contributions, and reba-lance your portfolio with a long-term perspective.

Source: Shiv, Babe et al, *Investment Behavior and the Negative Side of Emotion, Psycological Science*, Vol. 16, No. 6, 2005

- **Average Cost**

  Another method for specifying which shares will be sold is the average cost method. The investor calculates the average purchase price of the shares being sold. The result becomes the basis used to calculate capital gains or losses on the redemption. This method is useful if the shares were purchased regularly over a period of time with dollar-cost averaging and/or if fund distributions such as dividends were reinvested.

EXCHANGING MUTUAL FUND SHARES

Instead of collecting cash when an investor redeems shares, he can *exchange* them for other shares of a fund in the same fund family. Most mutual fund companies will facilitate this exchange at no extra charge to the investor as long as both of the funds are part of the same family of funds. The shares must be exchanged for shares of the same class. For example, Class A shares of fund ABC can only be exchanged for Class A shares of fund XYZ. The exchange is executed at the NAV of both of the funds. The exchange is not subject to any sales charges, allowing all of the money to be invested immediately.

The ability to exchange fund shares allows investors the flexibility they need when their investment needs change. For example, as a couple nears retirement and needs steady income, they may want to switch some of their assets from an equity fund to a bond fond, or from a growth equity fund to a value equity fund. Or, investors in bond funds may switch to equities while interest rates are low in an effort to achieve a higher return.

Exchanges involve the sale of shares and the purchase of new shares, so the gains made may be subject to taxes. These exchanges may also be subject to administrative fees and trading fees, which are outlined in the fund's prospectus.

NEWS CLIP
BUY THE MANAGER OR BUY THE FUND? A FUND'S PERFORMANCE RECORD MAY NOT REFLECT CURRENT MANAGEMENT

SAN FRANCISCO (Market Watch) — A fund's record doesn't always speak for itself. Funds are ranked, rated and rewarded on the strength of returns over several years. But those numbers may not reflect what the current leadership has done. So what's more important — the fund or the manager?

Fund companies tend to spotlight the overall quality of an offering rather than superstar managers, as they did in the 1990s.

"Fund companies would like you to believe that the fund is an institution and carries on regardless, but I don't think that's consistent with the real world," said Roy Weitz, publisher of the watchdog Web site FundAlarm. com. "Funds are people. It ultimately comes down to the quality of the talent."

But others will tell you that while long tenure is welcome in a manager, it isn't as crucial when a fund is managed by a team or when a successor carries a solid track record from another portfolio. Fund managers stay on the job about four years, on average.

One reason for a diminished emphasis on individual managers is the fact that management teams now are the norm. About two-thirds of broadly invested US stock funds have multiple managers, according to investment researcher Morningstar Inc.

More commonly, a team of managers make collective buy and sell decisions, although sometimes the "team" is actually one leading player with a supporting cast.

So ask a fund company for the new manager's background, or better yet, scout that information on the Web — it's in the fund's prospectus. See how a manager performed in up and down markets, making note of any outsized gains or losses against a benchmark that may offer clues into risk-taking.

"Generally you go with a manager who has a meaningful track record somewhere," Morningstar's Kinnel said. "It doesn't guarantee this is a smart or good manager, but at least it said I've got a few years and I can learn a lot from that."

Source: Jonathan Burton, *MarketWatch*, Apr 23, 2006

SUMMARY

Buying and selling open-end mutual fund shares differs significantly from trading equities or other securities because mutual funds set their prices just once a day. They are not traded on an exchange. Instead they are purchased from and redeemed by a mutual fund company.

Mutual fund prices are set according to forward pricing, the calculation of net asset value of mutual fund shares after stock markets close each day. Orders received before the close of trading receive the price set at the end of the day. Orders received afterwards receive the price set the following day.

Dollar-cost averaging is a regular savings strategy that allows investors to average out their purchase price by spreading out investments during different market cycles. The cost of each share is often lower than the average price during the same period. Many mutual fund companies offer automatic investment plans to facilitate this strategy.

Market timing is used by some investors who try to pinpoint the best time to buy and sell to maximize their returns and reduce losses. While investment professionals may adopt this strategy because of their expertise and access to specialized information and analysis, individual investors are generally advised to follow a buy-and-hold or dollar-cost averaging approach to ride out market fluctuations.

Dividends and capital gains can be reinvested into a mutual fund automatically to increase the number of shares that can be purchased without investing new money.

Mutual fund shares can be purchased directly from a fund company or through discount brokers, mutual fund supermarkets, a financial adviser or a full-service broker. Each option has its benefits and depends on the investor's individual needs for additional services. Another major source of mutual funds is employer-based retirement accounts. The employer often matches contributions made by its staff, increasing retirement savings.

Instead of redeeming mutual funds for cash, they can be exchanged, sometimes at no additional cost, for other shares within the same fund family.

Investors sometimes redeem shares when their investment goals change, when they rebalance their portfolio and when the mutual fund changes its strategy or fund manager, or shows sustained poor performance. There are three methods of deciding which funds to sell and how to account for them for tax reporting purposes. Investors can specify which shares to sell based on their cost or date of purchase. They can also decide to sell the first shares that were purchased. Another method is to have the fund calculate the average purchase price of the shares being sold to create the basis for calculations of capital gains or losses.

QUICK QUIZ

1. When an investor places an order to buy mutual fund shares at 18:00 on Monday, which price does he receive, Monday's NAV or Tuesday's NAV? Why?

2. Two investors buy into the same fund during the same year. Investor A buys 400 units at $25/unit. One year later, he sells all the units at $28.75/unit. Investor B invests on a quarterly basis. First he buys 100 units at $25/unit, then 138.9 units at $18/unit, then 156.3 units at $16/unit, and finally 87 units at $28.75/unit. Which investor has the best return? (Value for investor A = 400 units x $28.75 = 11,500. Value for investor B = 482.2 units x $28.75 = 13,863)

3. If an equity fund is volatile for a 12-month period, who would probably make the best returns: a market timer, a lump-sum investor, or a dollar-cost averaging investor? Why?

4. Why are investors often advised to reinvest dividends and other distributions?

5. Name the advantages of buying funds directly, using a fund super-market and using a financial adviser.

7

BUILDING MUTUAL FUND PORTFOLIOS

DEFINING GOALS

Investors use mutual funds as tools to fulfill many different financial goals. Perhaps it is a plan to buy a new house in five years, send children to college in 10 years, or retire comfortably in 20 years. Each goal requires a different type of portfolio, or collection of funds.

Key considerations when creating a mutual fund portfolio to meet a financial goal can include:

- Time horizon
- Risk tolerance
- Investment goal
- Inflation

Time Horizon

An investor's particular type of goal determines how long the money will be invested, also known as the *time horizon*. It also helps set how much risk is appropriate. The shorter the timeframe, the less risk an investor may be willing to take because of the need to preserve the gains already achieved or to limit future losses.

Risk Tolerance

Before creating a portfolio investors should examine their feelings about market volatility and the amount of risk they are comfortable taking. How would you respond if the value of your investment suddenly declined? Would you be tempted to sell to prevent further losses or would you stick with the investment strategy?

Investment Goal

The time horizon is critical to the decision regarding how much money the goal requires. Some retirees can live comfortably on a fraction of their previous income. Others dream about round-the-world trips or working on improving their golf handicap.

No one wants to guess when their time on earth is up, but when it comes to life expectancy, it is better to plan for a long life than run out of cash. In the US, average life expectancy is about 74 years for men and almost 80 years for women. But in most industrialized countries, life expectancy is increasing.

Inflation

Another important consideration is inflation. Many financial advisers assume an annual inflation rate of between 2% and 4% for retirement planning. College costs tend to increase by much more than the inflation rate but those numbers could be too low.

Many investors need to set aside money to meet more than one goal at a time. Creating a separate portfolio for each goal may help simplify the planning process.

THE REWARDS OF STARTING EARLY

Saving towards specific goals by investing in mutual funds early in life can take advantage of the benefits of compounding. Simply put, compounding is when your interest earns interest. Compounding has a snowball effect with money. Every year, the earnings made and reinvested contribute a little more to the earnings made the following year. As time goes by, additional earnings contribute more and more to the value of the investment.

Figure 7.1 illustrates the effects of reinvesting a hypothetical 4% return on a $15,000 money market investment.

The amount of interest increases each year by a slightly larger amount because the interest rate is applied to a bigger amount each year. Over 30 years, the $15,000 investment earning 4% in interest can almost triple in

Figure 7.1 — How a Money Market Investment Compounds

Year	Value	Interest Earned at 4% Interest	Additional Interest Earned from Prior Year Due to Previous Year's Interest Added to the Fund
1	$15,000	$600	
2	$15,600	$624	$24
3	$16,224	$649	$25
4	$16,873	$675	$26
5	$17,548	$702	$27
6	$18,250	$730	$28

For illustrative purposes only; assumes all interest is reinvested. The concept of compounding is presented by using a hypothetical money market fund.

value to $48,651. After a while, the reinvested interest becomes greater than the initial investment. If the fund's share price rises, then that growth is added on top of the income earned from compounding.

Starting early can make a significant difference in returns. Consider the stories of Kelly and Jennifer, who are the same age. Kelly starts investing $100 in a mutual fund every month starting at age 25. She then stops contributing to the fund after ten years because she needs the money for mortgage payments. She doesn't touch her retirement account until she stops working at 65. At age 35, Jennifer starts contributing $100 every month to her retirement fund. She continues these investments until she retires at age 65.

Let's compare the returns on both investments assuming a 10% annual return: Kelly contributed to her fund for only 10 years, while Jennifer contributed for 30. Kelly contributed just $12,000, while Jennifer contributed $36,000. Kelly's is worth $357,433, while Jennifer's is worth $226,049. Why is Kelly's worth more?

Compounding is the answer to the difference. Time makes a huge difference in the growth of the investment. By starting 10 years earlier, Kelly gave compounding more time to take effect.

Specific attitudes to risk can be balanced with objective investment criteria — such as time frame, goals and the availability of emergency money — to create a portfolio with an appropriate balance between risk and return through diversification and asset allocation.

The right amount of risk gives the investor the confidence to stick with a specific investment strategy even when there is a market decline.

"My dad's mutual funds outperform your dad's mutual funds."

RISK QUIZ

The following quick risk quiz can shed some light on your attitude and whether your portfolio should be more aggressive/growth-oriented or conservative/income-focused.

I'm looking for long-term growth rather than current income. T/F

I have money set aside for large expenses or a financial emergency. T/F

I can ride out significant fluctuations in the market without feeling very anxious. T/F

I prefer an investment with a 50% chance of losing 10% and a 50% chance of gaining 25% in a year rather than an investment with a steady return of 5% a year. T/F

I am comfortable waiting more than 10 years to achieve the returns I expect. T/F

I am well versed in the facts about risk and potential rewards associated with investing in various types of securities. T/F

If you answered "True" most of the time, then you are a rather aggressive investor who is most likely comfortable with a portfolio mostly comprising equities. Your investments may be geared towards aggressive growth, small-cap, and international investments. Aggressive investors are typically younger or are more experienced investors who are comfortable with risk and have a long time horizon for meeting their financial goals. They can tolerate higher degrees of market volatility.

If you answered "False" more often than not, you have a more conservative investment attitude. Conservative investors need more current income from their investments and may be willing to accept just a small amount of risk or volatility. They may be more cautious or first-time investors. They also may have five or fewer years before they need the money invested to meet their financial goals. Their investments may be concentrated in money market funds, bonds and large-cap equities.

NOTE
AGGRESSIVE OR CONSERVATIVE?

The following are some of the characteristics typically found in aggressive and conservative investors.

Aggressive Investor:

- Focused on equities

- Funds may include aggressive growth, small-cap, emerging markets.

- Younger or more experienced investors

- Longer time horizons to goals — more than 10 years before needing the money invested

- Can tolerate higher market volatility

- Have higher expectations for returns

- Desire returns that outpace inflation

Conservative Investor:

- Needs current income from investments

- Willing to tolerate only low amounts of risks or volatility

- Older or less-experienced investor

- Has five or fewer years before money needed for financial goal

- Investments may be concentrated in money market funds, bonds, large-cap equities

INVESTMENT GOAL

While most homeowners know the level of their mortgage and monthly repayments, few individuals have the same clear picture about their retirement goals.

To do a quick check on how far you are on your way to meeting your future retirement liabilities (or other similarly large expenses), here are a few easy calculations to complete:

- What do you need for your retirement each month?

- What have you saved so far for this purpose and what is the future value likely to be?

- What is the possible shortfall and how much do you need to save on a monthly basis to reach your goal?

A good question to consider is: "In today's money, how much money do you need per month during your retirement?"

Let's take an example of someone who needs $5,000 per month for living, clothing, car, travel, insurance, medical costs, club memberships, gifts, etc. This equals $60,000 per year. We are assuming that no money needs to be put aside for housing as the home will (hopefully) be fully paid off at the time.

Now $60,000 in today's money does not have the same value as it will in 20 or 30 years when you may actually be retiring. Inflation will erode the value of your savings. We have to adjust the figure to ensure the buying power remains constant.

We could assume, for example, that inflation will amount to 3% per year for the next 20 years until retirement. Adding 3% per year to $60,000 gives us a final value of approximately $108,000.

According to this example, in 20 years time, $108,000 will buy the same amount of goods and services as $60,000 buys today.

You could now try to speculate how long you are going to live in order to find out how big your capital pool needs to be in 20 years. The problem is that nobody knows how old they will be when their time is up. Taking into consideration the pace of medical and health care innovations, 20 years down the line, we could be living until we are 100 years old!

A more conservative strategy is to work with the idea of creating a large capital pool from which you can draw an annual "salary" in the form of dividends and returns from your investments.

DIVERSIFICATION

Diversification is the mantra of the mutual fund industry. The ability to spread your investments over a wide range of securities is one of the main attractions of investing in mutual funds rather than in individual securities.

Many people do not have enough time or money to invest in a wide variety of individual stocks, bonds or other assets.

Most mutual funds are diversified. A single fund can own securities from hundreds of issuers. The objective is to protect investors from major price declines in any one sector at any given time.

NEWS CLIP
US RETIREMENT SAVINGS LIKELY TO FALL SHORT OF NEEDS

NEW YORK (AP) — The majority of American workers think they'll be able to retire comfortably, but most aren't saving nearly enough to meet that goal, according to a new study.

The Employee Benefit Research Institute's annual retirement confidence survey found that about 68% of workers are confident about having adequate funds for a comfortable retirement, up slightly from 65% in 2005.

At the same time, more than half of all workers say they've saved less than $25,000 toward retirement, according to the Washington, D.C., based research group. Even among workers 55 and older, more than four in 10 have retirement savings under $25,000.

"'Overconfidence' is the word that comes to mind," said Jack VanDerhei, co-author of the study.

He said that the poor savings performance was especially troubling because it comes as many of the nation's employers are eliminating the defined benefit plans — better known as pensions — that have buoyed the retirements of current workers' parents and grandparents. Many companies also are eliminating retiree health care coverage or asking retirees to contribute more for it.

"It's clear that people currently working should factor into their retirement planning the long-term trend away from traditional defined benefit pensions," VanDerhei said. "That means people need to be saving more than they are."

VanDerhei believes that people would save more if they took the time to project what their costs in retirement are likely to be. But just 42% of workers say they've done such a calculation.

"But some people are absolutely clueless about this and frozen into inactivity as a result," he said. "They really should find a fee-based professional to help them out. It's going to cost a couple of hundred dollars, but you'll make that amount up many times in the future."

Source: The Association Press

Mutual funds allow investors to diversify across different asset classes (bonds, stocks and money market) as well as many types of subsets within a group of securities (large/small-cap stocks, growth/value equities, government bonds and international bonds).

- **Among asset categories:** Choose funds from several asset categories, such as stocks, bonds, money market and even real estate, for example. This can reduce the risk that an entire asset category will do poorly over a period of time.

- **Within asset categories:** You can reduce the impact on your investments that a specific underperforming type of security could have. Diversifying is not simply owning many bonds, it is owning different types of bonds, such as long-term, short-term, corporate, government, and, possibly, high-yield (See Figure 7.2 on page 131).

- **Global investing:** Investing outside the domestic market expands the investable universe and reduces the risk if local financial markets go through an extended bear market. This can help offset overall portfolio volatility.

Figure 7.2 on page 131 shows the annual returns of 50 stock markets all around the world for 10 years from 1996 to 2005. As the chart shows, no one market is the best performing year after year. In fact, during that entire 10-year period, only two markets, Turkey and Russia, were the best performing for two of the ten years. Also, only eight markets of the total 50 markets were the best performing. Of course, these findings are no guarantee that in the future the performance pattern will not change. However, one thing is very clear: If you want to have an opportunity to find the best performance, you must look globally at all markets and you must diversify.

ASSET ALLOCATION
The process of choosing investments among these different groups of securities is called asset allocation. The reasoning behind this strategy is that different groups of equities and bonds or other securities offer better returns at different points in a market cycle.

For example, in the 1990s large-cap stocks had the best performance, while in the mid 1980s small-cap stocks showed impressive returns. Allocating some assets in different sectors allows you to reap some of the most significant returns and avoid major losses across your portfolio.

Ideally, one would keep all investments in bonds when they are doing well and switch to equities when they are offering better returns. But the reality is that market timing is usually not effective. Instead of trying to predict the future, it is advisable to hold investments in various types of assets. No matter what is going on in the market, chances are that at least part of the portfolio will register decent returns.

Figure 7.2 — Yearly Returns in Percentage for Markets Around the World

	2005	2004	2003	2002	2001	2000	1999	1998	1997	1996
Argentina	63	26	101	-51	-18	-25	34	-24	25	20
Australia	18	32	51	0	3	-9	19	7	-10	18
Austria	25	72	58	17	-5	-11	-9	1	2	5
Belgium	10	45	37	-14	-10	-16	-14	69	14	13
Brazil	57	36	115	-31	-17	-11	67	-40	27	43
Canada	29	23	55	-13	-20	6	54	-6	13	29
Chile	22	29	84	-20	-3	-15	39	-28	6	-14
China	20	2	88	-14	-25	-31	13	-42	-25	37
Colombia	108	133	67	25	46	-39	-14	-42	42	11
Czech Republic	46	87	66	44	-2	2	5	1	-23	31
Denmark	25	32	50	-16	-14	4	12	9	35	22
Egypt	162	126	92	2	-41	-44	88	-27	31	59
Finland	18	7	20	-30	-38	-14	153	123	18	35
France	11	19	41	-21	-22	-4	30	42	12	22
Germany	11	17	65	-33	-22	-15	21	30	25	14
Greece	16	46	70	-25	-30	-42	50	78	36	7
Hong Kong	8	25	38	-18	-19	-15	60	-3	-23	33
Hungary	19	92	32	31	-9	-27	12	-8	95	107
India	38	19	78	8	-19	-22	87	-21	11	-2
Indonesia	16	52	78	43	-8	-62	93	-32	-74	28
Ireland	-2	43	44	-26	-3	-13	-13	35	16	32
Israel	27	20	58	-31	-31	28	60	-5	25	-2
Italy	3	34	39	-6	-26	-1	0	53	36	13
Japan	26	16	36	-10	-29	-28	62	5	-24	-15
Jordan	74	61	58	5	35	-23	6	-11	2	-8
Korea	58	23	36	9	49	-50	92	141	-67	-38
Malaysia	2	15	27	-1	5	-14	115	-31	-68	26
Mexico	49	48	33	-13	19	-20	80	-34	54	19
Morocco	14	23	49	-8	-14	-22	-12	25	35	36
Netherlands	15	13	29	-20	-22	-4	7	24	25	29
New Zealand	3	38	58	26	10	-33	14	-21	-13	19
Norway	26	54	50	-7	-12	0	32	-30	7	29
Pakistan	65	18	42	156	-23	-12	50	-57	28	-17
Peru	35	3	96	29	20	-24	19	-40	21	0
Philippines	24	27	43	-29	-19	-45	3	13	-63	18
Poland	25	62	35	1	-27	-4	32	-7	-22	59
Portugal	-1	26	44	-13	-22	-10	-8	28	47	36

Figure 7.2 — con't

	2005	2004	2003	2002	2001	2000	1999	1998	1997	1996
Russia	74	6	76	16	56	-30	247	-83	112	153
Singapore	14	22	38	-11	-23	-28	99	-13	-30	-7
South Africa	28	45	46	28	-17	-17	57	-28	-8	-18
Spain	5	30	59	-15	-11	-16	5	51	26	41
Sri Lanka	34	11	46	35	44	-41	-6	-26	13	-15
Sweden	11	37	66	-30	-27	-21	81	15	13	38
Switzerland	17	16	35	-10	-21	6	-7	24	45	3
Taiwan	7	10	43	-24	10	-45	53	-21	-6	40
Thailand	9	-1	145	28	5	-56	47	12	-73	-37
Turkey	57	42	126	-36	-33	-46	252	-53	118	37
United Kingdom	7	20	32	-15	-14	-12	12	18	23	27
USA	6	11	29	-23	-12	-13	22	31	34	24
Venezuela	-24	56	42	-16	-7	4	9	-49	28	131

Source: MSCI

That is why choosing the right mix of assets is essential. Equities offer the best returns over time, but also carry more risk. A stock-heavy portfolio is usually one that has a longer timeframe. If planning for a shorter-term goal such as buying a house, investors may instead rely more on bond funds, which could provide income while taking less risk.

Younger investors can afford to take more risk because they may have more time to save to meet their financial goals, such as retirement. Middle-aged investors are more risk averse, and retirees focus on preserving the wealth they have built over the years.

Figure 7.3 — Different Investing Strategies

Consider the following three scenarios, illustrating different investing strategies. While these returns cannot guarantee future results, asset allocation, in this particular example, was the most successful strategy during the noted time period.

Asset Allocation Can Impact Returns	
Returns on $10,000 invested annually in stocks and bonds 1984-2004	
Strategy	Average Annual Return
Chasing the winners Investing in previous year's best performing asset class	9.55%
Chasing the losers Investing in previous year's worst performing asset class	8.12%
Allocating among asset classes Investing evenly across asset classes	10.65%

Source: S&P Micropal, 12-31-2004

Although asset allocation plans will be different for different investors, a hypothetical asset allocation can be illustrated with a pie chart as follows.

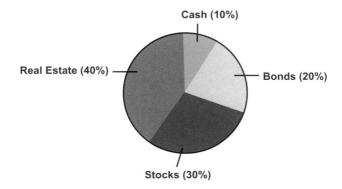

Some typical mutual fund asset allocations for these three groups of investors by age are:

- Young professional: at least 80% in stocks

- Middle aged: 60% stocks, 40% bonds

- Retired: 20-40% stocks, remainder in bonds

There are many different ways to allocate money among asset classes. The following are examples of hypothetical asset allocation portfolios for investors focusing on aggressive growth, growth, moderate growth, conservative growth and income. Stocks are represented by the S&P 500 index, bonds by long-term US government bonds, and cash equivalents by US Treasury bills.

Aggresive growth: Stocks 100%

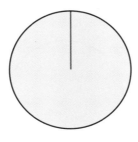

Stocks 100%

Growth: stocks 80%, bonds 20%

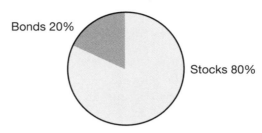

Bonds 20%

Stocks 80%

Moderate growth: stocks 60%, bonds 40%

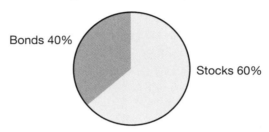

Bonds 40%

Stocks 60%

Conservative growth: Stocks 40%, cash equivalents 20%, bonds 40%

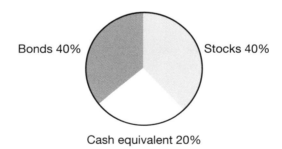

Bonds 40%

Stocks 40%

Cash equivalent 20%

Income: stocks 20%, cash equivalents 20%, bonds 60%

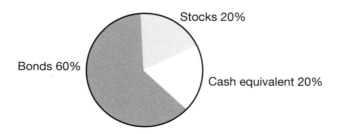

Stocks 20%

Bonds 60%

Cash equivalent 20%

These models are by no means prescriptions. They are merely typical suggestions made by mutual fund companies and advisers. They should be adjusted to match specific objectives, risk tolerance and time horizons.

CREATING A PORTFOLIO

How much should an investor allocate to each category? To simplify the selection process, some advisers recommend first selecting a core mutual

OPINION
ARE YOU OVERDIVERSIFIED?

If you put all your money into just one or two investments — stocks, bonds, or anything else — you run the risk that something will go wrong and wipe out a big chunk of your nest egg. By spreading out your investments, you smooth out returns and lessen the effect that any one holding can have. Modern portfolio theory has shown that a diversified portfolio has a better expected return, for a given level of volatility, than a portfolio that's concentrated in just a few issues.

Mutual funds offer automatic diversification, which is one reason they've become so popular. It's still a good idea to diversify among different funds, though, in order to prevent one fund or asset class from dominating a portfolio.

But is it possible to be too diversified? Absolutely. After a certain point, adding more funds to your portfolio just creates additional bookkeeping and tax headaches, while doing little or nothing to increase returns or lower risk. When dozens of mutual funds are

thrown together, the result tends to be indistinguishable from that of an inexpensive index fund, because any differences among the funds become diversified away.

So what can you do to prevent overdiversification in your own portfolio? The first thing to do is to make a list of all your investments, organized by asset class. This will make it easier to look at your whole portfolio and decide whether you really need everything that's there. If you've bought funds and stocks through a variety of different channels there may be more than you realize.

If you own too many funds in one asset class, it's a good idea to think about trimming that number, as doing so will make your portfolio a lot easier to manage and will also reduce the likelihood that you've built a costly, yet index — like, portfolio.

Source: *David Kathman, CFA,* April 25th, 2006 *www.morningstar.com*

NEWS CLIP
THE IMPORTANCE OF DIVERSIFICATION

As the red-hot California real estate market sizzled in recent years, National Consumer Mortgage looked like just another residential mortgage company successfully riding the boom. It had lush offices in downtown Orange; the former baseball great Steve Garvey promoted its products in radio spots; and its founder, Salvatore Favata, a former local baseball hero himself, lived in a $1.7 million mansion in tony Yorba Linda and zipped around in a Mercedes roadster. An annual "Favata Fest" at the founder's home featured live music and photo ops with Mr. Garvey.

The little mortgage company was also ambitious. N.C.M. ran an investment arm that offered high-yielding notes to preferred clients, promising to use customers' funds to make short-term, high-interest loans to individuals and companies that needed money quickly. For customers like Bryan F. Downey, a 41-year-old father of three, it was a tantalizing pitch. Mr. Downey had a $125,000 inheritance that he wanted to put to work, and his younger brother had already invested his inheritance with N.C.M.

In April 2005, Mr. Downey invested the entire $125,000 in N.C.M. notes guaranteeing annual interest payments of 12.5 percent for two years. After the contracts were signed, Mr. Downey recalls, Mr. Favata, 46, tan and trim, glided into the conference room, which had a view of Angel Stadium, nearby in Anaheim. Mr. Favata greeted him like an old friend and shook his hand, saying, "Welcome to the family." It's a relationship Mr. Downey now wishes he could disown.

Earlier this spring, Mr. Downey, along with more than 200 others living mostly in California and Colorado, found out they were victims of a long-running Ponzi scheme that pulled in about $30 million before N.C.M. sought bankruptcy this spring, according to a Securities and Exchange Commission civil complaint and filings in a federal criminal case, both filed in United States District Court for the Central District of California in Santa Ana. Rather than using the money to make loans, authorities say, Mr. Favata wagered away about $10 million of it in Las Vegas and plowed through much of the rest in his business dealings and lavish lifestyle.

Source: Julie Creswell and Vikas Bajaj
New York Times, 2006

fund that is a relatively stable investment. The core takes up at least 50% of the holdings and is geared towards helping achieve specific goals. The remainder of the portfolio's assets are held in non-core funds such as specialty funds, which may not be as stable as the core fund, but enhance returns and add variety.

Core Funds

Core funds are often large-cap domestic stock funds because they are a reflection of economic performance. They also can be more stable than small-company shares. Core funds could be large-cap blend funds, which hold companies with both growth and value characteristics.

Some conservative investors focus on large-cap value funds, which invest in established companies that are deemed inexpensive compared with their peers. More aggressive investors may focus on large-cap growth funds. Some may decide to include an international fund as part of the core, to avoid investing too much in a particular market. These international funds typically focus on developed countries, where markets are less volatile.

For shorter-term goals, bond funds may form the focus of core holdings. These should be funds that invest in high-quality debt and intermediate maturities. Funds that focus on lower quality debt carry more risk, while bonds with longer maturities can be more volatile.

Non-core Funds

The remainder of the portfolio can go into non-core investments, which help make the portfolio more diversified. These can include small-cap or foreign funds with a good performance compared with their peers. Non-core funds also may include specialty funds that focus on a specific sector or region such as emerging markets. These can create the possibility of higher returns, but also have more risk. But since they do not form the major portion of the portfolio, a significant downturn in these funds is unlikely to put reaching specific goals into jeopardy.

HOW MANY FUNDS?

Some investors like to cover all of their bases by investing in funds in dozens of categories. They choose one large-cap, one small-cap, one growth fund, one value fund, one international fund, one pharmaceuticals fund, one technology fund, one emerging markets fund, one Asian fund, and on and on.

It is good to spread risk across various types of funds, but there are disadvantages to over-diversification and owning too many funds. With so many funds to monitor, it is easy to lose track of how they are helping an investor achieve certain goals. It is difficult to keep track of performance and how all of these investments work together.

So what number of funds is ideal? One Morningstar study created hypothetical portfolios containing one to 30 funds each, using every possible combination of funds, to explore this issue. The study found that the single-

Fig 7.4 — How the Number of Funds in a Portfolio Affects Standard Deviation

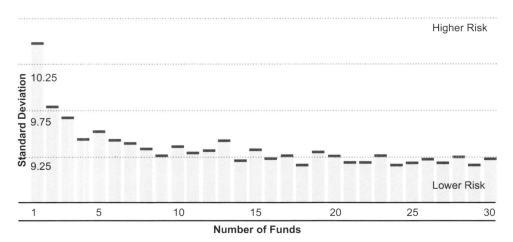

Source: Morningstar, Inc. 2003

fund portfolios had the highest standard deviation, meaning they produced either the biggest gains or losses. With each additional fund in a portfolio, the standard deviation declined. This meant that returns were lower, but so were the losses.

Still, after four funds, the effect of adding another fund on standard deviation declined. After seven funds, changes were slight, and after 10 funds the portfolio's standard deviation stayed the same no matter how many more funds were added. Therefore, after owning seven to 10 funds, it may be unnecessary to add more to a portfolio.

In the end, it is not the number of funds that makes a difference; it is how well the portfolio is diversified. For that, an investor must know what each fund owns, whether the various fund holdings overlap and whether there are holes that need to be filled.

Overlap

Having more than one fund that focuses on the same types of stocks can dampen returns as the fund that has inferior performance chips away at gains. Overlapping funds can also inadvertently increase risk by decreasing the level of diversification. These issues often are not obvious until the market starts to decline. Suddenly the portfolio's assets shrink much faster than expected.

Overlap is common with large-cap funds. Only about 250 US stocks can be classified as large-cap, according to Morningstar. As a result, many large-cap, blend, and hybrid funds hold some of the same equities. If you hold several large-cap stocks, it is likely some of the holdings overlap.

To avoid overlap, it makes sense to invest in funds that have a different focus and style. For example, large value, large growth, small value, and

NEWS CLIP
MY PORTFOLIO IS ON AUTOPILOT.
WELL, PART OF IT IS.

Every once in a while, the mutual fund industry manages to mass-produce a newfangled product that's actually useful for a broad swath of the investing public. An example is found in asset allocation funds — premixed portfolios that give investors instant exposure to stocks and bonds through a single fund.

Rudimentary forms of asset allocation funds have been around for years, but these offerings have grown in sophistication and popularity since the bear market that began in 2000. The funds have nearly tripled in number — to 775 — since the start of the decade, while their assets have grown from $58 billion to $160 billion, according to Lipper, the mutual fund information company.

These portfolios are geared to hands-off investors having neither the time nor the interest in selecting and rebalancing individual funds. Many of the funds invest in other stock and bond funds, as opposed to making decisions on individual issues; managers choose the funds and the allocations to each. Asset allocation funds run pretty much on autopilot and are designed, in theory, to be single-fund solutions for all of your investment needs.

But in reality, the vast majority of people who invest in asset allocation funds do not use them the way they were intended, said Lori Lucas, director of retirement plan participant research at Hewitt Associates, the consulting firm. "People understand they're not to put all their eggs in one basket but don't seem to realize that these are well-diversified baskets," she said.

A recent study by Hewitt found that only 15% of 401(k) investors who hold an asset allocation fund put all of their money in that portfolio. The typical investor who uses these funds actually invests in more than four other mutual funds.

To be sure, asset allocation funds can be used in a "core and satellite approach," said Joseph C. Flaherty Jr., senior vice president at MFS, an asset management firm in Boston that offers four variations of the funds — for conservative, moderate, growth and aggressive-growth investing styles.

Investors may make an asset allocation fund their core holding by putting, say, 75% of their money into it. Then, Mr. Flaherty said, "if they have a certain view about the market or an asset class they favor, they can tilt their portfolio in that direction by layering some funds on top of it." ....

Source: Paul J. Lim, *New York Times*, August 7, 2005

small growth funds tend to have little correlation with one another. They all produce different returns within a given time period.

Another strategy is to avoid investing in more than one fund run by the same managers. Fund managers tend to stick with a certain style even when managing more than one fund. Some smaller fund management companies, sometimes known as boutiques, also focus on either growth or value or another segment of the market. Larger fund families tend to offer more diversified choices.

Fund analysis websites have tools which help identify overlap or gaps in a portfolio. These tools can be easier to use than trying to track all of your funds' holdings independently.

Morningstar, Value Line, and Standard & Poor's, as well as mutual fund company websites, list the 10 to 25 top holdings in a particular fund's portfolio. Take note that the same company could appear in funds categorized with different styles. For example, a software company could be found in a large-cap fund, a growth fund, and a technology fund.

When analyzing a portfolio, the information about a fund's holdings should be as current as possible. Some fund companies only give holding information in their annual report. Others distribute this information semi-annually or quarterly. Monthly updates are most often available on the companies' websites or via fund analysis websites.

REBALANCING A PORTFOLIO
While an asset allocation plan reduces the number of decisions related to owning a portfolio of investments, it should never be set in stone.

Regular reviews to monitor and rebalance positions can help make sure an investor stays on track to meet specific goals. They assure that the portfolio does not become unbalanced as some asset classes appreciate or depreciate. Periodic check-ups also help keep investors focused on their strategies and goals rather than seeking out the latest hot investment.

Financial advisers can provide many types of graphs, calculations and risk analysis or tax advice. They can also provide different types of simulations based on various assumptions to see if an investor is on track to meet their financial goals.

Do-it-yourself investors who opt not to use an adviser can set up their own monitoring system by scheduling specific dates to review their investments. They can use online tools to help with calculations and download retirement planning software on the Internet.

One simple way of analyzing a portfolio is listing all the funds by style, such as growth, value, small-cap or large-cap. Comparing funds with similar styles in terms of costs, performance and holdings can uncover weaknesses or overlap in the portfolio. Investors should identify the reasons for owning each fund and know which constitute the core of the portfolio. The number of funds should be reduced to a figure that is easy to track.

Another consideration is changes in an investor's risk profile. Investors may set milestones for shifting asset allocations to more conservative

"To hell with a balanced portfolio. I want to sell my Fenwick Chemical and sell it now."

investments as they come closer to deadlines for fulfilling financial goals.

It is also important to get the maximum return for the level of risk you have chosen. This can be achieved by selecting better performers within asset classes or changing the asset allocation of a portfolio. Check the fund's ratings, standard deviation and beta. Then compare those risk measurements to the fund's historical returns. If a fund is taking on above average risk, is it paying back with higher returns?

 ## SUMMARY

The funds that make up an investor's portfolio vary according to the investor's specific goals, time horizon and comfort with risk. It is also important to consider the effects of inflation on the value of savings.

By starting investing in mutual funds early, you can benefit from the effects of compounding. Earnings made each year and reinvested in the portfolio contribute more to the earnings made the following year.

An investor's attitude towards risk helps determine whether a portfolio should be focused on growth or on income, depending on how aggressive or conservative an investor is. Diversification is a hallmark of mutual funds. It helps create the right balance between risk and return. This means spreading investments over a wide range of securities to protect investors from major declines in any one sector. Assets may be diversified within asset categories and among asset categories.

The process of dividing up assets among these different groups is called asset allocation. Portfolios with longer timeframes tend to focus on equities, while those with a short deadline for meeting financial goals tend to focus on bonds or cash equivalents.

When creating a portfolio, some advisers recommend first selecting a core, relatively stable, mutual fund. The core takes up at least 50% of the holdings and is meant to help achieve specific goals. Core funds are often large-cap domestic equity funds for longer-term goals and high-quality bond funds for shorter-term goals. The remainder of the portfolio assets can be invested in non-core funds, such as specialty funds, to add variety. These can include small-cap funds, foreign funds, or funds focusing on a particular industry or region.

Funds with overlapping assets can inadvertently increase risk by decreasing the level of diversification. Many large-cap funds hold the same equities. To avoid overlap, investors should invest in funds with different focus and styles, such as large-cap value, large-cap growth, small-cap value, and small-cap growth.

Portfolios require regular review to monitor and rebalance positions and make sure an investor is on track for meeting certain goals. This can be achieved independently or with a financial adviser.

 QUICK QUIZ

1. Why is it that investors with a long time horizon of more than 10 years are more likely to benefit from an investment into equities than investors with a short time horizon (less than three years)?

2. How does a typical asset allocation look like for a young professional? And for a retired individual?

3. Owning a large number of mutual funds from several different asset classes may not necessarily help to diversify your portfolio. Why?

4. Name two ways of diversifying a mutual fund portfolio.

5. What types of securities do conservative investors tend to buy? Why?

6. Name three factors that determine whether an investor is more aggressive or conservative.

8

THE MUTUAL FUND INDUSTRY: TRENDS AND GROWTH DRIVERS

The $17.3 trillion global mutual fund industry has developed into one of the most competitive businesses in the world after 20 years of explosive growth at the end of the 20th century. Even after weathering the challenges of trading scandals, a stricter regulatory environment, and a bear market, the industry is poised for further expansion.

The next decades promise to bring interesting product innovations and original services as mutual fund companies compete for new investors. With increasing access to information and analysis, some investors will choose to run their own portfolios, selecting and buying mutual funds themselves. Others will tap the expertise of investment advisers who will help them choose the funds best meeting their investment requirements.

Many factors are coming together to fuel the industry's growth. They include:

- The growth of individual savings

- Aging populations fostering the growth of pension funds and such structures as 401(k) plans

- Personal income growth in China, India, Russia and other emerging markets

- Liberalization of various government savings schemes, such as Japan's postal savings system

AGING POPULATION FUELS AND FUNDS DEMAND

One of the biggest drivers for industry growth is the simple fact that the population around the world is aging. Demographic factors are likely to drive industry growth in the next decade, considering the "stickiness" of retirement planning assets.

The growth of an older population has increased the pool of savings available for investment and the need for increased funding of pension plans. In the US, 82 million Americans of the "baby boomer" generation were born between 1946 and 1964, comprising 30% of the US population according to research by Banc of America Securities. The fastest-growing age segment is the 55- to 64-year-old group. Figure 8.1 shows that a significant percentage of this segment owns mutual funds. This segment's holdings are also expected to grow the fastest, as indicated in Figure 8.2 on page 145.

In the US, a large pool of money is also expected to shift out of 401(k) plans as baby boomers retire. About $3 trillion in client assets will move from 401(k) accounts into individual retirement account (IRA) rollovers or other self-directed plans over the next 10 years. In addition to planning for their own retirement, this segment of the population will also need to invest the money they are inheriting from their parents.

"Winning is crucial to my retirement plans."

Figure 8.1 — US Households Owning Mutual Funds by Age, 1998-2004

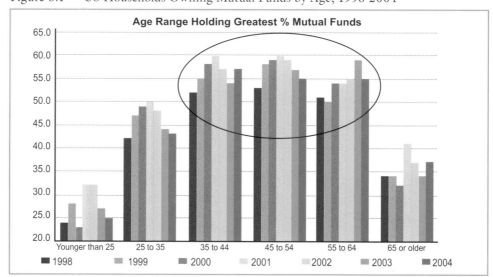

Source: US Census Bureau, Investment Company Institute (www.ici.org) Household Ownership of Mutual Funds 2004 report, Banc of America Securities LLC estimates. Reprinted with permission.

Figure 8.2 — Expected Growth in US Mutual Funds by Age, 1998-2004 Cumulative Annual Growth Expected Rate

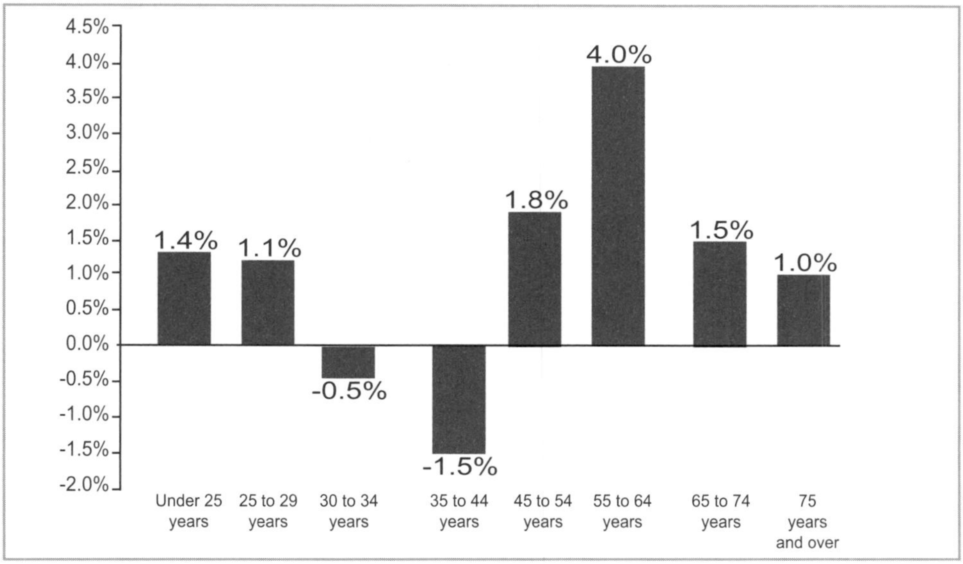

Source: US Census Bureau, Investment Company Institute Household Ownership of Mutual Funds 2004 report, Banc of America Securities LLC estimates

GOVERNMENT PENSIONS SWITCH TO PRIVATE PLANS

This trend is likely to repeat itself around the world, where governments and citizens worry that state pension plans will be unable to support the needs of the increasing number of retirees. The development of the industry worldwide may mirror its expansion in the US in the 1980s, when it was fueled by the widespread adoption of defined contribution plans.

In many developed countries there is now also a growing realization that individual savings, rather than programs sponsored by companies or governments, will be playing a much greater role in funding retirements than in the past. Some governments are considering transferring their public pensions to private managers.

TERMINOLOGY

DEFINED CONTRIBUTION PENSION FUND — *The amount placed in the fund each month or any other time period is "defined," or recorded, so that the pensioner receives only what he has put into the fund plus investment returns.*

DEFINED BENEFIT PENSION FUND — *The amount the pensioner receives when he retires is defined or guaranteed regardless of how much he contributed.*

COMPETITION AND CHOICE BENEFIT SHAREHOLDERS

Shareholders are the main beneficiaries of the competitive environment of the industry, which drives firms to innovate and differentiate themselves. The ability of shareholders to redeem their mutual fund shares daily allows them to "vote with their feet." As a result, fund management companies must provide excellent performance, service and fees.

Consider the number of choices available to investors. "There are over 55,000 different 'products' (funds) in this industry — a staggering sum compared to almost any other industry," notes a study of the global fund industry by Khorana, Servaes and Tufano.

The $9 trillion US market is the largest in terms of assets held and the number of available mutual funds. In the US, more than 600 organizations offer more than 8,000 funds that post performance figures daily.

The industry is very dynamic, with companies changing their ranking in the industry regularly. Out of the top 10 players in 1985, only five remained in the top 10 in 2005. With such a large number of firms, no one company can dominate the market. In 2005, the 10 largest firms managed 48% of assets. The top five firms controlled less than 40% of assets, according to the ICI.

Mutual fund companies compete not only among themselves but also with banks and insurance companies, as well as separately managed accounts,

Figure 8.3 — Access to mutual fund information is increasing via the Internet

Source: AFP Photo

exchange-traded funds, hedge funds and a number of other investments. As a result, mutual fund shareholders are demanding superior investment performance and services at competitive fees, an ICI study showed. This, in effect, makes industry costs self-regulating.

Access to Information Increases
The competition is fueled by the vast amount of information available from a wide range of sources. Investors are making informed decisions with information obtained at low or no cost. Sources of information include fund websites, fund supermarkets, 401(k) plan sponsors, advertising, independent analysts such as Lipper and Morningstar, and online newsletters, newspapers and magazines.

Access to information will only increase in the coming decades, as more and more people use the Internet as a resource. About 90% of mutual fund investors have access to the Internet, according to the ICI. About three-quarters of mutual fund investors that go online use the Internet to access their financial and investment accounts.

Pressure to Perform
Investors armed with information are clearly choosing the best funds the industry has to offer. Pressure on mutual funds to perform will intensify in the future as people gain the tools to easily compare different types of investments. An ICI study showed that investors tend to choose funds that are ranked among the top half in their peer group in terms of performance.

Mutual fund assets are already concentrated in funds with a long track record and above-average performance histories. About three-quarters of stock and bond fund assets in the US were in funds that have operated for at least 10 years (see Figure 8.4). Those stock and bond mutual funds ranked in the top half in terms of 10-year performance manage more than three-quarters of the assets held by funds with a 10-year track record or older, as shown in Figure 8.5 on page 148.

Figure 8.4 — Percent of Stock and Bond Fund Assets Invested in Funds that Have Operated for at least 10 years, 1995-2005

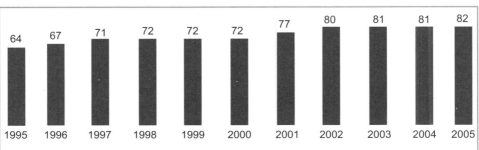

1995	1996	1997	1998	1999	2000	2001	2002	2003	2004	2005
64	67	71	72	72	72	77	80	81	81	82

Source: Research Commentary, "Competition in the Mutual Fund Business." Copyright © 2006 by the Investment Company Institute (www.ici.org)

Figure 8.5 — Percent of Assets of Long-tenured Stock and Bond Funds in Top Performing Funds, *1995-2005

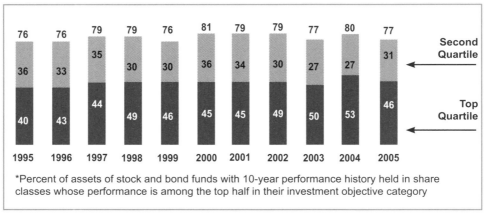

*Percent of assets of stock and bond funds with 10-year performance history held in share classes whose performance is among the top half in their investment objective category

Source: Research Commentary, "Competition in the Mutual Fund Business." Copyright © 2006 by the Investment Company Institute (www.ici.org). Reprinted with permission.

SERVICES

While performance will always be an important criterion used by investors, clients are also demanding better service.

The mutual fund industry has responded to demands for convenience and accessible information and invested billions of dollars in websites, telephone and in-person service representatives, and other services (see Figure 8.6 on page 149). To differentiate themselves from other types of investments, mutual fund companies are stepping up efforts to keep investors informed about current investments, making it simple to invest more money, and providing detailed research and performance statistics.

As the industry grows, the increasing amount of information and choice may be welcomed by do-it-yourself investors who want to choose their own funds. Many others may get "information overload" and instead use an adviser.

Services Offered by Fund Firms

Not all funds offer the same types of services. The following is a list of some typical shareholder services:

- Automatic investment
- Check writing
- Dividend reinvestment
- Exchange privileges
- Information via the telephone or the Internet

Figure 8.6 — Percent of Services Available from Leading US Mutual Fund Companies in 1990 — 2005*

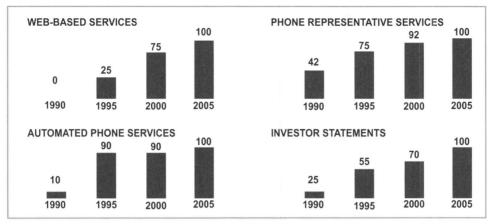

* Scope for each year is in relation to 2005 as 100%.

Source: Research Commentary, "Competition in the Mutual Fund Business." Copyright © 2006 by the Investment Company Institute (www.ici.org). Reprinted with permission.

- Investment adviser services
- Low minimum investment amounts
- Reinstatement privileges
- Shareholder reports
- Simplified record keeping
- Systematic withdrawal plans
- Tax-deferred retirement accounts

Automatic Investment
Investors can arrange an automatic monthly deduction from a bank account in order to make regular investments in a mutual fund. Each fund has a minimum requirement and the arrangement can usually be changed or altered with 30 days' notice. In another type of arrangement, an investor signs a contract with a mutual fund to invest a specific amount in regular installments over a set period of time. The amount of the debit cannot be changed during the contract period.

Check Writing
Many money market funds and some bond funds allow shareholders to write checks, stipulating a minimum sum, such as $100. Each check written results in the redemption of shares.

Dividend Reinvestment

Mutual funds offer the option of automatically reinvesting dividends and capital gains distributions in the same fund or in another fund within the same fund family. This gives the advantage of compounding — earning interest on interest.

Exchange Privileges

Investors in a particular fund can often exchange their shares for shares of equal value in another fund within the same fund family. The shares can only be exchanged for shares within the same class (A, B or C shares). This gives investors the flexibility to change their portfolio when their investment objectives change or the returns from a particular fund do not match their requirements. When exchanging A type shares (which normally carry a front-end sales commision), there is no front-end charge on the new shares. If exchanging B shares (which have a required holding period in order to escape a sales change), the holding period related to the back-end load is applied to the new shares.

Information Services via Telephone or Internet

Fund prices are available over the telephone or the Internet at any time. Customer service representatives and brokers can respond to queries and take orders to buy and sell over the telephone. Almost all mutual fund companies and supermarkets maintain websites. Performance histories, annual reports, prospectuses and other information are usually available online.

Advice and Asset Allocation Models

Investors can access analysis directly from mutual fund companies or from outside sources such as Morningstar or Standard & Poor's. Funds also often provide asset allocation models for investors with different goals and risk profiles.

Low Initial Investment

Many mutual funds offer access to shares for low initial deposits, allowing smaller investors to benefit from professional management and diversification. Some mutual funds allow entry for as low as $50. Still, lower entry levels may come with higher costs. To accommodate more shareholders than do similarly sized funds with fewer investors and larger balances, mutual funds must devote more resources for staff and other services.

Reinstatement Privileges

After selling shares in a fund, investors can often reinvest in the same fund shortly thereafter with no additional fees charged. This so-called reinstatement privilege applies to all of the proceeds of the redemption as long as the reinstatement occurs within a period of time set by the fund. The repurchase must be for the same class of shares. If an investor repurchases Class A shares, then there is no sales charge on the new shares. If the investor reinstates shares with a back-end load, he will receive a credit for the sales charge paid at the time the shares were redeemed.

Shareholder Documents
Mutual funds must send reports to their shareholders. These reports disclose the portfolio's specific shares, provide information about the board of directors, and give specific financial details. All mutual fund investors can also vote on fund changes via written proxy, telephone or website.

Simplified Record Keeping
For record keeping, a mutual fund investment is treated as an investment in a single security. At the end of the year, the fund provides a detailed statement of purchases, sales, capital gains distributions and dividends. A fund company often provides a single tax statement to help file returns easily.

Systematic Withdrawal Plans
Mutual funds often can arrange regular withdrawals once a certain amount of money has been accumulated. This is an especially attractive service for retirees. There are several ways to structure fund withdrawals.

1. *Fixed dollar*: An investor specifies an amount required each payment period and the fund redeems as many shares as necessary to meet that amount.

2. *Fixed shares*: An investor specifies a fixed number of shares to liquidate each payment period. The proceeds vary according to the net asset value of the shares in each time period.

3. *Fixed percentage*: An investor decides a fixed percentage of his total mutual fund holdings to liquidate each payment period. Each payment will vary according to the net asset value of the shares at the time.

4. *Fixed time*: An investor can set the number of years over which the total holdings will be liquidated. This option is often used for funds set aside to pay for education.

Tax-deferred Retirement Accounts
Most mutual funds allow investors and corporations to set up tax-deferred retirement accounts. The minimum investments for these types of accounts are usually lower than those set for non-retirement accounts. They may be subject to an annual service fee.

COMPETITION FUELS INNOVATION IN NEW PRODUCTS AND SERVICES
Increased competition ultimately breeds innovation. Investment companies are creating new products and services to retain existing clients and attract

new ones. Consider some of the latest developments in the industry.

New products or new versions of old products are emerging that some analysts say may divert attention from traditional open-end mutual funds. At the same time, mutual funds themselves are adopting some of the strategies of alternative products, while offering the transparency and regulation inherent in the mutual fund environment.

Some of the products gaining popularity include:

- International funds such as emerging market funds

- Hedge funds and hedge-like mutual funds

- Passively managed funds such as index funds and ETFs

- Closed-end funds

- Separately managed accounts

International and Global Equity Funds
International equity funds are becoming increasingly popular as investors seek to increase portfolio diversification and gain access to newer economies as well as the possibility of higher returns. International and Global funds attracted more than $140 billion worth of inflows in 2005, according to mutual fund asset-flow tracker Financial Research Corporation. International investment has also become more accessible through the growth in the number of international mutual funds and exchange traded funds (ETFs) now available.

Most US investors concentrate their portfolios on domestic securities. By adding foreign stocks, many investors are improving their diversification. But, to be sure, investors should be aware of the risks involved.

Region-specific funds are usually concentrated in just a few countries and carry more risk and volatility than truly international funds. Often, they are also subject to the cycles created by the booms and busts of prices for commodities such as oil, iron-ore and copper. The increase in these prices often fuels fund flows into countries like Brazil, Russia and South Africa, for example.

Hedge Funds
Hedge funds, which were earlier only available to extremely wealthy investors, are starting to become more mainstream. These are funds that use derivatives to offset investment risk and gain from market inefficiencies. Put options, call options and short-selling are widely used hedging tools. The hedge fund market grew to more than $1 trillion in global assets in 2005. The number of hedge funds grew to about 8,100 worldwide in 2005. Much of the attraction has been due to impressive returns. The CSFB/Tremont Hedge Fund Index outperformed the S&P 500 index by about 64% from

NOTE
HEDGE FUND STRATEGIES

Hedge funds use trading strategies that are usually not permitted by more traditional funds. For example, they can short-sell stock, meaning they may borrow shares to sell them, with the intention of buying them back later at a lower price.

Some other hedge fund strategies include:

- **Funds of funds:** investing in a basket of hedge funds. Some funds of funds use many different strategies while others focus on a single strategy. These funds carry additional fees.

- **Long-Short:** taking strategic positions in markets by going long or short to various degrees.

- **Market neutral:** equal amounts of money are invested long and short in the market, with the intention of neutralizing risk by buying undervalued securities and taking short positions in overvalued securities.

- **Convertible arbitrage:** buying convertible securities such as shares or bonds that are exchangeable for a certain number of another form of security, such as common shares, at a preset price. At the same time the fund shorts the underlying equities.

- **Global macro:** investing in shifts among global economies. The fund often uses derivatives to speculate on currency or interest-rate movements.

These sophisticated techniques come with a higher price tag than regular funds. Hedge funds typically charge a 1% to 2% management fee, plus 20% of any gains over the initial investment.

Source: "Growing Pains — What's in a Name" *The Economist*, March 4, 2006.

OPINION
INVEST AT YOUR OWN RISK

NEW HAVEN - The current mania for hedge funds reaches into every corner of the investment world. As is often the case with financial excesses, what began as a reasonable opportunity for sophisticated investors has become a killing ground for naïve trend-followers, with scandals and frauds prompting predictable calls for increased regulation of hedge funds. But if Congress and the Securities and Exchange Commission really want to protect individual investors, they should prohibit unsophisticated players from participating in hedge funds.

Although the roughly 8,000 hedge funds now in existence pursue so many strategies that hedge funds almost defy definition, generally they promise to deliver every investor's dream — high returns with low risk. In some respects, hedge funds are like mutual funds on steroids: they pursue complex investment strategies, charge huge fees and reward only those few investors able to identify funds that are worth the money they charge....

Hedge funds typically add a "profit participation" fee, say 20% of any gains, to the already-too-large base fee. Portfolio turnover often surpasses the feverish pace posted by mutual funds, generating soft dollar kickbacks — basically hidden credits granted by brokers for trading securities — that line the manager's pocket at the investor's expense. In

the zero-sum world of active portfolio management, where every winning position requires an offsetting losing position, over-the-top hedge fund fees virtually guarantee subpar results for investors....

Less informed investors rely on an intermediary (often a fund that invests in a variety of hedge funds) to make fund choices. The best fund managers avoid these "funds of funds," which operate with shorter time horizons, in favor of a direct relationship with big long-term investors. Of course, the funds of funds add more fees to the already overburdened hedge fund investor, further reducing chances for success....

First, hedge funds should be required to have direct relationships with their investors, eliminating the use of funds of funds. Second, hedge funds should be obliged to demonstrate that their investors have sufficient expertise to participate in this treacherous arena. Third, the existing net worth and investment portfolio size standards should be increased substantially to weed out inexperienced or smaller players.

Only by restricting hedge fund access to large sophisticated investors can regulators ensure a fair fight when the hedge fund manager lines up across from the hedge fund investor.

Source: David F. Swensen, *New York Times*, October 19, 2005

December 1993 through August 2005. Hedge fund assets have grown at an average annual rate of 18% since 1990 and about 15% per year since 1999 However, recently this bright picture has begun to fade.

Diversification is another reason institutions are getting involved, since hedge funds often have low correlations with other investments. One popular hedge fund product style is a multi-manager, multi-strategy style that aims to provide consistent returns with low volatility.

Today, hedge funds are being used more and more by pension funds, endowments and foundations. About half of hedge-fund assets now come from institutions, according to Oliver Schupp, president of the CSFB/Tremont index. As a result, hedge funds are coming under pressure to ensure less volatility and more moderate returns.

Stricter regulations may be inevitable as more investors and institutions get involved. In 2004, the SEC passed a new rule requiring hedge fund advisers to register.

Mutual Funds with Hedge Fund Strategies

A small number of mutual funds are starting to adopt some hedge fund strategies and behaviors, such as the use of leverage, short-selling and derivatives.

This may appeal to investors who long for the benefits that hedge funds can provide, such as further diversification and better performance, without sacrificing the greater transparency of mutual funds, which are more tightly regulated than hedge funds.

Some funds are developing strategies that will allow them to short-sell exposure to companies in an index that are not attractive to them, rather than just underweighting them.

These funds are more expensive than traditional mutual funds, but far cheaper than the average hedge fund. Some service firms have developed rankings to track these hedge-like mutual funds, since indexes that are used for comparisons with traditional mutual funds do not work well for those that mimic hedge funds.

Exchange-traded Funds (ETFs)

An increasing number of investors are turning to exchange-traded funds (ETFs) instead of individual stocks or sector funds. ETFs are preassembled portfolios that model a composite benchmark or index. They can be bought by an investor in a single transaction and traded on exchanges like stocks. They are often attractive to investors because they have lower costs than actively managed funds. ETFs do not charge back-end redemption fees that have become more commonly used by mutual funds to discourage frequent trading. They can be bought and sold throughout the market day at known prices, while mutual fund prices are only set once a day after the close of markets.

By the end of 2005, the number of ETFs reached about 200 and assets rose to almost $300 billion. While ETFs comprise 2.9% of total investment company assets, they are attracting an increasing proportion of net flows in recent years. They may be diverting some investment away from mutual funds.

For example, ETFs had $54.6 billion in inflows in 2004, compared with $57.1 billion for mutual funds. ETFs have grown at an average annual rate of 55.5% since 1998. Mutual fund assets have grown 6.6% on average in the same period. One area of particular growth has been in international segment ETFs, which make up about 17% of all ETF fund assets.

Institutional investors initially led the growth in ETFs. They used ETFs for many reasons, including-hedging, short-selling and as substitutes for investing in individual stocks.

In a sign that ETFs have gained a significant market share, rating services have begun rating ETFs on the market, based on their risk-adjusted returns in their respective peer groups, as well as their expense ratios. The ratings help investors compare ETFs to one another as well as to regular mutual funds.

Figure 8.7 — Net Assets of ETFs (millions of dollars, 1993–2005)

Year	($) Total	Investment Objective				Legal Structure	
		($) Broad-Based Domestic Equity	($) Sector-Based Domestic Equity	($) Global International Equity	($) Bond Index Funds	($) Open-end	($) UIT
1993	464	464	–	–	–	–	464
1994	424	424	–	–	–	–	424
1995	1,052	1,052	–	–	–	–	1,052
1996	2,411	2,159	–	252	–	252	2,159
1997	6,707	6,200	–	506	–	506	6,200
1998	15,568	14,058	484	1,026	–	1,510	14,058
1999	33,873	29,374	2,507	1,992	–	4,499	29,374
2000	65,585	60,530	3,015	2,041	–	10,257	55,328
2001	82,993	74,752	5,224	3,016	–	22,865	60,128
2002	102,143	86,985	5,919	5,324	3,915	35,983	66,160
2003	150,983	120,430	11,901	13,984	4,667	68,306	82,677
2004	226,205	163,730	20,315	33,644	8,516	132,013	94,192
2005	296,022	186,832	28,975	65,210	15,004	200,958	95,064

Note: Components may not add to the total because of rounding.

Source: 2006 Investment Company Fact Book, Copyright © by the Investment Company Institute (www. ici.org). Reprinted with permission.

UIT=Unit Investment Trust

New innovative types of ETFs are frequently being introduced. Traditionally, ETFs tracked specific indexes or lists of stocks. The newest products are exploring uncharted territories such as tracking the price of gold or the value of the euro. They give investors access to currency and commodities markets without having to open a specific trading account for that purpose.

Passively Managed Funds

There has been a significant shift to passively managed funds in recent years with the development of ETFs and index funds. These are funds with a portfolio of equities with the same weighting as a specific index in order to mirror the index's performance.

Since 1993, equity index funds have grown at an average annual rate of 32%, compared with 15% for actively managed funds and 16% for total equity funds (active and passive) according to Banc of America Securities. Passive equity index fund net assets make up about 11% of total equity fund assets in the US. If we add ETFs, which have grown to about 3%, the total of passive managed equity fund assets equals about 14% of fund assets.

By 2005, assets in index mutual funds and ETFs totaled $865 billion, which is about 9% of the total assets managed by all registered investment companies. Much of the growth has been in funds that track broad market indexes.

Figure 8.8 — Assets of ETFs and Index Mutual Funds

(billions of dollars, 2005)

- Assets of ETFs and Index Mutual Funds
- Assets of Actively Managed Mutual Funds

Category	Index/ETF	Actively Managed	Total
Large-Blend Domestic Equity	445	764	1,209
Other Large-Cap Domestic Equity	71	1,648	1,719
Other Domestic Equity	149	1,160	1,309
Foreign Equity	117	868	985
Hybrid	8	559	567
Bond	75	1,297	1,372

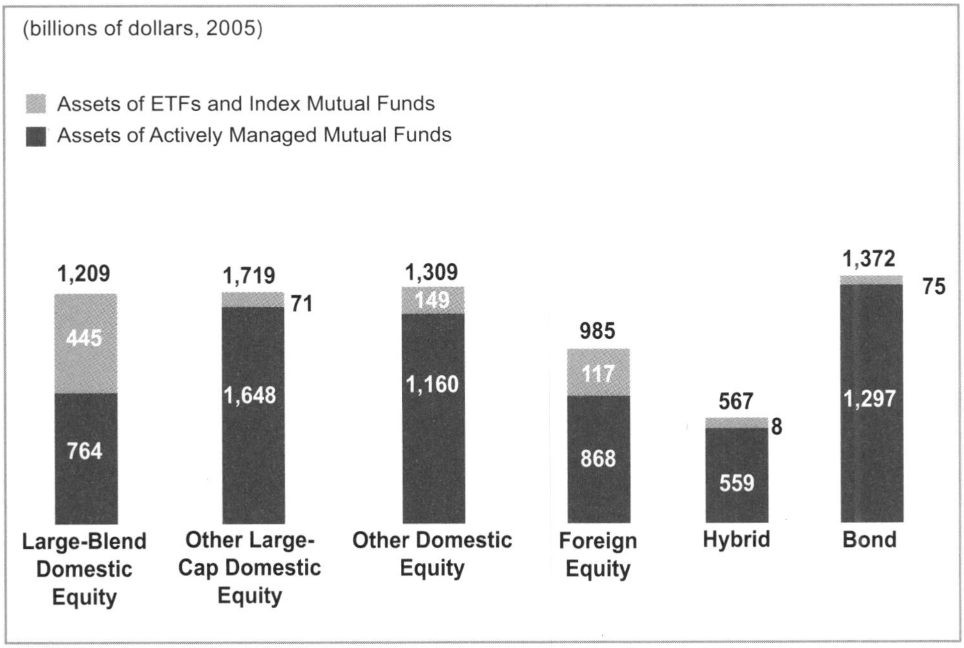

Sources: Investment Company Institute and Federal Reserve Board

To be sure, the market is large enough to accommodate both active and passive funds, and there is likely to be continued demand for both types. Active managers can prove their worth through performance, while passive funds can differentiate themselves through costs.

Closed-End Funds

Closed-end funds are also attracting more investors because of their unique features. As we have said, closed-end funds do not continually issue new shares like open-end mutual funds. Instead, they are traded on an exchange like stocks. The market sets the price of closed-end fund shares, and as a result the price may differ from the NAV.

Since closed-end funds do not need to maintain cash reserves or sell securities to meet redemptions, they have the flexibility to invest in less liquid securities such as those issued by very small companies, municipal bonds that are not widely traded, or securities traded in countries without fully developed securities markets.

Assets in closed-end funds grew to $276 billion by the end of 2005 (See Figure 8.9). They have increased 93% since year-end 2000. Closed-end fund assets have grown at an average annual rate of 8.5% since 1998, compared with 6.6% for mutual funds, Banc of America Securities research shows.

While the majority of these types of funds are concentrated in bond funds, a shift is developing towards equity funds. From year-end 2000 through 2005, assets in closed-end equity funds rose by 186% while all closed-end funds grew by 93%.

Figure 8.9 — Closed-End Fund Assets

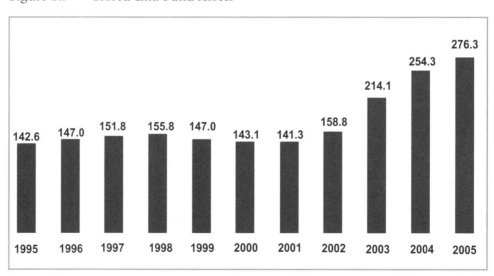

Source: Fundamentals, Vol. 15, No. 3, Copyright © 2006 by the Investment Company Institute (www.ici.org).

During the same time period, there was a significant increase in the number of closed-end fund offerings to 643 at the end of 2005 from 482 at the end of 2000. They are gaining a greater share of the investment marketplace, and are owned by as many as two million US households.

Separately Managed Accounts (SMAs)

For some wealthier investors, mutual funds are competing with the development of a relatively new sector: SMAs.

These accounts can be designed to meet the specific needs of an investor, such as creating a portfolio of securities with maturities that will coincide with specific life milestones. They can also take into account the specific tax consequences for an investor and take capital gains or losses to meet those needs. Clients usually pay a percentage of the assets under management.

Unlike mutual funds, separately managed accounts offer direct ownership of the equities or bonds in their portfolios. In contrast, mutual fund investors buy a share of an entity that owns a portfolio of equities securities.

SMAs also typically offer updates on their holdings more frequently than mutual funds, which disclose their holdings quarterly.

Still, these products are not accessible to everyone. Most require at least $100,000 to start, with many traditionally beginning at a minimum of $250,000. However, these minimums may come down as the industry develops. While these services are often offered via a bank's trust department, mutual fund companies may end up participating in this business if they are able to develop and offer products and services to meet the needs of more affluent clients.

"If we take a late retirement and an early death, we'll just squeak by."

STRICTER REGULATIONS AND INDUSTRY CONSOLIDATION

While competition is intense in the mutual fund industry, there are some signs that larger fund companies may be more resilient than smaller competitors in the face of a harsher regulatory environment. The investment management industry may see consolidation, as the costs of increased regulatory scrutiny are more difficult for smaller investment companies to bear.

Competition was often fueled by the low barriers to entry. For example, at the end of 2004, at least 200 different managers each had fund groups with total assets of $100 million or less. Establishing a fund itself required less than $200,000. But because of new industry regulations, smaller boutiques may find it harder to operate. A whirlwind of new legislation has resulted in additional costs for compliance efforts. Fund companies are creating new databases and tracking systems to meet audit requirements, and, consequently, these new systems are causing costs to mount.

GLOBAL GROWTH DRIVERS

With heavy competition and the development of elaborate shareholder services in the US, where are the opportunities for industry growth globally? While few markets offer the breadth of the US market, many international markets still represent significant opportunities.

Globally, mutual fund assets have grown by 9.5% per year since 1998. Outside of the US, other countries are developing mutual fund industries with varying degrees of growth.

The countries with the largest proportions of the worldwide fund industry in 2001 were the US (60%), Luxembourg (6.5%), France (6.1%), Italy (3.1%) and Japan (2.9%). Assets under management as a percentage of the country's GDP range from a high of 3,991% for Luxembourg and 186% for Ireland to a low of 0.011% for Bangladesh. Of course Luxembourg and Ireland are fund management centers for funds that are sold to investors all over Europe and the world.

What are the elements needed to develop a robust mutual fund industry? In a 2004 study, Khorana, Servaes and Tufano concluded that four main factors contribute to growth:

- The mutual fund industry is larger in countries with stronger rules and regulations, especially pertaining to the protection of shareholders' rights.

- Industry growth is stunted in countries in which barriers to entry are higher, measured by the effort needed to set up a fund, in terms of both money and time.

- The industry is larger in countries with a wealthier and more educated population, and where the industry is older.

- The fund industry is more developed in countries in which defined-contribution plans are popular.

NEWS CLIP
BRITISH PENSION PROPOSAL WOULD
SEND MILLIONS TO FUND MANAGERS

LONDON — If proposals announced on Wednesday to revamp the British pension system become law, some of the biggest beneficiaries would most likely be money managers.

British companies like Schroders and fund units of banks like HBOS stand to gain £250 billion, or $432 billion, of assets over three decades from proposals that would automatically enroll all British employees in savings plans.

The plan, the National Pension Savings Scheme, proposed by a commission led by Adair Turner, would seek managers to oversee investments in about 10 areas, including British bonds and domestic and international equities.

The government would offer contracts for funds with management charges of no more than 0.3%, Turner, a Merrill Lynch vice chairman, said at a news conference.

Turner's report capped a three-year study into how to plug a £57 billion gap in annual pension savings in Britain. The provisions could bring in as much as £10 billion a year in new funds for asset managers, the report said.

Under the pension proposals, all employees in Britain would have 8% of their salaries invested each year in savings plans.

The National Pension Savings Scheme would invest 4% of an employee's salary. Employers would pay the equivalent of 3%, while 1% would come from tax relief.

Source: David Clarke, *Bloomberg News,* December 1, 2005

SUMMARY

Mutual fund industry growth will be fueled by demographic factors as the world's population ages. Government-run pensions around the world are increasingly unable to meet the needs of growing numbers of retirees. As a result, individual savings will play a greater role in retirement planning.

The mutual fund industry is characterized by intense competition. This will result in product and service innovation as well as lower costs to ultimately benefit shareholders. There are more than 55,000 mutual funds available worldwide and hundreds of firms that must post performance figures daily. The ability of shareholders to redeem shares at any time drives the competitive environment.

Investors will make more informed decisions as access to information and analysis at low or no cost increases. This increases the pressure on mutual funds to perform. Investors are choosing funds with a long track record and above-average performance histories.

Besides top performance, investors are also increasingly demanding better service. Mutual funds offer services such as automatic investment plans, check writing, information hotlines, simplified record keeping and systematic withdrawal plans. Service offerings are bound to become more sophisticated as mutual funds compete to retain and attract customers.

Increased competition also promotes innovation. New products are emerging that will both attract new investors to mutual funds and divert some to alternative types of investments.

International equity funds will become increasingly popular as investors seek to increase diversification and gain access to the possibility of higher returns. Hedge funds are becoming more accessible and have attracted wealthier investors because they are uncorrelated to other types of investments. Some mutual funds are adopting hedge fund strategies such as the use of short-selling and derivatives. Closed-end funds and ETFs are also rapidly growing sectors.

Passively managed funds such as index funds and ETFs have been gaining ground as investors seek to match market performance and reduce fees. The market is large enough to accommodate both passively and actively managed funds. Each suits different types of investors.

Mutual funds will also compete with the growth of the separately managed account (SMA) industry. This relatively new sector designs portfolios to meet the specific needs of an investor and takes into account their specific tax environment. SMAs will likely be an option for wealthier investors with at least $100,000 to invest.

Increased regulatory scrutiny and restrictions may force consolidation in the industry as smaller mutual fund companies find it more difficult to bear the increased costs of ensuring compliance.

QUICK QUIZ

1. What is the problem with state-sponsored pension plans that countries like Germany, France and Italy are facing today?

2. What are some of the factors that are likely to influence the growth of the industry in the future?

3. To meet the demands of clients, what services are some mutual funds offering today?

4. Mention some of the reasons why hedge funds have attracted both private and institutional investors.

5. Explain what an ETF is and what are some of its attractions compared to traditional mutual funds.

GLOSSARY

12b-1 Fee
The annual charge deducted from fund assets to pay for distribution and marketing costs.

401(k) Plan
An employer-sponsored retirement plan that helps employees defer taxes on a portion of their salaries by earmarking that portion for the retirement plan.

Active Management
Ongoing management and trading of a portfolio by a fund manager, with the aim of achieving maximum results and outperforming market indexes.

Administrative Costs
These fees pay for employees, rent, benefits, equipment, and other aspects of running the offices of the fund management company. They are often grouped as "other expenses" in a prospectus.

Adviser
The investment company that manages a mutual fund. The adviser receives an annual fee for this service, which is usually a percentage of the fund's total assets. Also known as the fund manager, the adviser invests the fund's assets according to the fund's stated investment objectives by researching and choosing the specific securities that will be bought or sold in the portfolio. As a professional money manager, the fund manager provides knowledge and expertise beyond the scope of the average investor.

Aggressive Growth Fund
A fund with the investment objective of rapid growth of capital. Aggressive growth funds usually include funds that invest in smaller companies, funds that invest a majority of assets in a single industry, and funds that employ riskier investment techniques.

Alpha

Alpha tries to measure the difference between a fund's expected return and its real return, taking into account the amount of risk it takes. A positive alpha means that the fund manager produced a higher return than expected, while a negative alpha indicates that the fund did not get enough reward for the amount of risk it took. It must be analyzed in the context of the fund's beta and R-squared.

Annual and Semi-annual Reports

Reports issued once or twice a year to a fund's shareholders detailing the fund's performance, portfolio holdings and current investment strategy.

Asset Allocation Fund

A fund that invests in many types of asset classes, such as domestic and foreign stocks and bonds, money market instruments, precious metals and real estate. While some asset allocation funds maintain a fixed allocation between asset classes, others actively alter the mix as market conditions change.

Assets

A fund's investment holdings and cash.

Automatic Investment

A service that allows shareholders to regularly withdraw a specified amount from their bank account to be invested in a mutual fund account.

Automatic Reinvestment

A service that automatically reinvests dividend and capital gain distributions to buy more shares of a mutual fund.

Automatic Withdrawal

A shareholder service that entitles an investor to fixed payments every month or quarter. The payments come from the dividends, income and/or realized capital gains on securities held by the fund. This service is often chosen by retirees who want to receive a regular income supplement.

Average Annual Total Return

A measurement of fund performance that includes gains, dividends, and changes in share price.

Average Maturity

The dollar-weighted average of the maturities of a fund's fixed-income holdings. Maturity is the date on which a bond's principal is to be repaid.

Back-end Load

Also known as a contingent deferred-sales charge, a back-end load is a fee charged when the fund's shares are sold. The amount of the fee usually varies depending on how long the investment is held. When the fund is held for a longer time, the size of the fee is reduced and can disappear after a number of years. Shares sold with a back-end load are usually known as Class B shares.

Backdating

Backdating allows fund holders to use an earlier date on a promise to invest a specified sum over a specified period in exchange for a reduced sales charge.

Balanced Fund

A fund with an investment objective of both long-term growth and income. To achieve this objective, the fund invests in both stocks and bonds.

Benchmark Index

An index used as a reference point for analyzing a fund's performance.

Beta

A measure of an asset's sensitivity to the movements of the market. The market's risk is represented as 1.0. A fund with a beta of 1.30 is 30% more volatile than the market, while a fund with a beta of 0.70 is 30% less volatile than the market.

Bid Price

Also known as the "sell" price, the bid price is the price at which a fund's shares are bought back by the fund. The bid price of a fund share is usually its net asset value.

Blended Fund

A mutual fund that invests in both growth and value stocks.

Board of Directors

Shareholders elect a board of directors to oversee the management of the fund and the work of the portfolio manager. The board makes sure the fund manager's investments adhere to the fund's objectives and votes on renewing the fund manager's contract and any changes to his fees.

Bond Fund
A fund that invests primarily in bonds, which could be issued by corporations, the government or related agencies.

Breakpoint
Dollar levels of investment in a fund that qualify you for reduced sales charges. The purchases may either be made in a lump sum or by accumulating shares.

Capital Appreciation
The profit made on an investment, which equals the increase in a fund share's value from the time of purchase to the time of sale.

Capital Appreciation Fund
A capital appreciation fund tries to make money by investing in stocks whose prices are expected to rise due to a wide variety of factors (e.g. earnings growth), or simply because the shares are trendy among investors. Managers of these funds trade frequently and use riskier strategies such as buying *options* which are exchange-traded contracts that give the buyer the right to buy or sell an asset at a set price on or before a given date.

Capital Gain Distribution
The distribution of profits realized from the sale of securities in a fund's portfolio. Capital gain distributions are usually paid to shareholders once a year and may be subject to tax.

Classes of Shares
Different mutual fund shares are categorized into classes according to their various load structures. Whether they are Class A, B or C shares, all of the share classes of a particular mutual fund are backed by the same portfolio of securities. Typically, Class A shares have a front-end load, Class B shares have a back-end load, and Class C shares have an ongoing charge, such as a 12b-1 charge. A fund's performance and net asset value will be different for various share classes.

Closed-end Fund

Closed-end funds issue a *fixed* number of shares and do not issue new or redeem old shares. They thus are not as liquid as open-end funds. While closed-end funds no longer sell shares at the net asset value of the fund's assets, investors can still buy shares in these funds on a stock exchange or over-the-counter market. The market price of closed-end fund shares fluctuates like other publicly traded securities. The assets of the fund are professionally managed and invested in stocks, bonds or other securities according to stated objectives.

Closed To New Investors

A fund can become closed to new investors and refuse to accept any new investments. This can be a temporary situation brought about because a very large amount of money has been invested in the fund during a short period of time, raising concern that the fund manager will not be able to find enough appropriate securities to add to the portfolio.

Compounding

Earning interest on the returns made previously and on reinvested distributions.

Contingent Deferred Sales Charge

See "Back-end Load."

Corporate Bond Fund

A fund that invests primarily in corporate bonds. Corporate bond funds usually aim for income rather than growth.

Country Fund

A fund that usually invests in the securities of a single country or region.

Country Risk

The risk that stock prices in a particular country will fluctuate because of specific political or economic events in that country.

Credit Rating

A measure of a bond issuer's creditworthiness and likelihood of default as rated by an independent agency, such as Standard & Poor's (S&P), Moody's or Fitch. Bond funds rated Baa or higher by Moody's or BBB or higher by S&P are considered "investment grade." Bonds rated BB or lower by S&P or Ba or lower by Moody's are known as junk bonds or high-yield funds. These bonds see a higher number of defaults but offer higher yields as compensation for the risk.

Credit Risk
The possibility that a bond issuer will default and not pay the principal or interest as agreed.

Currency Risk
The possibility that prices of international equities will fluctuate in terms of their dollar value because of changing currency exchange rates.

Custodian
An organization, usually a bank, which holds and protects the securities and other assets of a fund. These securities must be separated from the bank's assets to protect them in case the custodian goes bankrupt. If the management company were to shut down, the fund's assets would be liquidated by the bank and distributed to shareholders.

Defined Benefit Plan
A defined benefit plan offers a participant a specific monthly benefit at retirement, possibly stated as an exact dollar amount. Monthly benefits could also be calculated through a formula that considers a participant's salary and service. A participant is generally not required to make contributions in a private sector fund, but most public sector funds require employee contributions. Unlike defined contribution plans, the participant is not required to make investment decisions.

Defined Contribution Plan
A defined contribution plan provides an individual account for each participant. The benefits are based on the amount contributed and are also affected by income, expenses, gains and losses. Examples of defined contribution plans include 401(k) plans, employee stock ownership plans and profit sharing plans.

Diversification
Investing in different securities to reduce risk. Ideally, losses incurred by securities falling in price are offset by gains of those rising in price. Mutual funds are inherently a diversified investment.

Dividend
Short-term profits, stock dividends or interest income that funds distribute to shareholders.

Dollar Cost Averaging
A style of investing in which a specific amount is invested at regular intervals, without taking into consideration the fund's share price. More shares can be purchased when prices are lower than when prices are higher. As a result, the investor's average cost per share is reduced over time.

Emerging Markets Fund
A fund that invests primarily in the stocks of companies in, or doing business in, developing countries and emerging markets. Emerging market funds usually have an investment objective of long-term growth and are generally considered aggressive stock funds. Definitions of "emerging markets" vary, but the most commonly used defines them as all countries designated by the World Bank as "low and middle income," based on per capita income. Countries with per capita incomes of less than about $10,000 per year are normally included in this category.

Equity Income Fund
A fund that largely invests in stocks seeking to provide relatively high current income and growth of income.

Ethical Fund
A fund that invests in the securities of companies that meet certain ethical standards. The fund may exclude companies that produce specific products, such as alcohol or tobacco, or companies that harm the environment.

Exchange Privilege
A service that allows shareholders to move their money from one fund to another within the same fund family. Shareholders are not usually charged additional fees for this service.

Ex-dividend Date
The date on which a fund's net asset value will decline by an amount that is equal to a dividend or capital gains distribution.

Expense Ratio

Total operating expenses divided by total net assets. Operating expenses include: management fees, administrative service fees, custodian and transfer fees, shareholder service fees, director's fees, legal and audit fees, interest costs, and 12b-1 fees. Operating expenses exclude brokerage costs and front-end and back-end loads. The lower the expense ratio, the higher the amount of return that will be paid to shareholders. The higher the ratio, the lower the return.

Family of Funds

An investment management company that sells funds with many different types of investment objectives. Fund families usually permit investors to transfer money between funds at no additional cost.

First-in, First-out (FIFO)

One of three methods to determine the cost basis of the mutual fund shares you sell. Under FIFO, the first shares purchased are the first shares that will be sold. Since the first shares purchased tend to be the ones with the lowest price, this method usually results in a higher gain.

Forward Pricing

A system in which mutual funds calculate and report the net asset value of their shares after the stock markets close every day. The price at which investors buy shares is set at the end of each day, regardless of the time of day when the purchase order was received.

Front-end Load

A sales fee charged during the initial purchase of fund shares. Funds that offer several sales charge options usually call the shares that are sold with a front-end load "Class A shares."

Fund of Funds

A fund that invests only in the shares of other funds.

Fund Manager

The fund manager invests the fund's assets according to the fund's stated investment objectives by researching and choosing the specific securities that will be bought or sold in the portfolio. As a professional money manager, the fund manager provides knowledge and expertise beyond the scope of the average investor.

Fund Supermarket

A brokerage, usually accessible via the Internet, that provides access to a variety of mutual funds from different fund families at a central location. The main advantage of using discount fund supermarkets is the reduction of paperwork needed to buy and sell mutual funds. The supermarket sends investors one statement that consolidates all mutual fund transaction and records. Switching assets among different funds is easy with a fund supermarket.

General Bond Fund

A fund that invests in bonds without any quality or maturity restrictions.

General Municipal Bond Fund

A fund that invests mostly in municipal bonds in the US. These funds are exempt from federal income tax.

GNMA (Government National Mortgage Association)

Also known as Ginnie Mae, the Government National Mortgage Association is a government-owned corporation that can guarantee the full and timely payment of all monthly principal and interest payments on the mortgage-backed securities collateralized by registered holders.

Global Mutual Fund

A mutual fund that invests in securities sold in any country, including in the US.

Growth

An objective of many equities funds. Growth occurs when the market value of a fund's holdings rises. This raises the net asset value per share.

Growth Fund

A fund that invests mostly in the stocks of companies whose earnings are expected to grow significantly compared with those of their peers. Growth funds seek capital gains rather than regular income from dividends. Growth funds buy stocks the manager believes will rise in price, even if the current price is high relative to its assets.

Growth and Income Fund
A fund that aims for capital gains as well as regular income. This is achieved by investing in shares of companies with growing earnings and a record of paying regular dividends to shareholders.

Hedge Fund
A fund that uses derivatives to reduce investment risk. Put options, call options and selling short are tools often used by hedge fund managers. Hedging is also widely used by international funds to minimize currency risks.

High-yield Bond Fund
A fund that invests primarily in high-yield bonds, also known as junk bonds. High-yield bond funds are typically riskier investments.

Inception Date
The date a fund was first made available for sale to investors.

Income
The payment of dividends, interest or capital gains earned by shares held by a fund.

Income Fund
A fund that invests mainly in fixed-income securities or shares that pay dividends.

Index
A measure of performance of a group of stocks or bonds. A fund's performance is often evaluated by comparing it to a relevant index. Common stock indexes are the Dow Jones Industrial Average and the S&P 500 index. Fixed-income funds are often compared with the Lehman Brothers Aggregate Bond Index.

Index Fund
A passively managed fund that seeks to mirror the performance of a particular index.

Individual Retirement Account (IRA)
A US savings plan that provides tax advantages for retirement investing. Contributions are usually at least partially tax-deductible.

Inflation Risk

The risk that the value of assets or income will decline because of inflation, which is the rising cost of goods and services. Fixed-income funds may be subject to inflation risk.

International Fund

A fund that invests in securities sold outside of the US.

Investment Company Act of 1940

US legislation that sets the structure and regulatory framework for the mutual fund industry. It requires that mutual funds keep detailed records, safeguard the securities in their portfolio and file semi-annual reports with the SEC.

Investment Grade

Investment rating of a bond as given by a rating agency.

Junk Bond

Bonds rated below safe standards by Standard & Poor's, Moody's or Fitch rating services. Junk bonds are usually more volatile and offer higher yields than high-quality bonds.

Junk Bond Fund

A fund that invests primarily in lower-rated bonds called junk bonds. These funds tend to seek high returns by taking greater risk.

Large-caps

Shares of companies that generally have a market cap of more than $10 billion. The largest and most successful companies are often called "blue chips," named after the most valuable chips in a casino poker game.

Letter of Intent

An agreement requiring an investor to invest a specific amount in a fund during a specific period of time to qualify for lower sales charges.

Level Load

Funds with level loads do not charge front- or back-end loads. Instead they charge ongoing 12b-1 fees. Funds with level loads are often called C shares.

Liquidity
The ability to convert an investment into cash. Mutual fund shares are usually highly liquid because they can be sold on any business day.

Load
A sales charge levied by mutual funds. A front-end load is charged at the time of purchase. A back-end load is charged at the time of sale.

Load Fund
Mutual fund that has a sales charge.

Management Fee
The payment a fund makes to an investment adviser for services such as investment research and portfolio management. This is usually a fixed percentage of the total value of the fund that is set once a year.

Market Timing
Efforts to time the purchase and sale of securities during the right market conditions to achieve the best possible returns. Investors may switch among bond funds, money market funds and stock funds as economic conditions and interest rates change.

Mid-caps
Shares of medium-sized companies with a market capitalization of between $2 billion and $10 billion.

Money Market Fund
Money market funds seek to maintain a stable net asset value by investing in the short-term, high-grade securities sold in the money market. These are generally the safest, most stable securities available, including Treasury bills, certificates of deposit and commercial paper. Money market funds limit the average maturity of their portfolio to 90 days or less. They seek to generate monthly income, and to maintain a stable $1.00 per share net asset value.

Mortgage-backed Security

A security that returns principal and interest monthly as payments are received on the underlying mortgages. These securities are made of individual home mortgages backed by government agencies such as the Government National Mortgage Association (GNMA), Federal National Mortgage Association (FNMA), and the Federal Home Loan Mortgage Corp. (FHLMC).

Mutual Fund

An open-end investment company that pools the money of thousands of shareholders and invests it in securities in order to achieve a specific investment objective. Mutual funds offer diversification, liquidity and lower costs of professional management.

Maximum Sales Charge

A combination of the highest possible deferred fees and front-end sales charges a fund can apply. The amount is generally relative to the amount of the investment — larger investments incur smaller charges.

Net Asset Value (NAV)

Mutual funds calculate and report the net asset value of their shares after the stock markets close every day. Net asset value is the current market value of all of the fund's assets, minus liabilities, divided by the outstanding number of shares.

No Load Fund

A fund that sells its shares directly to investors without a sales charge.

Objective

The financial goals a mutual fund has, such as growth or income.

Offering Price

The price at which a mutual fund's shares can be bought. Also known as the "ask" price. The offering price equals the fund's current net asset value per share plus any applicable sales charge.

Open-end Fund

An investment company that invests money from many shareholders in a range of securities such as stocks, bonds and money market instruments.

Also known as a mutual fund. An open-end fund sells and redeems shares on an ongoing basis.

Operating Expenses
Operating expenses are the annual, ongoing costs of running a mutual fund. Unfortunately, these simply cannot be avoided. Every fund must charge fees to pay for its day-to-day costs. Operating expenses are used to pay the fund manager and research analysts, maintain customer hotlines and websites, and cover the cost of printing and mailing documents.

Passive Management
An investing strategy that aims to mirror a market index.

Payment Date
The day on which a mutual fund pays income dividend or capital gains distributions to its shareholders.

Periodic Payment Plan
An agreement by a mutual fund shareholder to make regular investments over a longer period of time. This plan results in dollar cost averaging.

Portfolio
A collection of securities owned by an individual or organization such as a mutual fund.

Price/Book Ratio
A ratio of the price of a stock to its company's book value per share. Companies that have a low price/book value grow more slowly or have lower prices because of poor earnings.

Price/Earnings Ratio
A ratio of the price of a stock to its earnings per share. The P/E ratio is calculated by dividing the price of a company's stock by its earnings during the past 12 months. A high P/E ratio indicates that investors are willing to pay more because they expect the company will increase its earnings. A low P/E can mean investors do not believe the company can increase its earnings. It may also be a sign that the company's shares are undervalued compared with its peers and may rise in the future.

Principal
The amount invested, excluding earnings.

Prospectus
An official document that provides detailed information about a mutual fund. In the US, it includes information required by the Securities and Exchange Commission, including the fund's investment objective, investment style, past performance, services and fees. A prospectus is given to all investors of the fund.

R-squared
R-squared measures whether the fund's price movements are correlated to the benchmark index on a scale from one to 100. A fund that mirrors the movements of the S&P 500 index, for example, would have an R-squared of 100, because 100% of its fluctuations are determined by the S&P 500. A low R-squared number means that the fund is moving out of sync with the index.

Real Return
The return on an investment after factoring in the rate of inflation.

Redeem
Selling shares back to the mutual fund. Mutual fund shares can be redeemed on any business day.

Redemption Fee
A fee charged by some funds when shares are bought back by them. It is often a fixed percentage of the total value of the fund.

Redemption Price
The price at which a mutual fund's shares are bought back by the fund. The price is subject to the market value of the fund's portfolio at a specific time and equals the net asset value per share. It is also known as the bid price.

Reinstatement Privilege
The privilege of repurchasing mutual fund shares that were sold after an investor changes their mind about the sale. The purchase is made at net asset value with no sales charge and generally can be completed up to a maximum of 30 days after the sale.

Right of Accumulation (ROA)

A right given by some mutual funds allowing shareholders to count existing holdings in the fund together with new purchases to qualify for discounts on new shares.

Russell 2000

An index of 2,000 small-cap stocks.

S&P 500

An index of stocks that is often considered representative of the US stock market in general. The index is comprised of 400 industrial, 20 transportation, 40 utility and 40 financial companies.

S&P 500 Index Fund

A fund that invests primarily in the stocks included in the S&P 500 index.

Sales Charge

A fee for buying shares in many mutual funds sold by sales agents such as brokers. In the US the maximum sales charge is 8.5% of the initial investment.

Sector Fund

A fund that mostly invests in securities focused on a specific industry or geographical region. Sector funds carry more risk, but may offer higher returns.

Shareholder

The owner of shares of a mutual fund.

Small-caps

Also known as small capitalization stocks, these stocks have a market capitalization of less than $2 billion. They tend to be newer companies that grow more quickly than more established ones. Investing in them can carry more risk, because small-cap stocks are usually illiquid and therefore very volatile.

Sponsor

A financial services company such as a mutual fund company, a brokerage, a bank or an insurance company that makes the initial investment in a fund and assembles a group of third parties needed to operate the fund. In the US, the sponsor must register the fund with the SEC. This registration document will become the *prospectus* for the fund, which identifies the fund's sponsor, board of directors, investment objectives, types of permitted investments, fees and risks.

Standard Deviation
A statistical measure of the variability of a fund's returns that helps determine its potential for volatility.

Statement of Additional Information (SAI)
A document that contains additional details about a fund not included in the prospectus. The SAI can be obtained by request.

Switching
Moving assets from one fund to another. Switching can often be done by shareholders within the same family of funds at no extra charge.

Systematic Withdrawal System
A service allowing shareholders to redeem a fixed amount from a mutual fund at regular intervals.

Symbol
A five-digit code, or ticker, assigned to each mutual fund by NASDAQ, which is used to identify the correct fund in all transactions.

Specific Identification
A method of identifying the cost basis of the mutual fund shares an investor sells. The shares sold are identified by their date of purchase.

Tax-exempt Bond Fund
A fund that invests in municipal bonds. In the US, investors do not pay federal income taxes on the income from these funds, but they may be subject to state or local taxes.

Ticker
See "Symbol."

T-bill (Treasury Bill)
A fixed-income security issued by the US government.

Total Return
A measure of a fund's performance that takes into consideration capital gains distributions, share price changes and income dividends.

Transfer Agent
An organization hired by a mutual fund to prepare and maintain records relating to the accounts of its shareholders. Some funds serve as their own transfer agents.

Turnover Rate
The frequency with which the fund buys and sells securities each year. The lower the turnover rate, the less trading a fund does. The ratio generally represents the percentage of the portfolio's holdings that have changed in the previous year.

Underwriter
The organization that acts as the distributor of a mutual fund's shares to brokers/dealers and investors.

Unit Investment Trust (UIT)
An investment company that buys and holds a fixed portfolio of stocks, bonds or other securities. The trust sells units to unit holders who receive a share of dividends or interest paid by the trust's investments. UITs are terminated on a specific date, when investors receive a proportionate share of the trust's net assets. Like a mutual fund, shares of a UIT can be redeemed on any business day. A UIT has an unmanaged portfolio. UITs should not be confused with unit trusts, which is another term for mutual funds that is used in the UK and other countries.

Unit Trust
The term used to identify a mutual fund in the UK and some other countries.

US Treasury Fund
A fund that invests mostly in fixed-income securities issued or guaranteed by the US Treasury or its agencies.

Value Investing
An investment style in which a fund manager buys underpriced stocks with

the potential to increase in price. Value investors compare the share price with the company's assets, earnings or sales, or with similar companies in the same industry to find bargains.

Volatility
The amount by which the price of a security fluctuates as market conditions change.

Wilshire 5000
An index that represents the entire US stock market.

Yield
Interest or dividends paid by a fund, expressed as a percentage of the investment's price.

Yield To Maturity (YTM)
The annual rate of return earned by a bond if held to maturity. This rate takes into account the amount paid for the bond and the length of time to maturity, and assumes that coupon payments can be reinvested at the yield to maturity.

Zero Coupon Bond
A bond sold at a discount, which earns interest that is paid in full at maturity.

BIBLIOGRAPHY

Barney, Lee "Morningstar Begins Rating Exchange-Traded Funds." Money Management Executive (March 13, 2006). http://www.mmexecutive.com.

Benz, Christine et al., *Morningstar Guide to Mutual Funds*. Hoboken, NJ: John Wiley & Sons, 2003.

Damato, Karen "Morningstar Edges Toward One-Year Ratings." *The Wall Street Journal* (April 5, 1996).

Glover, Hannah, "Defined Contribution Plans Abroad Expected to Abound: Opportunities for International Markets Multiply." Money Management Executive (February 27, 2006). http://www.mmexecutive.com.

Gremillion, Lee *Mutual Fund Industry Handbook*. Hoboken, NJ: John Wiley & Sons, 2005.

Hall, Alvin D *Getting Started in Mutual Funds*. New York, NY: John Wiley & Sons, 2000.

Hecht, Michael, Avi Ghosh, and Robert Ristau "Asset Manager Coverage Initiation." Banc of America Securities (August 2005).

Hoffman, Ellen "Giving Your Plan Regular Tune-Ups." *BusinessWeek* online (May 6, 2005). http//www.businessweek.com.

Investment Company Institute 2005. Investment Company Fact Book Washington, D.C.: Investment Company Institute, 2005.

Investment Company Institute 2006. Investment Company Fact Book Washington, D.C.: Investment Company Institute, 2006. http://www.icifactbook.org.

Investment Company Institute "Exchange-Traded Fund Assets, January 2006." ICI Statistics & Research (February 24, 2006). http:www.ici.org.

Investment Company Institute "Competition in the Mutual Fund Business." Research Commentary (January 2006). http://www.ici.org.

Investment Company Institute "Worldwide Mutual Fund Assets and Flows, Third Quarter 2005." Key Issues (February 9, 2006). http://www.ici.org.

Investment Company Institute "Shareholder Assessment of Bond Fund Risk Ratings." (October 1997).

Investment Company Institute "Ownership of Mutual Funds Through Professional Financial Advisers." Fundamentals, volume 14, number 3 (April 2005).

Investment Company Institute "The Cost of Buying and Owning Mutual Funds." Fundamentals, volume 13, number 1 (February 2004).

Investment Company Institute "Mutual Fund Shareholders' Use of the Internet." Fundamentals, volume 9, number 3 (July 2000).

Investment Company Institute "Performance Fees and Expense Ratios." Fundamentals, volume 12, number 2 (August 2003).

Investment Company Institute "Frequently Asked Questions About Mutual Fund Fees." http://www.ici.org.

Investment Company Institute "Mutual Fund Shareholders' Use of the Internet, 2005." Fundamentals, volume 15, number 2 (February 2006).

Investment Company Institute "The Closed-End Fund Market in 2005." Research Fundamentals, volume 15, number 3 (March 2006).

Khorana, Ajay, Henri Servaes, and Peter Tufano "Explaining the Size of the Mutual Fund Industry Around the World." Darden Graduate School of Business, University of Virginia Working Paper No. 03-04 (January 5, 2004).

Kinnel, Russel "Rating the Star Rating." Morningstar (December 5, 2005). http://www.morningstar.com.

Kinnel, Russel "Fund Fees: The Silver Lining Has a Big Dark Cloud." Morningstar (April 7, 2005). http://www.morningstar.com.

Kinnel, Russel "Is Your Fund Too Fat?" Morningstar (November 1, 2004). http://www.morningstar.com.

Kinnel, Russel "Closed Funds Worth Waiting For." Morningstar (July 24, 2003). http://www.morningstar.com.

Lipper Inc "Global Themes in the Mutual Fund Industry — 2005." (February 2006).

Lyons, Gareth "International Investing Pitfalls." Morningstar (March 21, 2006). http://www.morningstar.com.

Opiela, Nancy "Promise Is in Europe, Not Japan, Study Says." Money Management Executive (May 10, 1999). http://www.mmexecutive.com.

Reid, Brian "The 1990s: A Decade of Expansion and Change in the U.S. Mutual Fund Industry." ICI Perspective, volume 6, number 3 (July 2000).

Rouwenhorst, K. Geert "The Origins of Mutual Funds." Yale ICF Working Paper No. 04-48 (December 12, 2004). http://ssrn.com/abstract=636146.

Rowland, Mary *The New Commonsense Guide to Mutual Funds.* Princeton, NJ: Bloomberg Press, 1998.

Shiv, Baba et al., "Investment Behavior and the Negative Side of Emotion." Psychological Science, volume 16, number 6 (2005).

Stevens, Paul Schott "The Success of America's Mutual Fund Marketplace: Benefiting Fund Investors." Remarks by ICI President Paul Schott Stevens in a presentation at AEI/Brookings Forum (March 15, 2006).

Stevens, Sue "How to Analyze Your Portfolio." Morningstar (December 28, 2000). http://www.morningstar.com.

Strauss, Lawrence C "Tailor Made." Barron's Online (February 20, 2006). http://www.barrons.com.

The Economist (March 4, 2006) "Growing Pains."

The Economist (February 23, 2006) "The Long and the Short of It."

Tyson, Eric *Mutual Funds for Dummies.* Hoboken, NJ: John Wiley & Sons, 2004.

U.S. Securities and Exchange Commission "A Plain English Handbook, How to Create Clear SEC Disclosure Documents." (August 1998). http://www.sec.gov/pdf/plaine.pdf.

Williams, Richard E., and Peter W. Bacon "Lump Sum Beats Dollar-Cost Averaging." Financial Planning Association Journal (April 1993). http://www.fpanet.org/journal/articles/2004_Issues/jfp0604-art11.cfm.

INDEX

A

Absolute value investing, 75

Active management, 27, 35, 154, 157, 162, 165

Administrative costs, 27, 165

Adviser, 3, 5, 9, 11, 12, 19, 35, 38, 40, 70, 73, 88, 103, 115, 121, 122, 143, 148, 149, 155, 165, 176, 177, 186, 91, 92, 95-100, 105, 113, 135, 115, 140, 190

Aggressive growth fund, 22, 165

Alpha, 78, 80, 84, 166

Annual and semi-annual reports, 166

Annualized total return, 67

Appreciation, 2, 19, 20, 22, 24, 43,58, 99, 168, 189

Asset allocation, 3, 25, 63, 116, 125, 130, 132, 133, 140-142, 150,

Asset allocation fund, 33, 109, 139, 166,

Assets, 1-3, 5-9, 11, 16, 18, 21, 23, 25-27, 28, 29, 33, 41-46, 48, 49, 50, 56, 58, 66, 73-75, 79, 81, 84, 85, 89, 90-92, 94, 95, 97, 99, 103, 114, 139, 141-144, 146-148, 152, 155-161, 165-167, 169, 100, 102, 105, 109, 113, 114, 116, 119, 129, 130, 132, 137, 138

Automatic investment, 3, 107, 121, 148, 149, 162, 166,

Automatic reinvestment, 3, 107, 110, 111, 123, 150, 166

Automatic withdrawal, 166

Average annual total return, 39, 53-55, 59, 166

Average maturity, 29, 167, 176

B

Back-end load, 93, 94, 106, 111, 150, 167

Backdating, 167

Balanced fund, 33, 117, 167

Bear market, 6, 69, 70, 139

Benchmark, 12, 22, 23, 27, 42, 45, 47, 50, 56, 62, 66, 68, 80, 83, 84, 97, 98, 117, 120, 155, 167, 179, 48,

Benchmark index, 27, 42, 68, 80, 83, 167, 197

Beta, 78, 80, 166, 167

Bid price, 167, 179

Blended fund, 167

Board of directors, 9-11, 17, 26, 50, 63, 91, 151, 167, 181

Bond fund, 6, 8, 19, 29, 30, 32, 33, 20, 35, 38, 49, 67, 68, 81, 82, 84, 87, 88, 139, 142, 147, 149, 158, 147, 148, 181, 187, 101, 102, 119, 132, 137, 174-176,

Breakpoint, 92, 93, 96, 99, 103, 106, 168

Brokerage fee, 90, 92, 103

Bull market, 8, 70, 76, 111

Buy and hold, 21, 49, 109

C

D

E

F

OTHER

MARK MOBIUS

MASTERCLASS SERIES

EQUITIES
AN INTRODUCTION TO
THE CORE CONCEPTS

MARK
MOBIUS
MASTERCLASS

ISBN: 978-0-470-821442-2

DEBT
MARKETS
AN INTRODUCTION TO
THE CORE CONCEPTS

MARK
MOBIUS
MASTERCLASS

ISBN: 978-0-470-82147-3

TECHNICAL
ANALYSIS
AN INTRODUCTION TO
THE CORE CONCEPTS

MARK
MOBIUS
MASTERCLASS

ISBN: 978-0-470-82148-0

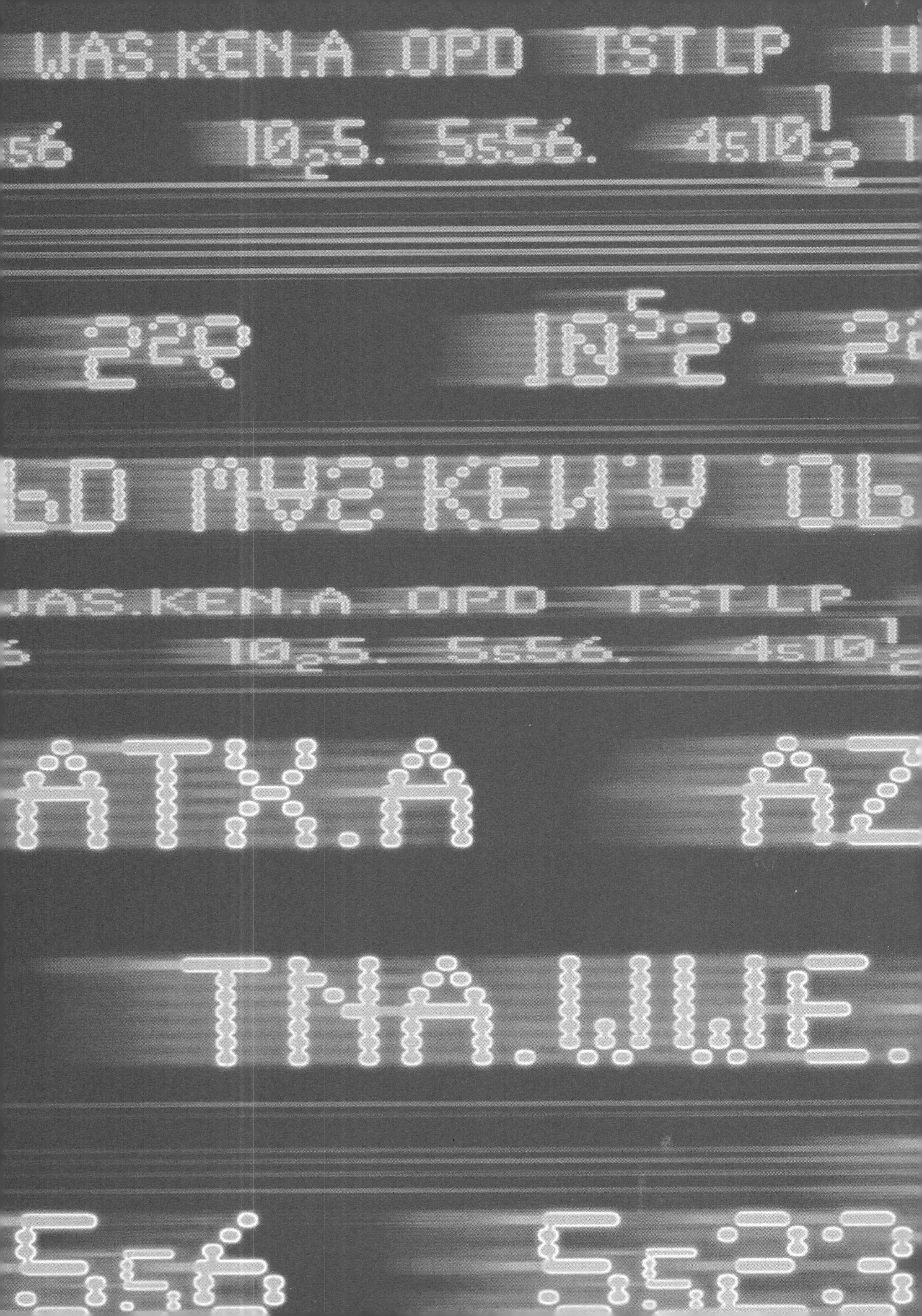
WAS.KEN.A .OPD TST LP
ATX.A
TNA.WIE.

Draw Buildings and Cities

in 15 Minutes

MATTHEW BREHM

Draw Buildings and Cities

in 15 Minutes

THE
SUPER-FAST
DRAWING
TECHNIQUE
ANYONE
CAN LEARN

ilex

An Hachette UK Company
www.hachette.co.uk

First published in the United Kingdom in 2017 by
ILEX, a division of Octopus Publishing Group Ltd
Octopus Publishing Group
Carmelite House
50 Victoria Embankment
London, EC4Y 0DZ
www.octopusbooks.co.uk
www.octopusbooksusa.com

Distributed in the US by Hachette Book Group
1290 Avenue of the Americas, 4th and 5th Floors, New York, NY 10020

Distributed in Canada by Canadian Manda Group
664 Annete St., Toronto, Ontario, Canada M6S 2C8

Publisher: Alison Starling
Editorial Director: Zara Larcombe
Managing Specialist Editor: Frank Gallaugher
Art Director: Julie Weir
Designers: Grade Design
Assistant Production Manager: Marina Maher

ISBN 978-1-78157-627-4

A CIP catalogue record for this book is available from the British Library.

Printed and bound in China.

10 9 8 7 6 5 4 3 2 1

Contents

INTRODUCTION

This book is for anyone with an interest in the visual character of the cities and buildings that frame our lives. It is intended to help you capture the life of the places where we work and spend our free time, and of the places we visit in our travels both near and far. The skills and strategies presented here will help you make a visual record of the urban places you experience, and help you learn about these places in the process.

Cities and Buildings

Cities, large and small, are a physical manifestation of the ways we organize ourselves as societies. They don't always work the way we would like, and they can remind us of our less effective attempts at planning and development. Nonetheless, cities bring together humankind in all its wonderful diversity; they act as an impetus for the arts, and are magnets for commerce and the leisure time that accompanies economic development.

Cities concentrate some of our most exalted achievements in architecture and planning, and their museums, theaters, restaurants, parks, and so on, are the venues for our cultural identity and advancement. Our cities express our ideals and aspirations as societies, and are the places where we determine who we are and how we create our successes in life. As such, cities are always worth our careful analysis and consideration. Drawing is one of the most direct and effective means by which we can achieve this essential and ongoing study.

Why Draw?

At least since the dawn of recorded history, drawing has been an essential form of expression. While digital technology has recently been distracting us somewhat from engaging in authentic, handmade arts and crafts, the computer will never fully replace the connections that occur between eyes, mind, and hand in the act of drawing from observation. We may also draw because it's an enjoyable thing to do. Drawing can be relaxing, as when we doodle mindlessly to pass the time, or it can be a great challenge, as when we attempt to draw what we see with a high degree of accuracy. This book is not about trying to create "picture-perfect" images, but it is about drawing what we see rather than merely doodling or drawing from the imagination. Drawing from observation is primarily about studying the things we see in the world, and only secondarily about producing polished works.

Certainly, the end products of our efforts—the finished drawings—can sometimes stand on their own as valuable works of art. To produce such works is often a motivating factor in attracting people to the practice of drawing in the first place. But most often, in the process of learning to draw we begin to sense that drawing is valuable because it forces us to really look at our surroundings, to spend time considering the way things are in our environment, and ultimately to understand the world around us more deeply than we would have without drawing. With this type of study as the goal, the drawings themselves—their quality or completeness—are often less important than the learning they represent.

For this reason, most artists draw in sketchbooks, with no intention to hang individual drawings on the wall, and the sketchbook becomes a storehouse of experience and memories regarding places visited, observed, and studied. With instruction and practice, the artist will see improvement in the quality of their drawings, and also in their ability to complete drawings in a relatively brief span of time. Such improvement ultimately makes drawing an ever more accessible and enjoyable way to learn about the world around us.

Time and Drawing

The ability to draw well is a skill that requires learning and practice. While we all seem to have an innate ability to be expressive with our hands, no one is born with the ability to draw with great skill. People who have an apparent "talent" for drawing are those who have invested the time and effort to build their skills for seeing and drawing well.

Some individuals are certainly more motivated than others to develop their skills, and these people are far more likely to make speedy progress. But everyone must go through the time and repeated effort to develop their abilities to the degree they desire.

Learning to draw takes time, of course, and in the process of learning it will often be necessary to spend more than 15 minutes on a single drawing. Practice sessions might last 45 minutes or one hour—as long as you feel you're being productive, and not becoming frustrated by the experience, feel free to keep practicing. The ability to capture an urban scene or a particular building in 15 minutes should be seen as one goal among many with regard to drawing.

We might feel that not having enough time to complete a drawing will be frustrating, and sometimes that's true. But, though it may seem a paradox, working within small windows of time is actually a good way to combat frustration. Brief drawings help us to stay focused on repeated, short bursts of practice rather than elaborately developed drawings that require far more time without necessarily producing better results. This idea is explored further in the section on Time, Scope, Size, and Medium later in the book. For now it will be helpful to understand 15 minutes as a valuable practice technique and as a potential goal for creating lively, energetic drawings down the line.

Drawing in Public

If our drawing subjects are buildings and cities, then it's most likely that we'll be doing our work outside and in public. A great many artists do their work indoors, in a private and protected studio. There's an obvious sense of security that comes with such a situation, and we might feel a bit exposed when we're actually out and in front of others. But drawing in public involves you directly with your subjects—not only the sights, but also the sounds, aromas, and other sensations that contribute to a fuller and more memorable drawing experience.

It makes sense to blend in as much as possible and avoid making a show of what you're doing, if only to allow yourself the freedom to focus on your task. But do try to be open to others on the street who might be interested in your drawings, and don't be shy about sharing your sketchbook with them.

Materials

Any type of paper and any type of common writing instrument is all you truly need to begin drawing. When you are just starting to learn, the most important thing to do is simply to draw as often as possible. Regular practice is far more valuable than spending time worrying you don't have the right materials. In other words, the "right" materials are those that are most immediately available to you, provided you're using them to draw often.

As you begin to develop your drawing skills, it's a good idea to experiment with a variety of materials and take notes along the way. Become your own judge of drawing instruments and papers, and try to find combinations that you find comfortable and that give you the results you're after. With time and testing, you'll begin to care more about the tools and paper you use, but again, the most important thing to do throughout this process is practice.

This book is focused on pencils and pens because they are the most commonly available drawing tools. Portability is also a factor—a single pen or pencil is easily carried anywhere, in a pocket or purse—as is the fact that pencil or pen can be used on virtually any type of paper. (Watercolor, by contrast, requires some specialized equipment and is best used with paper that's quite thick and has been treated with "sizing," a substance that affects its absorbency.)

Pens and pencils are also the most fundamental drawing tools in terms of technique. With a pen, you will be limited to making points and lines, with tones being created through "hatching" (consistent groups of roughly parallel lines). You can achieve the same results with a pencil, but pencils are also more responsive to varying pressure— light marks from a soft touch and darker marks from a heavier touch. Pencils can also be used to create smooth tones, without having to build up many lines to create a hatch pattern.

Sketchbooks and Paper

There are a great many types of sketchbook on the market, of different sizes, formats, and paper types. Look for something portable without being too small—I find that books no smaller than 8 inches (20cm) on a side give me the page space I need to develop my drawings without pushing the margins too much. For practice drawings, having a good large page is preferred—something around 10 x 12 inches (25 x 30cm) is ideal.

Hardbound books are more durable, and they allow drawing across the entire two-page spread, but they can be challenging to hold open while drawing; ring-bound books that open completely can be more comfortable. A standard portrait-oriented sketchbook is a good place to start, but there are also landscape-oriented books that can encourage you to experiment with other compositional approaches, such as extended horizontal or vertical drawings.

Ink pens are typically forgiving with regard to paper, with most working fine on almost any surface. Graphite is a bit more partial to a surface with at least a bit of texture, known as "tooth." You don't want the paper to be too rough, but if it's too smooth, the graphite won't adhere to the page very well.

Graphite Pencils

A basic #2 pencil is a fine place to start, though you'll eventually want to consider pencils with other levels of softness. Graphite is available in varying grades of density (soft versus hard) and in the amount of actual graphite contained in the core (dark versus light). The softer side of the range is designated with the letter "B" and a number from 1 to 9 (with 9 being softest) and the harder end of the spectrum has the letter "H" and a number from 1 to 9 (with 9 being hardest). So a "9H" is the hardest/lightest pencil available, and a "9B" is the softest/darkest option.

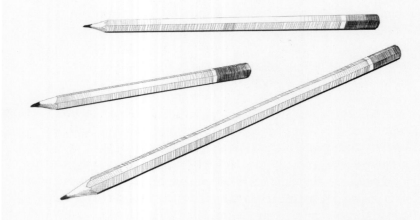

I typically work within a limited range of pencils, from about 2H to 4B. This so has helped me develop a sense of touch rather than being dependent on a wide range of drawing instruments. With practice, and by using a relatively soft and therefore responsive pencil (try a 2B), you should be able to achieve a complete range of values. In fact, in most drawings I only use one relatively hard pencil (2H) for the basic guidelines and one soft pencil (2B or 4B) for the shading.

Pencil Accessories

To get the most from your pencils, it's worthwhile to purchase one or two extenders. These have a stainless steel cuff with a sliding grip that can hold what remains of a pencil that's been sharpened down to the extent that it's too short to hold comfortably.

For sharpening, an inexpensive portable sharpener will work just fine. I sometimes prefer to use a small pocket knife, though, because this tool makes it easier to whittle away more wood without breaking the tip, or to shape the tip in a way that helps me to achieve a broader stroke.

Tracing paper and drafting tape can be useful to protect graphite drawings that might otherwise become smudged from pages slipping against one another. Cut a few pieces to size and keep these in the back of your sketchbook, then use small pieces of drafting tape to secure a sheet of trace to the page (drafting tape is less sticky than masking tape, so it's less likely to damage the paper when it's peeled off).

Binder clips can be used to hold sketchbooks closed when you're not drawing (preventing pages from slipping against each other) or open when you are.

A glue stick can be used to affix museum tickets, receipts, and other mementos related to drawing subjects, which can make your sketchbook a richer repository for your experiences.

A small pencil case is handy to keep your sketching gear together in a portable package.

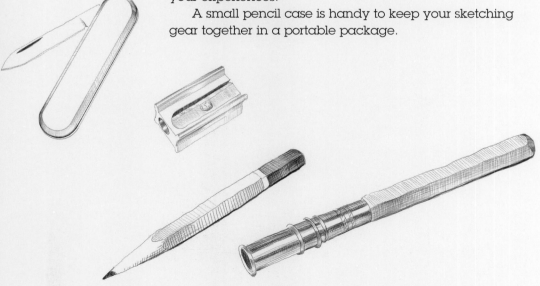

Erasers

The only reason I ever use an eraser is to clean up any smudges at the end of a drawing session. It's almost inevitable that you'll decide to carry one with you, but I strongly recommend against using it to erase any lines as you're drawing. Just keep your initial guidelines very light and don't worry about "mistakes"—by leaving an errant line on the page, you'll know better where its replacement will need to go.

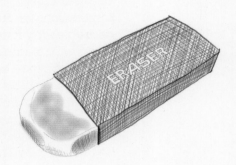

Ink Pens

There are many types of pen available today, from the most basic, inexpensive, and disposable "ball-point" pen to the most precious and expensive fountain pen, and a dizzying number of options in between. Most stores that carry a good selection will provide small pads of paper for you to test line size and quality, so spend some time making scribbles with different types of pens as you shop. Look for a pen that gives a clean and consistent line, and get a few different sizes—a pen with a very thin line, one with a wider or heavier line, and perhaps something between these two.

Digital Drawing

With the increased availability of tablet and smartphone applications for drawing, these tools have become a desirable way for many people to incorporate drawing into their increasingly digitized lives. If digital drawing appeals to you, there are a few things to keep in mind. First, try to find a tablet and/or stylus that supports pressure sensitivity, such that increased pressure will create darker or stronger marks. Without this feature, your ability to create subtle shades and graded tones will be severely limited.

When you are drawing on a tablet device, avoid frequent zooming in and out, and instead try to settle on a particular size for the view that is a compromise between stroke dimension and overall drawing size. Also, resist the urge to zoom in too far, thinking that increasingly fine levels of detail will improve the drawing—this usually leads to the sense of getting lost in the drawing and adding far too much unnecessary detail.

Finally, the size of the digital device should strike a balance between portability and a reasonably sized screen—if the screen is too small it will greatly limit your ability to draw freely and to view the entire drawing while it's being created. Incidentally, many of the drawings in this book were created using Autodesk Sketchbook Pro software and a Lenovo Tablet PC.

FUNDAMENTAL DRAWING SKILLS

The ability to draw well has nothing to do with "talent." It is instead a completely learnable skill, and the more you devote yourself to mastering fundamental techniques, the more effortless drawing will seem, to both you and the people who see your finished works. The fundamentals of drawing are not complicated, but they might feel somewhat challenging or uncomfortable at first. With thoughtful practice and a good deal of repetition, however, the basic techniques will become second nature, allowing you to focus increasingly on more complex subjects.

Attitude and Posture

The most basic "technique" for drawing relates to your attitude—how you approach the process and what's really important to you. As you continue to make marks on the page, begin to consider what you're trying to do—most essentially, try to cultivate the understanding that drawing

is more about a process than it is about a product. Let go of your expectations that any one drawing must achieve some arbitrary level of quality and instead learn to enjoy the simple acts of observing and drawing. If the process is engaged rigorously, thoughtfully, and repeatedly over an extended period of time, the resulting products will always be improving with regard to their perceived quality.

Do your best to be a good critic of your own development, rather than being "your own worst critic." This means that you care about the quality of your work, and you'll be honest with yourself about how you've succeeded and what needs additional work. But you'll also understand that not every drawing will be what you were hoping for, and take these bumps in your stride.

Posture

It might be assumed that you should draw in whatever position is most comfortable, but it's actually not quite so simple. While comfort is certainly important, there are other issues to keep in mind. One consideration is the amount of time you would like to spend drawing in a given session, another has to do with the way we perceive the urban spaces where we draw, and still another relates to the position of the sun. There is also the issue of how much—or how little—equipment you prefer to carry around with you.

I generally recommend trying to stand when you're out sketching, for several reasons. First, you'll be more free to really dial-in the best viewpoint for a given subject, and not be limited to places where there is convenient seating. Second, standing will usually force you to limit your time drawing—you'll be more likely to keep your drawings relatively brief and to the point, rather than getting too comfortable and spending too long trying to make the "perfect" drawing.

Standing while drawing also has the advantage of elevating your viewpoint to the height that most of us are at as we move through the urban space of the city. At the very least, I almost always stand while I'm setting up a drawing with light guidelines— then perhaps I'll sit somewhere within range of my original viewpoint to add value and complete the sketch.

Drawing on your feet might feel uncomfortable at first, but it does become easier with practice, and you can always use available props to your advantage.

It's generally better to draw with the sun at your back so the light is on your subject. It also means the sun isn't shining in your eyes, which can quickly cause fatigue. In hot climates, it's usually best to find a shady spot from which you can see a well-lit subject, but still remain reasonably comfortable and not have the sun glaring off the page.

Stairs are a great place to sit while drawing—you can usually determine your eye level by moving up or down the staircase, and they often provide a good vantage point in piazzas and public squares.

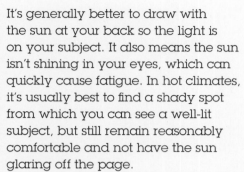

Many people like to carry folding stools, which allow them to sit just about anywhere comfortably. There are many types available, and some people even build their own.

Personally, I've never felt the need to carry the extra equipment—there are almost always some stairs or a low wall (or even the ground) if I really need to sit down.

Most often I tend to draw on my feet, and suggest that you give it a try at least several times before deciding that sitting is the best or only posture to adopt when you're drawing.

Seeing and Observing

There is a difference between "seeing" as it relates to our everyday experience and "observing" for the purpose of drawing. The difference has to do with how we perceive the underlying structure of a scene, and being able to translate what you observe into something that can be drawn in a relatively brief amount of time.

"Seeing" is a word we use frequently to refer to the act of using one's eyes, while "observing" might be a more appropriate word to refer to the act of preparing to draw, or what you do when you're trying to draw. "Seeing" suggests that you're taking in everything—all of the visual input your eyes can receive at any given moment—without very much in the way of discrimination. "Observing," on the other hand, has a stronger connotation toward being thoughtful and critical about visual information—certain elements of your view are receiving more or less scrutiny than others.

Stripping away extraneous visual information as a means to finding the essential structure of a view is a fundamental aspect of drawing. At the very least it allows us to complete a drawing in a reasonable amount of time, because we're not compelled to draw every single aspect of what we see.

Do your best to develop your ability to find the essentials of everything you draw—what is necessary to convey your interest in a given subject, and what is not. With practice, your skills for critical observation will contribute greatly to your ability to draw—you'll be able to size up potential subjects more effectively and then draw them more quickly and meaningfully.

The Brain and the Eyes

The single most significant impediment to drawing from observation is, paradoxically perhaps, the way our mind analyzes and interprets what we see. I first learned about this from Professor Francis D.K. Ching, who has been studying and writing about drawing for many years. In our daily lives, everything we observe is interpreted based on our past experience and our objective understandings of the objects and spaces we encounter.

When we see a scene like that shown above, we automatically and subconsciously convert the visual input into more "useful" or objective information—approximate geometries, dimensions, distances, and so on. In my experience with students, this most often takes the form of a quasi-omniscient point of view, as though we are seeing things from above and in an abstracted manner, like the image at upper right on the facing page. Of course there's nothing wrong with how we analyze and interpret what we see. The only problem is that, when we try to draw, the result is some amalgamation of what we see and what our brain is telling us we're seeing, like the sketch at right.

The solution is to learn to trust your eyes, and to use the techniques outlined in this book—measuring methods, basic perspective, and other compositional strategies. With practice you'll be able to translate what you see to the page with plenty of accuracy.

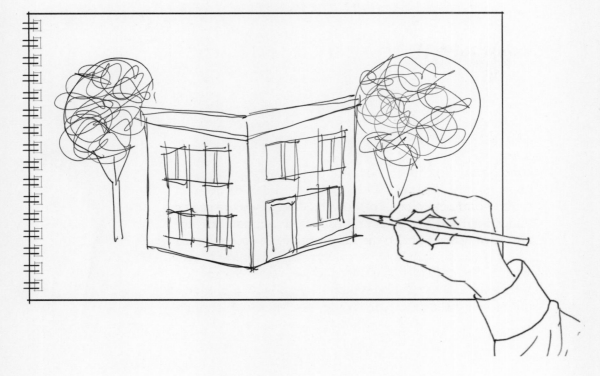

Selecting Subjects

It's most important that you draw what you find interesting. Whether crumbly old buildings are your thing, or you're only attracted to the latest shiny glass and steel skyscraper—draw what appeals to you. You'll have more motivation to draw frequently and more patience for the process of practicing than you would if your subjects are relatively uninteresting in your eyes. But if you only ever draw the same limited set of subjects, your skills might begin to stagnate, so try to challenge yourself occasionally and step outside your comfort zone by drawing subjects that you find less than completely compelling. At the very least, you'll be required to try some new techniques that might be more useful that you'd previously assumed.

When you're out looking for subjects—or even once you've found something you'd like to draw—move around before you begin. The same subject will appear different from a variety of angles, a point that is further discussed on the following pages, with regard to both point of view and proximity. But even slight movements on your part

can affect what you see. I will often find a subject that interests me, and that I plan to draw, but then I'll really get specific about a precise angle from which to sketch. The bell tower on these pages is, to me, a fascinating subject from almost any angle. It's at the church of San Rufino in Rome, and in all the many times I've drawn it, I've spent at least a few minutes moving around and thinking of what would make the most interesting sketch on that particular day and at that particular time.

One of the most important reasons to move around before starting to draw relates to sunlight. As the Earth rotates and the Sun appears to arc across the sky, the light is always changing. If you draw a subject that's in shade, it's very difficult to convey depth and volume through the use of value contrast—the entire subject is likely to come across as dark and muddy, like the drawing below right. If you really want to draw a particular subject, but the light isn't quite right, consider the time of day and the cardinal directions (North, South, East, West), and make a mental note, because you might need to return to draw at a different time of day when the sunlight will be better.

Point of View

It's very important to consider subjects from a variety of points of view before settling on the preferred position from which to draw. If you have ready access to an interesting drawing subject, try to approach it from a variety of angles and at different times during the day. Some factors to consider are the composition (a vertical or horizontal emphasis, for example), the particular lighting characteristics, the presence or absence of people, and the overall complexity of the view as it relates to the time you have available to draw.

The two views shown here were sketched from the same position, but the results are quite different from one another simply because I turned my head. The drawing on the left looks out through one of the major archways surrounding a plaza in Barcelona. It emphasizes the vertical orientation of a single arch and the light and activity out in the square. The second drawing (below), is a one-point perspective that emphasizes the interior of the arcade and the play of light and shade.

In each case, certain elements have been accentuated or suppressed, based on what I thought would add or subtract from my impression of each view. For example, the capitals on each pilaster were of interest to me in the view below, while I decided to edit out the same detail in the drawing opposite.

Proximity

An important aspect of selecting subjects for drawing
is proximity—that is, the distance between you and the
subject of the drawing. Proximity affects how much of a
particular scene can be included in the drawing and the
level of detail that can be achieved—both of which help
determine what the drawing is really "about" in terms of
scope, focus, texture, and so on. For example, all three of
these drawings are of the Reptile House at the National
Zoo in Washington, DC, but they begin to show the variety
that can be achieved by varying one's proximity to the
subject. In the drawing below, the central entry pavilion
of the building is shown "in context." We see how the
pavilion relates to the adjacent wings of the building,
get some sense of the surrounding landscape, and begin
to understand the size of the building as compared to the
human figures in the foreground. It could be said that this
drawing is about the pavilion as a whole, as we can
understand its general size, shape, and volumetric
characteristics rather than any particular details that
went into its construction.

By standing closer to the entry and facing it on axis, we're able to focus on the porch surrounding the door. At this distance, the rest of the building becomes less important, and we can give greater attention to the geometry of the porch and begin to suggest some of the details that provide its special character.

Getting even closer, some of the truly remarkable details become more apparent and more possible to draw with increased accuracy. In this case, the fantastical reptiles and amphibians that make up the corners and column capitals become the obvious focus—that is, what this drawing is about. It's often a good idea to combine a few drawings of the same subject—from varying distances—on the same sketchbook page, to give a more complete understanding of the building or other subject being drawn.

Measuring Methods

Sketching from observation isn't usually about achieving an extremely high degree of precision, but we'd typically like our drawings to be reasonably accurate depictions of what we see. Just a few easy techniques can help, but only if you make them part of your regular drawing routine. They'll require some practice and repetition before they begin to feel natural and you start to understand their value.

Sight Sizing

The simplest method, and the one most often overlooked, is called "sight sizing," and it's merely the act of holding your sketch right next to your subject in the distance. It's best if you move your sketchbook nearer or farther from your eye until the sketch and subject are as close as possible to being the same size. Then look carefully for mistakes in your drawing and try to correct them. This approach is best applied early and often—the more you catch big errors early in the process, the more easily and accurately the sketch will progress from there.

Sighting Angles

When trying to determine a particular angle in your view, you can use your pencil or pen as a baseline. Hold it horizontally or vertically, whichever is closer to the angle you're working on, and compare your pencil to the line in the distance. It helps to close one eye while doing this, so you can really compare one line to the other. If necessary, practice sketching the angle a couple times in the margin before adding it to your drawing, so that you'll be more certain to get it right. Use the sight-sizing method opposite to double check each angle as you add it to your drawing—especially for the major setup lines.

Sighting Proportions

Your pencil can also be used to measure relative sizes of elements in the view. Closing one eye, find one element (the space between the two columns, in this example) and compare it to another element (the height of the door). Look for situations where one element of the view is either equal to or some fraction (or multiple) of another, and use these proportional relationships to help establish the overall composition of the drawing. Note that it's important to hold the pencil the same distance from your eye during any related set of measurement.

Making Marks

Let's get started right away with some essential practice. You'll want to be skilled at making a wide variety of marks on the page, and it really helps to practice these skills repeatedly. In this way, you'll develop "muscle memory," meaning you won't need to think about it every time you need to make a particular set of marks, and your hand will more naturally make the marks necessary for sketching. This will allow you to draw with consistency and greater speed, regardless of the particular challenges you encounter in a given drawing situation.

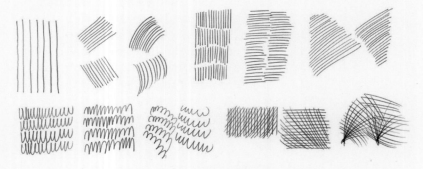

Start by making simple lines, trying to keep them reasonably straight, and mix it up with regard to speed. Make some sets of lines more slowly and deliberately, and others more swiftly. Notice the differences in the resulting lines—I find that the more swiftly I make the mark, the more smooth and clear is the result, but sometimes I might actually prefer a more wavering line. Also explore the variation possible between using the point of the pencil (above) versus the broad side (below), and experiment with varying pressure to achieve lighter or darker tones on the page.

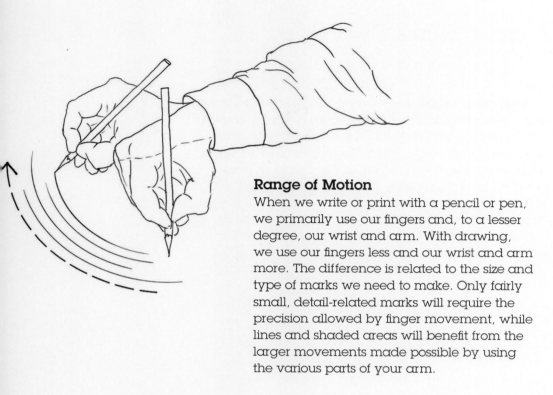

Range of Motion

When we write or print with a pencil or pen, we primarily use our fingers and, to a lesser degree, our wrist and arm. With drawing, we use our fingers less and our wrist and arm more. The difference is related to the size and type of marks we need to make. Only fairly small, detail-related marks will require the precision allowed by finger movement, while lines and shaded areas will benefit from the larger movements made possible by using the various parts of your arm.

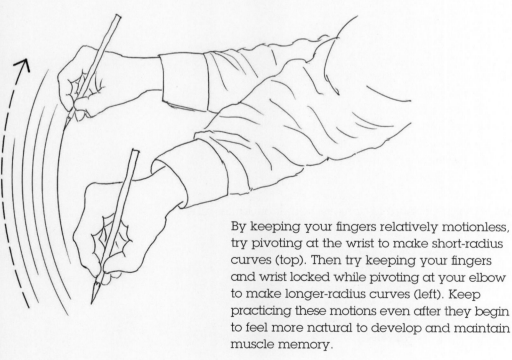

By keeping your fingers relatively motionless, try pivoting at the wrist to make short-radius curves (top). Then try keeping your fingers and wrist locked while pivoting at your elbow to make longer-radius curves (left). Keep practicing these motions even after they begin to feel more natural to develop and maintain muscle memory.

Lines

Making lines that are reasonably straight is an important skill to develop. Note that I've used the word "reasonably" rather than "perfectly." In freehand drawing, there's no need to make perfectly straight lines, or to be concerned about lines that waver. But you should be able to make lines that are straight enough to represent the edges and corners of buildings and other linear elements. Generally, the longer the line you'd like to make, the more you should try to use your entire arm in a smooth motion to move the pencil. It also helps to draw (or drag) the pencil across the page, with your hand leading the way and gliding on the surface, rather than pushing the tip of the pencil into the page. This has the added benefit of keeping the pencil pointed, particularly if you rotate it slightly as you go.

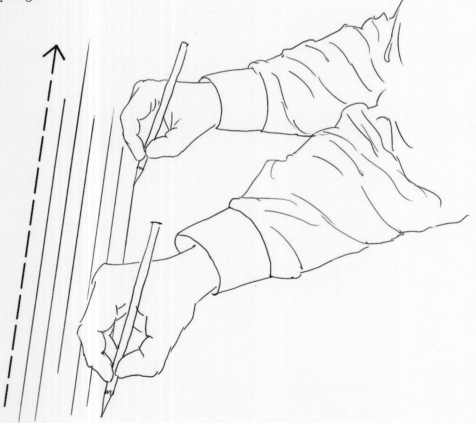

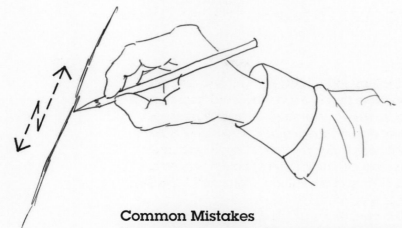

Common Mistakes

People will often make "sketchy" lines, as though moving the pencil rapidly back and forth is what they're supposed to do when "sketching." The result, however, is a fuzzy, indistinct line that leads to a fuzzy, indistinct drawing when every line is approached in this way. Strive instead to be decisive about where the line is going to go, and then draw it in a single, relatively swift motion. To do this well takes some practice, but the effect will be cleaner, less sloppy drawings.

Another mistake is to draw complete shapes in a continuous motion, especially with rectangular shapes (below left). It's far more effective to draw the lines individually, and to draw parallel lines in the same direction (below right), making sure that corners connect cleanly—even overlapping the corners slightly to create a definitive point where the lines meet one another. The result will be shapes that are clear and distinct, with lines that are more complete and straight.

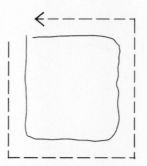 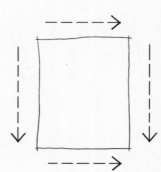

Hatching and Cross-Hatching

To develop consistent tone from lines, we use what are called "hatch" patterns. These are collections of parallel lines. To create uniform hatch patterns, the line lengths and the spaces between the lines should be as consistent as possible.

Avoid "scribbling" in both directions.

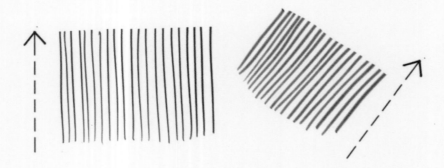

Instead, draw in the same direction, and strive for consistency.

Experiment with various densities and orientations.

Build up larger areas of tone with grouped patterns.

Create more density with crossing hatch patterns.

Graded Tones

While it's important to keep the value scheme of your drawings reasonably clear, there are often reasons to use graded tones. By "graded," we mean a tone that transitions gradually from one level of darkness to another—from a light tone to a dark one or vice versa. Pen and pencil require different techniques, because pen is a purely line-based, ink medium, while pencil is a dry medium.

As you saw on the preceding pages, pen can require multiple passes to build up tone through cross-hatching. If we were to try graded tones using only a single hatch pattern, we'd be limited to adjusting the spacing between the lines or the line thickness (or both). But the vast majority of ink pens provide only a single line thickness, and adjusting the spacing doesn't give a very convincing graded tone—it just ends up looking like widely spaced lines rather than a uniform tone (right). So we'll need to build up the darkness and control the gradation by using cross-hatching (below). It can be a challenge to maintain consistency with so many layers of hatching, and it can be a time-consuming process to achieve the desired levels of darkness, but with practice you can develop both consistency and speed.

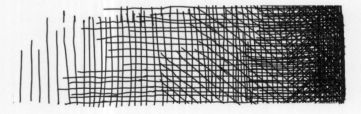

With pencil, we can use the broadside of the tip to achieve much wider marks with each stroke, and we can apply more or less pressure to adjust the relative values as we go (this versatility is one of the great advantages of graphite over pen and ink). It's usually best if you can apply the graded tone in one or two passes, rather than having to go over the area several times, but one or two additional layers of value applied as a cross hatch can greatly unify the tone. Practice making tones like the ones here—going from light to dark and back again—if only to develop a better sense of the varying pressure required to achieve smooth gradations. Learning to use fanning cross-hatch patterns (above, lower right) will be very useful as a way to reinforce the perspective of many architectural drawings.

Controlling Hatch Patterns

It can be difficult to keep hatch patterns consistent
and, at the same time, keep them within boundaries on
your drawing—especially if the patterns need to cover a
relatively large area. The technique shown here can help,
particularly with a good amount of practice over time.

Start with the pencil's tip at the most important
edge (the leading edge of a shadow, for example),
and make swift strokes away from this edge. You can
let the end of the strokes tail off by releasing pressure
at the tip, especially if it helps in keeping the repeated
strokes consistent—this part of the technique requires the
most practice. Make the strokes in whichever direction is
most comfortable, rotating your sketchbook if necessary.

In this example, the first pattern (below left) is being
made with swift strokes to the upper right. For the second
pattern (below right), the strokes can be made in the same
direction after the sketchbook has been rotated about a
quarter turn clockwise.

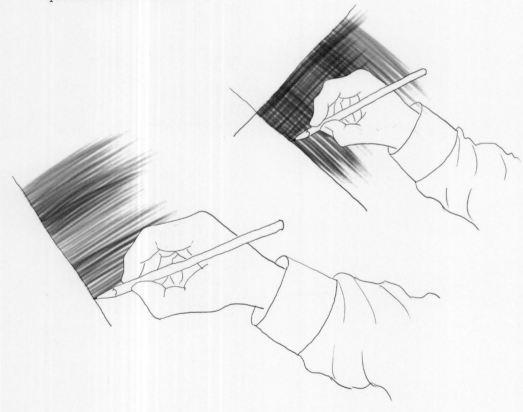

Strength of Contrast

The topic of value will be covered in greater depth later in the book, but don't be afraid to go "too dark" with your drawings. Quite often, beginners' drawings lack "punch" or drama, usually as a result of timidity when it comes to adding value. But the most effective way to create visual interest is to develop strong contrast between bright light and dark shadow, and it takes a strong and confident hand to apply enough darkness to overcome a weak drawing. Granted, these can be understood to be different approaches to the same subject—strong contrast versus more "subtle" contrast—and it's not as though one is right and the other wrong. However, it's generally a good idea to practice pushing your drawings farther than you think they can go with regard to contrast, if only to develop a sense of how to create drama and intensity in your work.

BEGINNING THE DRAWING

Perhaps the most common question I hear as a drawing teacher is, "where should I start?" As with many artistic pursuits, the answer could be, "start anywhere and see how it goes," but you're far more likely to feel a sense of accomplishment if you begin the process with some sort of plan regarding where and how to begin, and also how and when to finish.

At the most general level, I recommend a simple two-step process—making a reasonably complete "setup" sketch using light guidelines, followed by the addition of value (by drawing the darks and preserving the lights), with any development of detail being best approached as part of the value step.

Your first marks and lines are the most crucial elements in any drawing, though, as they will determine whether things go well or poorly for the duration. While it takes some patience and foresight to stick to this method, eventually the process will become easier and completed more swiftly.

Time, Scope, Size, and Medium

There is a variable relationship among the following factors: the amount of time you have to draw, the scope of the subject, the size of the drawing, and the tools you use to draw. The decisions you make about each of these factors should have some impact on the others.

With regard to time, for example, if you only have 15 minutes to sketch, it will affect what you'll be able to draw in terms of the subject matter and scope, the size of the drawing, and the medium you use. You'll be limited with regard to what you're able to accomplish in the available amount of time, and if your decisions about what to draw don't fit the allotted time, it's very likely to be a frustrating experience. If you have more time, you can spend it developing a more careful drawing with a fair amount of detail, such as the example being developed on these two pages.

The "scope" of the subject refers to how much or how little of a view you decide to include in your drawing. It can range from a wide-angle view of a cityscape at the

most ambitious end of the spectrum all the way down to a drawing of a simple detail such as a single window. The amount of detail you invest at either end of this spectrum will directly impact the amount of time the drawing takes to complete, and the size of the drawing will affect how much detail you're able to show in any case. In other words, a large scope in a small drawing will require a good amount of abstraction (like the example seen here), and vice versa.

With regard to media choices, graphite is usually the most versatile and quickest, while pen or marker are typically less versatile and take longer to build up the necessary amount of hatching for value. Watercolor usually takes the most time, unless it's used for a simple splash of color on a drawing that was first created with graphite or ink.

In the example shown here, the amount of time you have available for your drawing session should help determine what you decide to draw—all four houses, only one or two, or just a small portion of one? But the size of the drawing must be considered as well—perhaps a small drawing of all four houses could be achieved in a short time by drastically limiting the detail? These considerations might only require a minute or two of your time, and they should precede all of your drawings so that you're clear on what you're about to begin, how large or small it will be, and how long it will take.

Page Layout

Along with the considerations already mentioned, it helps very much to think about the overall arrangement of drawings and text on the page. You might not include any significant amount of text—perhaps the place and date are all that's needed. But if you're hoping to include more than just one drawing on a page, and more than the most minimal amount of written information, you'll want to plan the layout of the whole spread (that is, two facing pages) before you get started. If you plan to have a group of images and at least some narrative text, it's also wise to plan for a unifying title for all of your efforts. While all the components of a unified page spread might be developed on the fly, it's best to rough out some space-holders until you can get around to each drawing or block of text. Simple shapes like ovals and rectangles will do the trick, and if you draw them using very light graphite they'll remain flexible enough to evolve as the page or spread is fleshed out.

Keep in mind also that sometimes drawings will want to overlap each other in a collage fashion, so the boundaries between them might be a bit fuzzy or in some cases nonexistent. Especially appropriate for this treatment would be drawings at a variety of scales and sizes, and specific subjects that all contribute to the same story or experience of a place. Small key maps are also excellent candidates for inclusion, as they help to set the broader context for your observational drawings.

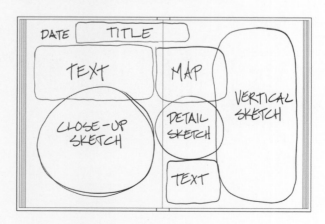

Initial Layout

Establishing the Elements: Example 1

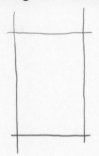

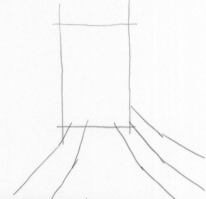

Start with the focal point: In this scene, from the Italian hill town of Assisi, the simple rectangular shape of the city gate is the first drawing element to be established, using very light lines.

Outline the foreground: Next, the basic outlines of the road and sidewalks determine the shape and extent of the foreground.

Balance the elements: Working from these guidelines, incrementally smaller elements of the drawing are added in a balanced way, without giving too much attention to any particular area.

Add detail: When the overall structure of the drawing has been established, the "initial layout" is complete. At this point, value and some detail may be added to create contrast and depth, thus finishing the drawing.

Establishing the Elements: Example 2

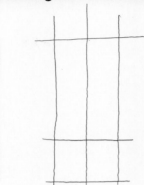

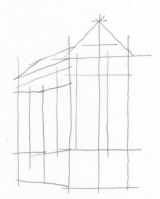

Start with the most basic shape: This grand old house on Embassy Row in Washington, DC, has an interesting circular corner tower. Start by drawing simple rectangular shapes that locate the major elements—don't worry about the curves yet.

Move to the next level: Using your first lines as a guide, and the measuring methods discussed on pages 30–31, arrange a few of the major angles of the view. With each step, start moving to the smaller elements, giving yourself small marks to identify locations.

Continue the process: With the overall guidelines mapped out, start developing smaller scale elements such as windows. This is also the best time to map out the lines of the street and outlines of any landscape elements.

Add value: Once you're confident that you have enough line work to serve as a guide, start to apply value (and therefore light and depth) to the drawing. Avoid getting too particular about little details, though.

Composition

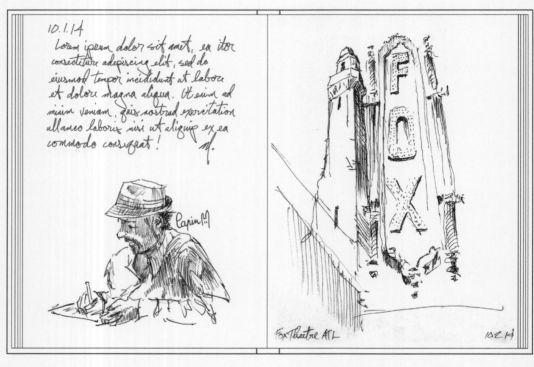

10.1.14

Lorem ipsum dolor sit amet, ea itor consectetur adepiscing elit, sed do eiusmod tempor incididunt ut labore et dolore magna aliqua. Ut enim ad minim veniam, quis nostrud exercitation ullamco laboris nisi ut aliquip ex ea commodo consequat!

Before starting a drawing, it helps to consider what might be the most natural organization of a particular subject. While it might seem that the majority of subjects can simply be placed on the page, some suggest (if not require) a different approach, or even a particular type of sketchbook that allows something other than the ordinary portrait orientation.

For example, some subjects are best drawn as a vertical composition, such as this street scene in Rome (left), while others will benefit from a horizontal orientation, such the broad view of Marina Bay in Singapore at the bottom of the page opposite. You may also want to think about space for text, whether it's personal notes or just the name of the place and the date of the drawing (opposite center).

As a way to arrange the major elements on the page, "composition" is the act of taking one element at a time and placing it with respect to a two-dimensional frame or organizing grid. You can use the edges of the sketchbook page as a frame, or you can draw a rectangle on the page and work within these boundaries. In either case, it's helpful to first visualize a frame around the subject by using a "viewfinder"—a piece of thick paper with a rectangular window cut out of it. You might create a few of these to carry in your sketchbook, each with a different set of proportions and with marks that divide each edge of the window into halves, quarters, and thirds.

The viewfinder can be used to determine how much of a particular subject will be drawn, and what the best orientation might be. Beyond these uses, the viewfinder can be used to locate major drawing elements within the frame (including their size, angle, and orientation), and then to help transfer these observations to the page. It should be obvious that each time you look through the viewfinder you need to hold it in the same place, so your references are consistent.

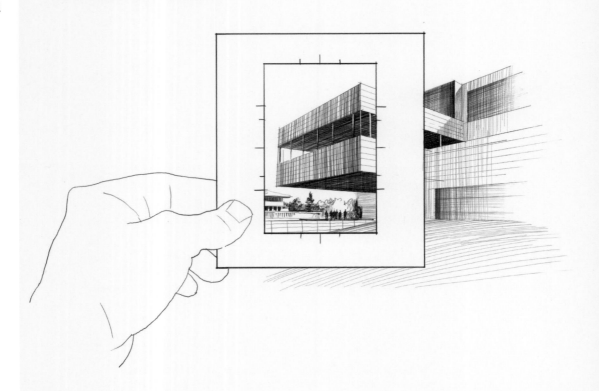

Draw a simple frame that corresponds to the proportions of your viewfinder (below). While the frame you draw doesn't need to be the same size as the frame in your viewfinder, it does need to be the same proportion—2 units wide by 3 units tall, or 2 units by 4 units, and so on.

Just having a frame like this on the page to work within can be enough to help you lay out the drawing, but it can also be helpful to add some grid lines that correspond to the marks on your viewfinder (below left), dividing the frame into quarters or thirds, for example.

Then, begin placing the major layout lines according to where they appear in relation to the viewfinder. In this example, notice how the line of the window sill crosses the very center of the frame—and how this location is clearly marked by the grid lines that cross at the center. These frame and grid lines can be extremely helpful as the major elements are arranged on the page.

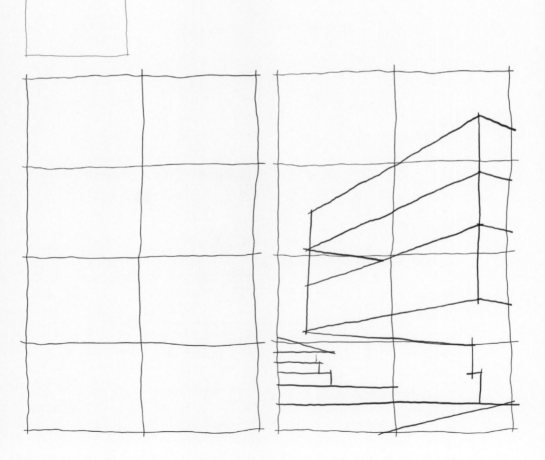

Perspective

Too often, the mere thought of perspective can instill a sense of fear in the beginning sketcher, because the subject is usually treated with too much complexity, or because it is assumed that a comprehensive understanding is necessary before one can use perspective to aid in the process of drawing.

The complete science of perspective is indeed fairly complex, and many excellent books cover the subject in detail. But for the purpose of drawing from direct observation, it's not necessary to have a very deep knowledge of every rule and technique. If you use the basics of composition as the primary means of laying out your drawings, then some limited knowledge of perspective can only help. These pages are intended to get you started with the most fundamental elements of perspective drawing, rather than attempt to cover the subject exhaustively.

Diminution

The most essential idea regarding perspective is that objects appear to diminish in size as their distance from the observer increases—in other words, the farther away something is from your point of view, the smaller it will appear to your eye. The lamp posts and wall shown here provide a simple example. The diagrammatic sketch below left shows that the lamp posts are all the same height, and the height of the wall and its openings are consistent along the entire length.

However, when viewed in perspective—that is, from the point of view of the human figure (below right)—these objects appear to be reduced in size as their distance from the viewer increases. It's quite a simple phenomenon once you understand it, but this rule (technically referred to as "diminution") determines how objects and spaces will appear in perspective.

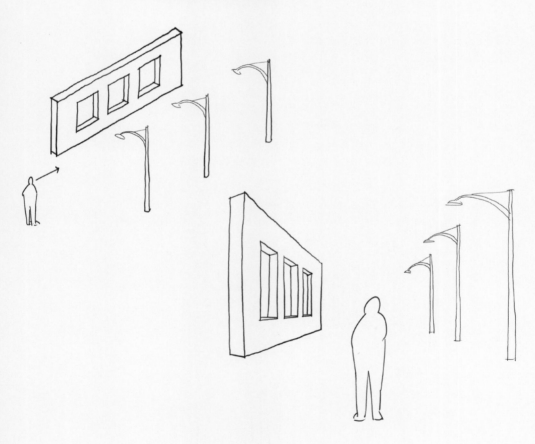

Convergence

The next most critical element of understanding perspective has to do with the way certain sets of lines appear to run toward each other when viewed from an angle. Groups of lines that are parallel to one another in space will appear to meet at the same point in the distance, a visual phenomenon known as "convergence."

This is reasonably clear with the wall shown here, and the tops and bottoms of the windows, because these are defined by a group of horizontal lines that are parallel to one another in space.

It's a bit less clear with the lamp posts, but the points at which these posts meet the ground, their tops, and the lamps themselves define an invisible set of lines in space, illustrated by the dashed lines running through the points.

It's important that you begin to see these lines of convergence in the architecture and other objects you're trying to draw, and that you use guidelines to define them on the page. Otherwise, elements of the view such as these lamp posts will likely be misaligned at the outset of the drawing.

Eye Level and the Horizon Line

The height of your eyes at any given time, known as your "eye level," helps determine how objects will appear from your point of view, and can be understood as an invisible, horizontal plane that intersects your eyes and extends outward before you. When we extend this plane to its greatest visible distance it becomes what we call the "horizon line." This is where all lines that are horizontal in space will appear to converge—every set of parallel, horizontal lines will have its vanishing point on the horizon line. Think of it as the line along which the earth or the sea meets the sky, assuming there's nothing to obscure the view—most of us have seen the horizon line when we've stood on a beach and looked toward the ocean.

In most drawing situations, however, the horizon line is not so clearly visible, although it's always there as an imaginary line at the greatest extension of our eye level. So the two terms (eye level and horizon line) mean almost the same thing, as they are so directly related to one another; I usually think of the latter as an extension of the former. With drawing, it can be very helpful to identify where the horizon line will be (related to the subject and also your drawing), and to build the sketch from this line.

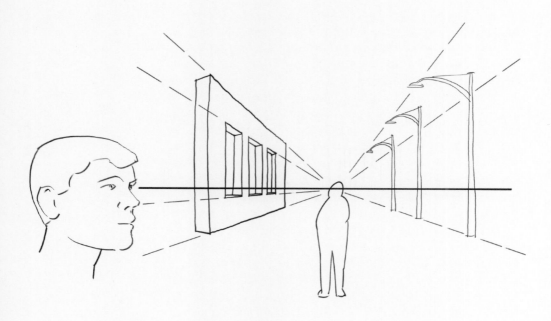

Multiple Vanishing Points

There are common expressions for a few types of perspective drawings—"one-point," "two-point," and "three-point"—that refer to the number of vanishing points that determine how converging lines are arranged in the view. The drawings on the preceding pages would be considered "one-point perspectives" because they are based almost entirely on a single vanishing point, with all the spatially horizontal lines converging on that point. The distinctions among these types of perspective can be useful, especially when drawing perspective views from your imagination—constructing views of a design project that has yet to be built, for example.

In reality, there are almost always going to be multiple vanishing points in a typical view. Take this simple drawing of a stair (below). The lines that are horizontal in space—the nose of each stair, and where the top of each stair meets the side of the staircase—will appear to converge on vanishing points on the horizon line, one point to the left and one to the right. However, because the sides of the staircase are not horizontal in space, and are instead sloping, they will appear to converge on a point well above the horizon line. So, even in this simple drawing, there are actually three vanishing points.

Once you have established the horizon line and one or two of the lines of convergence, the vanishing points can be used to draw additional converging lines with greater accuracy.

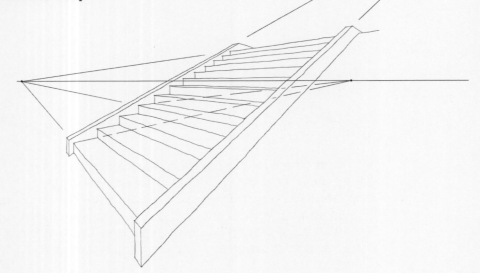

Applying Basic Perspective

I almost always use simple composition techniques to get a drawing started, but some very basic approaches to perspective can move things along while also ensuring a good amount of accuracy.

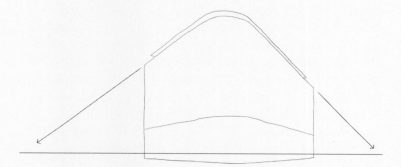

Start by establishing the horizon line, remembering that it will be at the same level as your eyes. In this case, the horizon line is about 6 feet (1.8m) above where the building meets the ground (my eye level as the viewer).

Then, establish one or more of the major angled lines in the view—the top left and top right lines of the building. By carrying these lines all the way to the horizon line, we find the left and right vanishing points.

Using the vanishing points as the start of additional guidelines, draw the tops and bottoms of aligned windows, doors, and so on. Complete the setup drawing by adding vertical lines as you go, then finish the drawing with value and entourage (see page 92 onward to read about entourage)—a process I've just started here.

COMMON CHALLENGES AND STRATEGIES

Every new drawing subject presents its own set of challenges, and this is one of the primary reasons I continue to draw—it simply never gets old. But there are numerous situations that tend to crop up repeatedly from one drawing to another.

Odd geometries and curvilinear elements are quite common, but very challenging to draw with a reasonable level of accuracy. Good examples are visible in several places in this sketch of Old St. Patrick's church in Chicago. It's always a good strategy to work out specific problems in the margins of your sketchbook, as I've done here at lower right. Make as many partial drawings, at a slightly larger scale, as you find necessary to understand the basic structure of any unusually challenging elements before working these into the overall drawing.

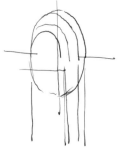

Structure and Value

While you should always develop a drawing's underlying structure thoroughly in light lines before adding value, try to keep from going overboard with the setup lines. It's during the initial setup that you'll work out the problems mentioned on the previous page, but knowing when enough is enough as a guide is a challenge in itself.

The key is to avoid trying to draw every little detail you see, because detail is usually only appropriate when you're drawing at a fairly large scale and at close range. You'll want just enough information to give you a clear understanding of where the value will go, and the value often ends up obscuring the finer details.

So be economical when laying things out, but generous with lines that will help you solve the types of problems mentioned on the previous page. This drawing is partially completed to give a sense of how much (or how little) I typically draw before jumping into value to complete the drawing.

Alignment of Windows

Windows are most often aligned
with one another in columns and
rows, or at least there is some
geometric relationship between
them that should be used to your
advantage in drawing.

Guidelines: Drawing each window
individually, one at a time, will
almost certainly weaken their
alignment as a group (upper right).
It's always better to start by drawing
a series of light guidelines that stretch
across the tops, bottoms, and sides
of as many windows as possible,
forming a grid as seen in this image.
If the guidelines are very lightly
drawn, they will be less apparent
in the finished drawing, once shading
is applied.

Using the grid: By establishing
an overall grid of guidelines, the
windows will be positioned more
accurately and they will come into
much better alignment with one
another. With a well-established grid,
drawing window outlines is seldom
necessary. They are only shown here
to emphasize the improved alignment
as compared to drawing windows
one by one.

Add detail: With the gridlines in place,
windows can be developed through
the addition of shading and hatching.
As the drawing nears completion, the
grid will recede to the background,
paling in comparison to the darker
shadows and detail elements.

Non-Linear Elements

It's generally an easier process to draw linear elements
in a view—the lines that are clearly straight. They may
be at angles that are challenging to capture, but the
techniques of composition and perspective can most often
assist in getting them down on the page with reasonable
accuracy. Curves, on the other hand—circles, ellipses,
and the like—are more difficult, but there are some basic
strategies that can make the process more manageable.

It's usually a good idea to begin with lines or other shapes to get the general forms into position, and then complete the curvilinear form by filling in between points. To draw a circle, for example, start by drawing a square, and then draw diagonals that connect the corners.

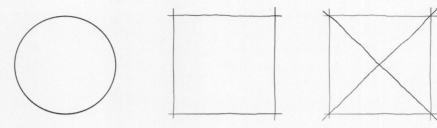

The diagonal lines will cross at the center of the square, which allows us to draw a vertical line and a horizontal line that subdivides the square into quadrants. If we measure the distance from the center with our pencil, along one of the vertical or horizontal lines, we can find the radius and transfer this measurement to the diagonals.

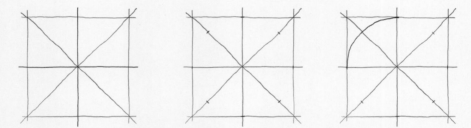

Then, draw an arc that connects these points, one quadrant at a time. If it helps, additional diagonal radii may be inserted to provide additional points before drawing each arc. Follow this process to complete the circle, or as much of it as is needed in your drawing.

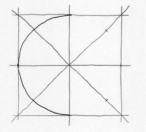
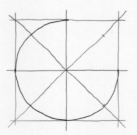
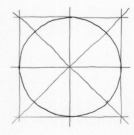

Ellipses: When a circular form is seen in perspective—that is, when it's being viewed at an angle, rather than straight-on—it will appear as an ellipse. Unlike circles, ellipses don't have a consistent radius, but instead have one long axis and one short axis. It's still best to start with bounding lines, as shown here, but it will take some practice to draw elliptical curves.

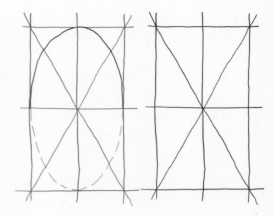

Arches: The practice of drawing ellipses really pays off when you're dealing with arches. Notice how the form of the ellipse is still clear, and is still constructed the same way as above. Also notice how the back side of each arch is also defined by an ellipse. Of course, the ellipses will get smaller as they become more distant in your view. If you're viewing the arches at a sharper angle, the columns would be closer together and the short axis of each ellipse would be shorter—making the ellipse narrower from side to side.

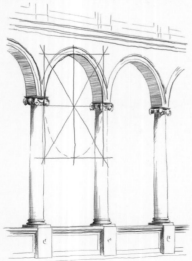

Horizontal ellipses: The same
technique for constructing ellipses
can be used whether they are
oriented vertically or horizontally.
As seen in the previous examples,
when a circular form is oriented
vertically in space, and we view it
from an angle, it will appear as an
ellipse with its long axis oriented
vertically. When a circular form is
laid flat (oriented horizontally in
space), the long axis of the resulting
ellipse will be oriented horizontally.
When there are numerous circular
forms in the view, there will be just
as many ellipses in the drawing.

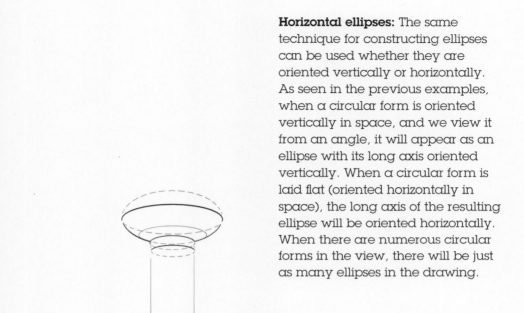

Reflections

Pools of water—or even wet pavement—will create
reflections that can add considerable interest to the
foreground of a drawing, which might otherwise be quite
empty. Try to understand how reflections will appear in a
structural sense. The vertical lines in the view will simply
appear to extend straight down into the reflection, while
the more challenging lines to understand are the angled
lines of convergence. These are merely an extension of
the perspective, with the reflected lines converging on the
same vanishing points as their counterparts in the view. In
this example, which is effectively a one-point perspective,
the converging lines of the wall on the right meet at the
vanishing point, on the horizon line. The horizon line and
its associated vanishing points are not reflected, but rather
serve as the source of the reflected lines of convergence.

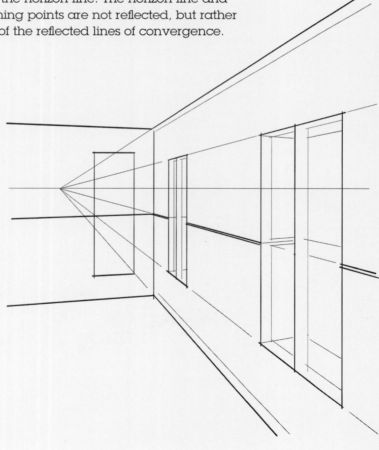

Rendering Reflections

As with any drawing, it helps to apply hatching in a way that reinforces the lines of convergence in perspective. But water, and particularly water that isn't perfectly calm, will affect the consistency of the lines and other marks used to render light and shade. The edges between dark and light areas of the reflection will often be broken up slightly by the ripples of the water's surface. This will tend to increase as the reflection nears your position and becomes more distant from the objects being reflected. In this example, the shading closest to the building is a fairly accurate reflection, while the reflection of the roofline becomes more broken. When rendering this slightly choppy water, it's best to keep the pencil strokes horizontal, to represent the horizontal orientation of the uneven water surface.

Calm Water

If the reflections are in still water, there will be very little difference between the way the view and its reflection are rendered—one is effectively a mirror image of the other. It can often help to develop the drawing somewhat, and then turn your sketchbook 90 degrees in one direction or the other. This allows you to see the objects in the view and their reflected image side by side, making it easier to see the direct similarity between the two. Try to mirror the hatch patterns and landscape elements to really reinforce the mirrored effect.

Reflections in Cityscapes

Modern glass buildings can be a bit tedious to draw,
but they often reflect adjacent buildings in their facades.
There's no need to be overly precise, as these reflections
are usually a bit inconsistent based on the imperfections
in the glass facade—the reflections frequently appear
quite wavy or even a bit random. There is often a shift
between the structure and the glass, depending on
whether the building being reflected is in sun or shade.
When it's in shade, it will be likely that the structure of the
glass (the mullions) will be light, and when the reflected
building is in sun, the mullions will typically be seen as
dark. Using reflections like this is an excellent way to
break up an otherwise monotonous facade—another
example can be found on page 74.

Developing Interest in Repeating Elements

There are often elements of buildings that appear repeatedly—windows, in particular. After establishing the overall layout of the drawing by outlining the major elements in a light hand (upper right), it's time to add shading and depth.

A common problem arises when repeated elements are handled in a very uniform manner—using the same hatch pattern, for example (right). This has the effect of creating a rather flat and monotonous rendering of the subject, and doesn't begin to suggest the differing levels of light and depth that are most often seen in groups of windows, doors, or other elements.

A better strategy is to strive for variation in the way shading and detail are applied—even if there isn't so much dramatic variation visible in the subject. Changing the directions and densities of the hatch patterns is a good way to begin this approach. Observe how reflections—of sky, trees, or adjacent buildings—tend to create variable patterns within each window, and how shades or drapes on the interior will make some windows much lighter than others. Be bold in drawing the alternating contrasts, and have some fun with the process of making the image sparkle and vibrate.

Glass and Steel

Even sleek modern buildings will benefit from variation, especially if it's based on careful observation of the building's reflectivity. At close range, and if you're looking at the shaded side of a building, you'll most likely see some blinds or drapes, but beyond that the interior will almost always appear to be very dark. When viewing a glass building from an oblique angle, especially if your line of sight is aimed upward toward the sky, you'll see almost nothing—only the seams of the building's exterior will cast very fine-lined shadows. Between these two extremes—close up and oblique toward the sky—it's very common to see other buildings reflected in the facade.

Being Selective

When you're faced with an interesting building, but the wealth of detail or repetition of windows seems too daunting to attempt a sketch, being selective about what you draw can be an excellent strategy. After laying out the entire subject in light lines, decide what aspects of the subject you find most interesting, or what parts of the building say the most about its character. Then do your best to add only enough additional information—usually in the form of varied value on the windows and other details—to provide some suggestion of three-dimensionality. Try to avoid getting locked into drawing everything with the same level of attention, and the viewer's eye will complete the scene.

LIGHT AND SHADE

Reserving Light

In direct combination, light and shade in a drawing make it easier for the viewer to understand three dimensions, depth, and the turn of one surface to another along corners and other building edges. Rather than seeing lines that define these edges, a more powerful and clear image can be made by defining edges as changes in light.

To produce the clearest contrast in your drawings, it's very important to reserve light on the page. Too often, there's an impulse to cover every square centimeter of the page with marks. If we were to follow this impulse to draw everything we see—every brick or stone or shingle on a building—we would significantly diminish the opportunity to show light. This is especially true when using a monochromatic medium such as graphite or ink, as opposed to colored pencils, markers, or watercolor.

The logic of the light needs to be consistent—such that it's clear where the sun and resulting shade are located—but within those parameters, you should be free to show the light/shade in a way that brings some emphasis to certain parts of the drawing, and perhaps less to others.

In this example of a Victorian Gothic building in Portland, OR, the area at the base is drawn loosely, but with strong darks, to represent the dappled shade from the trees. The upper portion of the building is more controlled and crisp, to represent the intensity of the sun and its effect on the complex architectural elements of the facade.

Developing Contrast

The process of adding value to a drawing can take some time, but the result is well worth the effort. If you get in the habit of planning what you're going to do before starting, you'll be more efficient with your time. In this series of images you'll see how I work in layers of value to develop contrast in a methodical way. Always keep in mind that the main area of focus should have a greater amount of contrast, which means that the darks should be darker and more crisp than in other parts of the drawing.

   The first step is to create a reasonably thorough line drawing of the subject—one that's not too heavy on detail but that identifies the various surfaces to be rendered. As part of this step I usually give myself at least a few lines that will define the edges of the shadows, so when the sun changes position I'll have guidelines that show the shadows where they were when the subject first caught my eye.

Begin layering the value, from the lightest tones to the darkest. Try to work with one level of tone at a time, and do your best to be consistent with the hatch patterns. In this step, I'm working only on the tones that are just a shade darker than the parts of the subject that are in full sun. I typically begin with vertical hatch patterns, concentrating on the vertical surfaces.

Try not to jump ahead too much, and add any of the darkest darks at this stage. If you know that there will be darker parts of a particular area, that's fine—just make one pass with a consistent vertical hatch, knowing that you'll be adding more layers of darkness as you go.

Create additional layers of hatching, but in opposing directions—either horizontal patterns or as directional patterns that follow the lines of perspective. The areas that are only as dark as the previous pass of hatching can be left alone, but the next level of darkness can be developed at this stage with an eye toward developing the central focus of the drawing. You can also make additional passes with hatch patterns in the same direction as those that came before, to add greater density (and therefore greater darkness) or to clean up any rough edges of the preceding hatch patterns.

The final level of value will require still more hatch patterns, often at an angle to complete patterns that are vertical and/or horizontal, as well as heavier pressure on the pencil. This stage is where the real visual depth comes from, with the darks becoming quite dark. The intensity of contrast should increase around the main area of focus— in this case the central part of the drawing. As you complete the drawing, try to reinforce the edges defining the greatest shifts between dark and light, and touch things up such that all the patterns are blended into tones rather than appearing only as groups of lines.

Small, Quick Studies

An excellent way to develop your eye and hand for seeing and sketching dramatic contrast is to practice small, quick value studies like those shown below. All four are views of streets in Rome, each of which was completed in just three or four minutes at a quite small size (about 2–3 inches/5–7.5cm maximum dimension).

Whereas the drawings on the preceding pages show a methodical approach to building value, almost the opposite is shown here. Both approaches are important to practice, as quick studies have some unique advantages.

While long studies will allow you to indulge in a penchant for detail (if that's something you enjoy), brief studies can help you learn how to focus on the big picture, using more energetic strokes in far less time, but still arriving at a truly compelling image. They limit your ability to become bogged down in detail—if the sketch is very small and very fast, there is simply no time or space to draw insignificant elements in the view. Instead, your focus will be on big, bold strokes that are only about applying darkness in ways that relate fundamentally to the perspective and the character of light in the scene.

Forcing Shadows

Drawing is about editing—emphasizing some aspects of your view while de-emphasizing or even eliminating others—for the purpose of creating a compelling or informative image. When it comes to value, this is often achieved by "forcing shadows," which is an old expression that means accentuating the direct contrast between dark and light edges in a drawing. With a too-consistent pattern of hatching and cross-hatching, as seen in the image on this page, there is little indication of the variable character of light that is usually present in shadows.

Seeing this in your subject can require careful observation, but there is usually some gradation to cast shadows and surfaces that are in shade. It can help to exaggerate this variation—at least a bit—to give a better, more interesting sense of depth in the drawing.

The greatest contrast in a drawing should be along the lines where dark meets light. In areas away from the leading edge of a shadow, there is often some light being reflected from other surfaces and lightening the deeper parts of the shaded area. To represent this phenomenon in a drawing, we "force" the edges of the shadows and grade away from the edges.

More specifically, wherever the edge of a cast shadow or a shaded surface meets direct sunlight, emphasize the contrast as much as possible. Make this edge very dark, and then grade the darkness as you move away from this edge—that is, make it gradually lighter as you go. It might require a few layers of hatching, and a few passes over the same area to really build up the darkest edge and to ensure a reasonably smooth transition to the lighter areas of the shading.

Value and Distance

As objects recede into the distance, they will typically show less value and distinction. This is known as "atmospheric perspective," because dust and water vapor in the air will diminish the sharpness and overall value of what we see far away from our drawing position. This can be especially apparent when there is a significant depth of field, with some objects relatively close to us, some in the middle-distance, and some quite far in the background.

In this example, the trees in the foreground are very dark and also clear with respect to detail. In the distance, we see more trees on a hillside, but these are relatively faint and show less detail. The objects in the middle distance—the buildings—show a more complete range of both value and detail. By adjusting the way objects are drawn, and particularly the strength of their respective values, we can accentuate their positions in space.

Increased Detail in Shade

A different strategy for applying value involves showing
a greater amount of detail in shaded areas of a building.
If we were to draw all the bricks in the example shown
here, the level of sunlight being shown would be greatly
diminished. Even if we only drew the mortar joints between
the bricks, the resulting lines would create a pattern that
would begin to read as shading, even if the surface is in
sunlight. By emphasizing the material surfaces that are
actually in the shade, it's possible to convey the nature
of the materials without compromising the brightness of
the parts of the building that are in direct sun.

It helps to practice drawing a variety of standard building materials such as stone, bricks, shingles, wood, and similar materials. Practice drawing them with varying dimensions and construction patterns, with a range of values for each; these practice patterns will come in handy when you're actually outside drawing.

Drawing at Night

At night, with only artificial light to work with, objects in view will be less clear, and the darks will tend to blend into one another, making it difficult to draw distinctions among elements. Nocturnal drawings also require a significant amount of graphite or ink on the page, because so much is in darkness and relatively little will be in light. Begin by laying out the drawing as usual—shown here on the left side of the image. Then use a much broader stroke to lay down the large areas of darkness, being careful to reserve the white of the page for the highlights.

An alternate way to approach drawing at night is to use dark or black paper with a white pencil. Once again, set up the drawing as usual, with light lines defining the major edges and composition of the view. A broad stroke is less necessary in this instance, because you'll be drawing only the elements that are illuminated—in this case from within the windows and from artificial lights shining upward on the architecture. A broad stroke comes in handy for the sky, though, to silhouette foreground objects like the trees and the building's profile, which would otherwise be indistinct due to a lack of contrast.

ENTOURAGE

The word "entourage" is used to refer to the elements
of architectural drawing that are additional to the
architecture itself—people, trees, street furniture, vehicles,
and the like. While our drawings are focused on buildings
and urban spaces, if we neglect to show any entourage
then our drawings will lack the life that permeates our
cities. This chapter is intended to help enliven your
drawings by providing some fairly simple ways to
draw the people and objects that surround us.

A Word About Editing

Always keep in mind that a significant aspect of drawing
from observation involves deciding, as you go along, to
leave some things out. Don't try to draw everything you
see. This is especially true if your interest is in the
architecture and the urban spaces of cities, in which
case you might begin to omit some of the extraneous
elements in your view as a way to emphasize the real
focus of your drawing. Lamp posts, benches, an
overabundance of trees and shrubs—these particulars
are certainly part of our environment, but they can be
a distraction from the more general elements of the view.
The drawing on this page shows enough entourage to
provide some context, without going overboard with the
cars, signs, and trees.

People

To give your drawings an appropriate sense of life, it's
often essential to include at least some human figures
in the view. For a variety of reasons, though, people can
be very challenging to draw convincingly. One of the
problems is that we often try to give them too much detail
by drawing faces or hands, rather than being satisfied
with indicating an overall shape that clearly represents
a human form. At the other end of the spectrum, we
sometimes don't provide enough visual information, but
try to get by with drawing "stick people." This section will
focus on striking a balance between too much and not
enough, giving you some shorthand techniques for
including figures that will add to the drawing rather
than detract from it.

Clyde Common 7.29.10

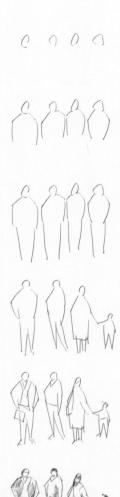

Basic forms: The human body is fantastically complex, yet it's important to develop some techniques for simplifying this form. The essentials of a standing figure can be boiled down to the head, the torso, and the legs. I typically think of this abstraction as seven individual marks on the page—a somewhat oval shape for the head, a pair of quick strokes for the shoulders, another pair for the sides, and two more that define the outline of the legs. The proportions can vary a bit, but it's usually assumed that the figure is roughly seven or eight head heights—this is one of the reasons I begin by drawing the head first, and then drawing the rest of the body to work proportionally from this starting point. Practice these simple shapes repeatedly, until you can very quickly sketch forms that are believable.

Developing variation: Another aspect of "believability" is variation—if all of the people look exactly the same, they will appear static and less human. It doesn't take much too suggest slightly different heights, weights, clothing types, or hairstyles, just by manipulating the basic seven strokes and adding just a few more marks before finishing with some hatching.

Groups versus individuals: I typically find it easier and more convincing to draw people in groups rather than trying to draw single figures. It's also a subtle way to indicate some sociability in your drawings—that people are meeting, talking, walking together, and so on.

Groups of people are drawn in much the same way as individuals, but with fewer lines because they can be blended together. In this way, drawing people in groups is both effective and economical.

People Viewed at Eye Level

Imagine all of the human figures in your view are standing on the same level surface as you, and you are all standing, as is often the case when sketching in cities. Begin by drawing the horizon line, which will coincide with the eye level of all the figures. Then draw rough circular outlines for the heads, followed by just a couple lines that suggest shoulders and torsos.

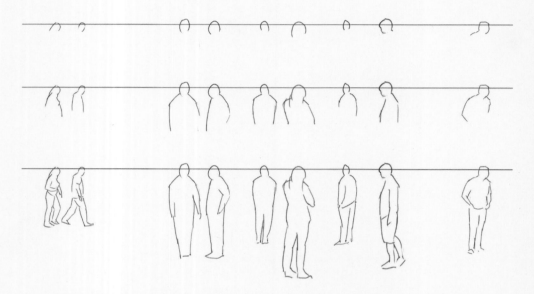

Complete the outlines by bringing their legs to the ground. By keeping all the heads roughly aligned along your eye level, you can indicate distance by making the figures larger (closer to your point of view) or smaller (farther away). Once the outlines have been established, a bit of value can be added to give the figures a sense of three-dimensionality.

People Viewed from Above

When you're looking downward, the heads of human figures don't align along the eye level, so you can feel free to distribute them in ways that add life to the scene. Just keep in mind that the farther away they are, the smaller and more abstract they'll appear (in other words, they will require less detail).

The same process for drawing the figures applies—start with a simple outline for the head, followed by the shoulders, torso, legs, and feet. Add value as necessary, but try to keep detail to a minimum (especially for faces and hands).

Counterpoint: As with all aspects of your drawing, it's a good strategy to consider contrasting lights and darks as you're developing the sketch. If the background is going to be light, make your figures dark, and vice versa, otherwise the people in your drawings will tend to get lost in their surroundings.

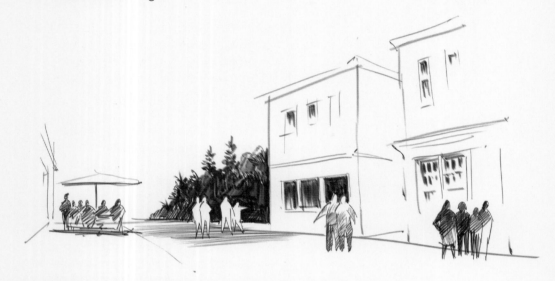

Indicating action: Just a few small gestures, props such as bicycles, or some indication of a striding figure can help to enliven a view by suggesting that you've captured a moment of action. It doesn't take much, so try not to overdo it. Also, a bold horizontal stroke or two at people's feet will ground them and indicate a shadow, even if the figures are kept very simple and without much indication of light and shade.

At closer range: While it's a good strategy to keep human figures relatively simple, or even somewhat abstract, there are times when a figure or two at close range will add something to the drawing—a sense of scale or distance with respect to the drawing subject, for example, or just a bit more specific character about the place. In these cases, it's usually wise to draw figures from behind, so you'll be less likely to get caught up in trying to create an accurate portrait, and less prone to the frustration of not capturing someone's likeness. In any case, strive to keep the forms and shading relatively simple.

Vehicles

As with buildings, drawing vehicles is much easier if you start with the basic outline and only fill in the smaller scale elements after the overall shapes are established. Although vehicles tend to have numerous curves, it's usually better to rough out their forms with relatively straight lines initially, and then develop the curving lines on this framework. Practice drawing vehicles from various points of view, and try to avoid getting into too much detail.

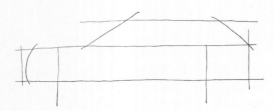

Begin with the major horizontals at the top, middle, and bottom of the vehicle.

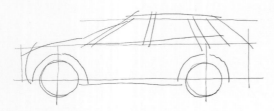

Continue with rough circles for the wheels and add diagonals to suggest the passenger compartment.

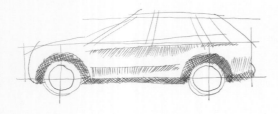

Use general hatch and cross-hatch patterns to clarify the darks, but leave most of the car light.

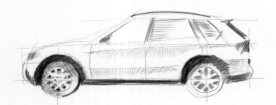

Finish with some strong darks around the wheel wells and undercarriage.

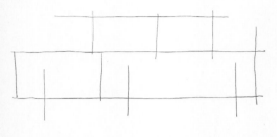

Always start with the basic framework, using lightly-drawn guidelines that will map out the entire image.

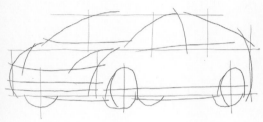

Develop the structure of the drawing by adding a second layer of guidelines, paying closer attention to the contours of the vehicle and the orientation of the wheels.

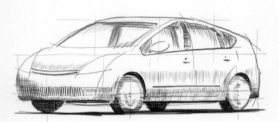

Add hatch patterns, making the strokes in the direction of the car's surface, using curving hatch patterns, if necessary.

When drawing groups of vehicles, see how little you need to put on the page to indicate their presence. Just a few lines, some simple hatch patterns, and a bit of strong darkness below—this is all that's necessary to convey the essential elements of cars and trucks. Keeping things simple like this will prevent the vehicles from overpowering the rest of the drawing.

Vehicles Aligned Along the Curb

It's very common to want to include a number of vehicles parked along the curb in a typical city street view. Here are some strategies to practice and keep in mind.

Guidelines: First, always try to begin with a simple set of guidelines that establish the locations of elements common to most (or all) of the vehicles in view. Here, I've drawn one line where the tires all meet the pavement, another that's roughly at the height of the roofs, and one more that's at the level where the windows meet the lower bodies of the cars. These three lines don't look like much on their own, but it's critical to draw them first as a way of unifying the row of vehicles.

Further form: In steps two and three (above and below), we begin to define the somewhat boxy shapes of the upper and lower bodies, while drawing another roughly horizontal line at the level of the undercarriage (making sure to leave space between this line and the line of the ground below). Notice that all of the vehicles in the view are being developed at the same rate—we're not getting into any detail yet, but instead we're drawing only the rough outlines of all the vehicles.

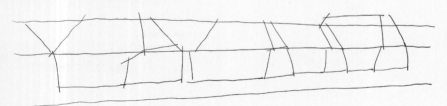

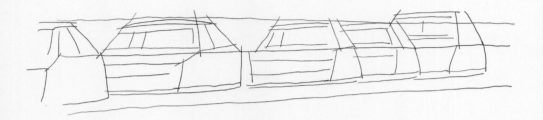

Additional form and adding the wheels: Continue the process of drawing lines to help flesh out the general forms of the cars, but don't go too far—keep them fairly simple and avoid detail. I typically add the wheels last, so they have somewhere to go—a framework into which they can be placed more accurately.

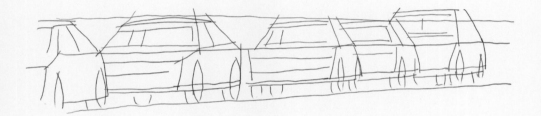

Finish with value: After patiently developing all of the vehicles at the same pace, we can finish the sketch by adding just enough value to give the image some three-dimensionality. Pay special attention to the darkness beneath and within the vehicles—the tires will be quite dark, while the undercarriage, ground, and interior of the roof can each be shown with a dark horizontal line.

Trees and Hedges

Landscape elements can add a lot of life to drawings of cities and buildings, but if they're not handled carefully they can also detract from an otherwise well-crafted image. The difference is made by applying simple yet convincing patterns rather than merely scribbling to indicate foliage. Practice drawing patterns like these (right), in various directions and at various densities, until it becomes easy to generate tones that can be combined into forms that read as trees and shrubs.

Mass and Light

Build up the masses of trees and hedges by repeating these patterns, but avoid filling in shapes with the exact same pattern at the exact same value, as this will detract from the sense of depth and light in your drawing. Consider the direction of sunlight and emphasize the three-dimensional forms of plants by keeping the upper portions light and adding darkness underneath. Hatch and cross-hatch patterns can be used to add additional value and unify the masses of foliage.

Basic Tree Forms

In drawing the basic tree shape, the stereotypical "lollipop" is actually a good place to begin, provided you don't stop there. Just a bit more information will go a long way toward a much more convincing image. Give the trunk some character and taper toward the top, then bring the limbs and smaller branches upward and outward to complete the form.

Pay attention to the essential differences between deciduous and coniferous trees, and the variety of species in each category. Develop some simple techniques you can rely on when you're out sketching—combining foliage and hatch patterns with basic tree forms.

Perspective

Trees and hedges, when arranged in rows, will conform to lines of perspective in your view. Use guidelines to link the tops of the canopies, the point at which trunks meet the ground, and where the trunks branch out into limbs. Hedges that have been trimmed into parterres will benefit from lines that define their edges and corners, and these will be related to the lines of perspective convergence.

Combining Elements

As you place landscape elements in your view, avoid drawing each tree or shrub as a complete object. Draw only enough to indicate its presence and how it relates to the rest of the view, and focus on variations in value and scale. Distant objects will appear more simple, while objects in the foreground will show increased detail— for example, try adding some close-up and silhouetted branches and leaves in the upper corners as a way to frame your view and give an added sense of depth. Most of all, have fun making marks that are loose and varied, and be patient as these marks build into a convincing image of foliage and landscape.

Street Furniture

When we pause to have a coffee or something to eat, the street becomes our social space. The furniture and decorations that compose these urban rooms can contribute greatly to the sense of life and scale in a drawing. Benches, tables, umbrellas, and the like can have similar lines to architecture, but they can also be somewhat more organic. Try to keep your focus on the general nature of the drawing, and don't feel compelled to draw every park bench or other bit of furniture you see—editing out some elements can be a good way to shorten the time spent on a particular drawing and also a way to keep the focus on the buildings and spaces. Even if you do try to include a good amount of street furnishings, see how little really needs to be drawn in order to get the point across.

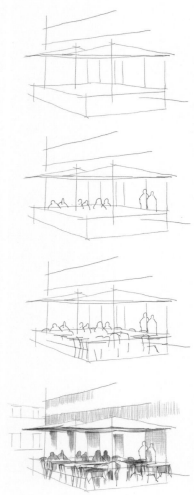

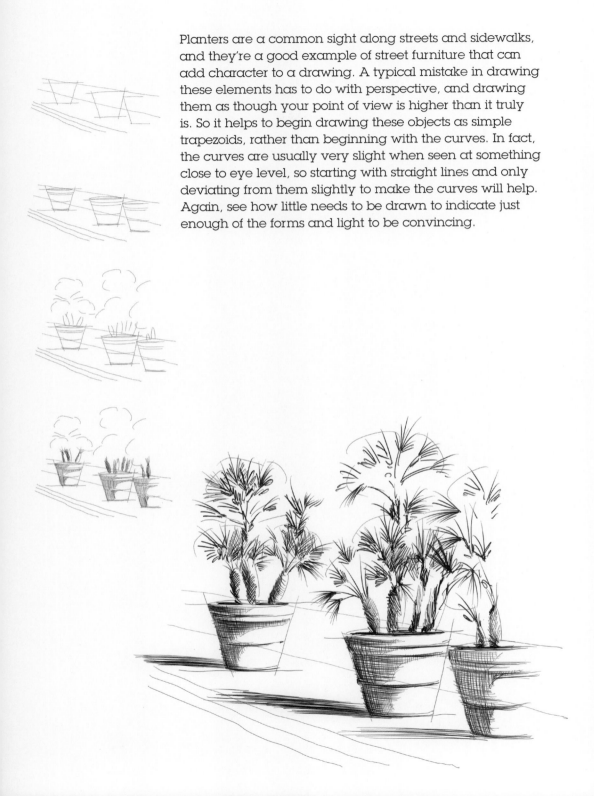

Planters are a common sight along streets and sidewalks, and they're a good example of street furniture that can add character to a drawing. A typical mistake in drawing these elements has to do with perspective, and drawing them as though your point of view is higher than it truly is. So it helps to begin drawing these objects as simple trapezoids, rather than beginning with the curves. In fact, the curves are usually very slight when seen at something close to eye level, so starting with straight lines and only deviating from them slightly to make the curves will help. Again, see how little needs to be drawn to indicate just enough of the forms and light to be convincing.

Signage

Our cities are littered with signs of all types. Trying to draw every sign as it appears would take much or all of our allotted drawing time, and it wouldn't necessarily make for a better drawing. At some point it becomes too much information, and can actually interfere with what we're trying to capture in the sketch. If your primary interest is in signs, then of course you should spend your time drawing them, but if you're trying to draw street scenes that include a balance of visual information, consider editing out some or all of the signage you encounter.

In the example on this page, I've tried to draw all the signs in a view of a street in Portland, and doing so took considerably longer than 15 minutes! It's an interesting drawing, if only for its abundance of detail—in other words, there's a lot to look at.

But to my eye, the drawing lacks focus—it's not clear what the intention is, or what is supposed to be the most important aspect of the view. But if we begin to edit, and be more selective about which signs we include, they no longer dominate the scene—allowing the drawing to develop a more apparent focus, such as the variety of buildings along the street. On this page I've eliminated all the signage, and even the telephone poles, from the view. Compare the two drawings and think about the effect of including or excluding signage.

If you do decide to include signage in your drawing, pay special attention to the character of the lettering, or fonts, that you see. They don't need to be perfectly precise in your drawing, but the distinctions between different types of text will make them far more believable.

CONCLUSION

Bringing it all Together

Each and every sketch, no matter how small and no matter the subject, is a step along the way toward developing the skill to draw with confidence in any given situation. Drawing is a practice, something you do frequently and repeatedly, that builds on itself over time. It's not about making pretty pictures, though you will do plenty of that as you go. It's much more about the daily observations you make through the act of drawing, and the more direct way of engaging with the world than most people experience.

Take the topics in this book individually, and practice them on a regular basis, such that you're improving in your ability to select appropriate subjects, deal with composition and perspective, apply value to describe light and shade, and enrich your drawings with entourage. Don't feel compelled to do all these things in every drawing, but do work toward an approach that will eventually bring these aspects of drawing together in a reasonable amount of time—perhaps only 15 minutes.

As a conclusion to this book, what follows are some ideas and tips that should help you develop drawing as a practice, and to continue and expand upon your own learning process.

Dealing with Frustration

One of the greatest killers of motivation to practice is the sense that you can't draw as well as you expect to. This frustration will always be part of drawing, but it should be matched by a sense of achievement along the way. This begins with the understanding that not every drawing will go your way—some will seem to work well, while others will not. This is actually one of the things that has kept me drawing for many, many years—that fact that it's not always easy. But there are proven strategies that will help you to succeed more often than "fail."

First, let's dispense with the entire idea of "failure" in the context of drawing practice, because it's simply not helpful. Whether or not you're happy with the results of any given drawing, it's still—always—a step toward improvement, particularly if you're thoughtful about how and why things may have gotten off track. Often, the best thing to do when frustration hits is to merely turn the page and start again, because no single drawing should be seen as being terribly important in itself, but rather in the context of your continued development.

However, it's even better to do some brief analysis, so if you feel dissatisfied with a drawing, get in the habit of asking yourself why. If you can begin to specify the reasons for your dissatisfaction, you'll be able to spend time working toward real solutions rather than just being frustrated in a broad sense. It also helps immensely to identify parts of the drawing that you feel are successful. I do this for virtually every drawing I create, and it really does help to offset feelings I may have about not making sufficient progress.

Much of your frustration will likely be related to the time you spend drawing, or the pressure you might feel regarding the time spent to achieve a drawing that satisfies.

Don't worry so much about not completing a given sketch or drawing. Always begin with the process described earlier in the book, with regard to time, scope, and size, and this will be less of an issue. But if you do get in over your head and take on too much in a given drawing, just do your best with it before you need to pack up and leave the scene. Also, don't feel compelled to continue working on an unfinished drawing when you've had to leave the subject's location. Certainly, if you have the time and motivation to keep working on it, go right ahead, but sometimes it's better to leave it unfinished and chalk it up to experience. You'll know better next time how to bite off what you can actually chew while you're on site.

Being decisive about what to leave out of a drawing can also help prevent frustration. In the drawing at right, my focus was on the towers above the theater entrance. The adjacent buildings are interesting, but not fundamentally what the drawing is about—so they're drawn very sparsely. Their essential outlines are visible, to provide some context for the central focus, but that's about it. This is the kind of decision you'll need to make almost every time you draw, and the more effectively you make little decisions like these, the more likely you'll be to feel satisfied with your effort.

Perhaps the most important overall strategy for working through frustration is to draw regularly, with a brief sketch or two every day if possible. If the individual drawings are of short duration, as suggested by the title of this book, you should be able to incorporate your drawing practice comfortably into your daily life and, most importantly, to experience some steady progress.

Date each and every sketch as a way to track this progress over the months and years. Challenge yourself to complete sketchbooks—that is, to fill the entire book— as a way to establish longer-term goals for the practice.

Part of your ongoing effort should be toward getting into regular, good habits, so focus on the fundamentals presented in this book, with as much repetition of the basic skills as possible, applied to a wide variety of subject matter. Another part of your effort should be focused on stretching your abilities further. What follows is a series of approaches to doing just that—continuing to learn as long as you continue to draw.

Continuing the Learning Process

While there is no substitute for frequent and diligent practice, there are strategies that will lead to ever-increasing levels of skill and ever-broadening approaches to technique. To continue developing your drawing ability, it's important to stay focused on the tasks of learning. If we only sketch without actually challenging ourselves to continually improve, then our ability is very likely to stagnate and perhaps lead to frustration or at least a sense of boredom. Not all who draw are very interested in constant improvement—some will be content with their skills just as they are. But if you'd like to work on developing your drawing abilities over time, here are some simple strategies that will help.

Stretch yourself in terms of subject matter or format. If you find yourself always drawing the same sorts of things in the same way each time, try to mix it up at least once in a while. Change your typical point of view, or the scope of your subjects, or the typical orientation of the drawing on the page. Whatever you find yourself doing out of habit, try doing it differently on occasion. The drawing on the page opposite is not my usual subject matter, or at least the point of view is more extreme than I would typically attempt. But it was a satisfying challenge to draw something new, to employ some perspective skills, and to avoid getting too bogged down in the detail.

Study the work of other sketchers, and try to apply their techniques to your own work as an exercise. This book would be the obvious place to start, but there are a great many books and other sources containing a wide variety of examples, in all sorts of drawing styles. If you only work from a single source, it may be true that your approach will become a bit too similar to that person's way of drawing. But as long as your source material is widely varied, there's absolutely no reason to fear developing an approach to drawing that isn't truly your own. This is an excellent way to learn new techniques and build your repertoire of sketching skills.

Carry images of sketches you would like to learn from, and keep a few of these in your sketchbook to refer to them while you're actually out sketching. If you find yourself struggling with particular elements of drawing, seek out examples of those elements that you think are worth emulating. Make some small copies of these references to carry with you—it might be several sketches of trees, for example, or cars, or whatever else you want to refer to when you're drawing.

Draw small, using preliminary thumbnail sketches to explore composition and value. More frequent, shorter duration sketches are generally better practice than larger, longer, less frequent drawings.

Try using media that you haven't used before, or haven't used in some time. When you begin to feel very comfortable with a particular medium, it may be time to try something else for a while. Transfer the knowledge you develop from one media choice to another. For example, when you begin to use color (and particularly watercolor), always strive to achieve the same levels of value that are possible, and relatively easy to achieve, with graphite or ink.

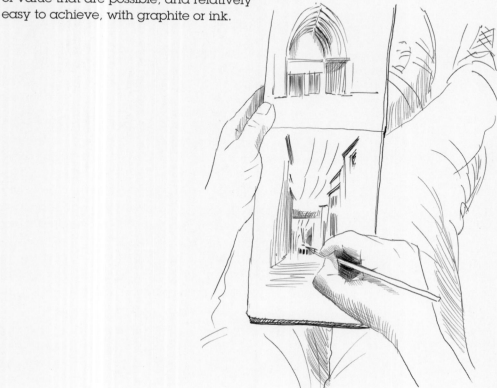

Finally, invite honest criticism of your drawings, and avoid the tendency to be protective or shy about your work. One way to make this happen is to attend local drawing events, sometimes called "sketchcrawls," where people of all experiences and abilities gather to draw in the same place and then discuss their drawings as a group. If this sort of event isn't available where you are, another excellent way to share your work is through the internet. The ease of communication provided by the web over the past decade or so has opened channels among sketchers around the world. There are many forums for sharing images and discussing the work, and in my experience, these forums are very "safe" places—full of support, generosity of spirit, and an abiding passion for drawing.

The more frequently you draw, the more you pay attention to the practice of drawing, and the more you get out there among other people who draw, the more swiftly and surely your abilities will advance.

References

Any single book about drawing can only cover so much ground, and will be limited to the author's knowledge and experience at the time of its publication. Hopefully this book has provided you with a strong start toward building your drawing skills and confidence. As you continue, there will be times when you'll need additional direction. The books listed here represent a selection of works that I've returned to on many occasions to push my own abilities further.

I've found that some of the most valuable texts are ones that have been long out of print. The books of Arthur Guptill, Ted Kautzky, and Ernest Watson, in particular, are an incredibly rich source of technique, inspiration, and examples, perhaps because they were written at a time when the general rigor applied to the practice of drawing was considerably higher than it has been for many years since. Although some of these books are out of print, copies may be found online, for sale through sellers of used books or for free in digital format.

Online forums are an excellent place to see and study the work of other artists, and also to share your own work as you develop your skills. Online video courses are becoming more widely available, particularly through platforms such as Craftsy, where the instructors are available for questions and feedback. There are numerous additional online venues where you can learn about drawing, view the work of others, and even find other people in your geographic area who enjoy drawing. Urban Sketchers is a non-profit organization "dedicated to fostering a global community of artists who practice on-location drawing," and it's really the most comprehensive site of its kind on the web. The Worldwide SketchCrawl is an event that happens a few times each year, and it gives people all over the world a chance to get out and draw together on the same day, then post their work in a geographically-arranged forum. The more you strive to participate in drawing and learning through these venues, the more connected you'll be to the ever-expanding community of artists around the world.

Graphic Journaling, Moh'd Bilbeisi
Kendall Hunt Publishing Company: Dubuque, IA, 2009.

Sketching on Location, Matthew Brehm
Kendall Hunt Publishing Company: Dubuque, IA, 2012.

Drawing Perspective: How to See It and How to Draw It, Matthew Brehm
Barron's Educational Series, Inc.: Hauppauge, NY, 2016.

Architectural Graphics, Francis D.K. Ching
John Wiley & Sons: New York, 2009.

Sketching and Rendering in Pencil, Arthur L. Guptill
The Pencil Points Press: New York, 1922.

Pencil Broadsides, Theodore Kautzky
Van Nostrand Reinhold Company: New York, 1940.

Architectural Sketching and Rendering, Stephen Kliment
Whitney Library of Design: New York, 1984.

Freehand Sketching, Paul Laseau
W.W. Norton: New York, 1999.

Architectural Rendering Techniques, Mike W. Lin
John Wiley & Sons: New York, 1985.

Basic Perspective Drawing: A Visual Approach, John Montague
John Wiley & Sons: New York, 1998.

Pencil Sketching, Second Edition, Thomas Wang
John Wiley & Sons: New York, 2002.

The Art of Pencil Drawing, Ernest W. Watson
Watson-Guptill Publications: New York, 1968.

Author Blog: brehmsketch.blogspot.com

Author Flickr Page: www.flickr.com/mtbrehm

Sketching Essentials Course: www.craftsy.com/ext/MattBrehm_10190_F

Urban Sketchers: www.urbansketchers.com

Worldwide SketchCrawl: www.sketchcrawl.com

Acknowledgments

Many thanks are due to all those who have helped me understand the process and value of drawing over the years, including numerous teachers and students. My colleagues and administrators here at the University of Idaho have been understanding and supportive as my time commitments have, at times, needed to be refocused on longer-term book projects such as this. My deepest thanks go to my family—my sons, Will and Sam, and my wife, Patty—who have provided their love, support, patience, and friendship over the years as I have developed my career in drawing and teaching.